COLLINS

Field Guide To

NEW ZEALAND
WILDLIFE

COLLINS

Field Guide To

NEW ZEALAND
WILDLIFE

Terence Lindsey
Rod Morris

HarperCollins*Publishers New Zealand Limited*

This book is dedicated to Ebony,
who helped the only way she knows, which was sufficient,
and to Erin and Sam with love.

TERENCE LINDSEY

ROD MORRIS

The authors and publishers wish to thank and acknowledge the following
individuals and organisations who have provided photographs:
Brian Chudleigh, p 52 (lower), p 64 (upper), p 67 (lower)
Department of Conservation, p145 (lower)
Doug Perrine/Auscape, p143
Rudie Kuiter, p162
Geoff Moon, p 24 (upper), p 65 (upper), p 66, p 67 (upper),
p 72 (lower), p 99 (upper), p 102
Gordon Roberts, p 136, p 137
Mike Soper, p 98, p 99 (lower)
Kim Westerskov, p 142, p 145 (upper).
All other photographs are by Rod Morris.

First published 2000
HarperCollins*Publishers (New Zealand) Limited*
P.O. Box 1, Auckland

ISBN 1 86950 300 7
Designed by Graeme Leather
Printed by Toppan, Hong Kong

Contents

Acknowledgements

The material in this book was drawn from three major sources: personal observations of New Zealand wildlife gleaned at various times over the past 25 years or so; uncountable conversations and correspondence with numerous New Zealand naturalists, zoologists and wildlife officials — a few regrettably forgotten and others unforgettable — over the same period; and from the pages of the *New Zealand Journal of Zoology* and related primary sources in the libraries of the University of Wollongong, the University of Sydney, the University of New South Wales and the Australian Museum, as well as numerous more popular accounts and texts.

I am grateful to all those who contributed in various ways along all three of these channels, as well as for the useful and constructive comments of Brian Patrick and Tony Harris. Ian McGee, Stan Nightingale, Margaret Mackay, Dr Richard Barnard and my agent, Sally Bird, provided much moral support and contributed in other ways too numerous to mention.

For anyone seeking Maori names for species we can thoroughly recommend Hirini Melbourne, Toby Rikihana, Wendy Pond and Andrew Crowe for their enthusiasm and encouragement. The photographs illustrating this guide relied heavily on the support of others, particularly the Morris/Anson family — thank you to Jamie and Sam, Rachel and Erin for finding the animals and sharing the adventures along the way.

Fellow photographers came to the rescue and filled in gaps, in particular Geoff Moon, Brian Chudleigh, Kim Westerskov, Gordon Roberts, Rudie Kuiter and Doug Perrine. Mrs Eileen Soper found two of the late Mike Soper's perfect bird portraits. Mark Bathurst first suggested the need for a field guide such as this — here it is at last Mark!

At HarperCollins Ian Watt, Sue Page and Lorain Day gently nudged the project along. Thank you to Ian for encouraging the inclusion of a Maori perspective, and special thanks to Hirini for writing it.

Oparara land snail, *Powelliphanta annectens*.

Author's introduction

One blustery spring day in 1975 I stepped ashore from a Zodiac onto tiny Rangatira Island in the Chathams with a team from the New Zealand Wildlife Service (as it was then) on a mission to census shore plovers, research the black robin, and generally participate in sundry other chores involved in the rescue from imminent extinction of some of New Zealand's most desperately threatened wildlife. A week or so later, I was not merely one of the very few sublimely privileged people on earth to have actually seen a shore plover, I had literally seen *all* of them (precisely 127 at the time, if I remember rightly), and was on even more intimate terms with many.

That sojourn was for me the beginning of a lifelong love affair with New Zealand and its wildlife. At one time or another I have wandered over most of New Zealand's varied landscapes. I've walked the Milford Track and dream of someday doing the Routeburn Track. I've watched Hector's dolphins and hand-fed takahe. I've been bullied by sea lions, marvelled at weta, spot-lighted kiwi and had my pocket picked by kea — but I haven't yet heard a kokako or seen a grasshopper ski. It seems to me, far too few people — New Zealanders and 'foreigners' alike — are aware of just how extraordinary New Zealand wildlife is. For any animal enthusiast with a global perspective, it's right up there on the billboard with its name in lights along with Hawaii, the Galapagos and Madagascar.

In writing books like this about animals, two perennial problems arise. The first is the question of scientific names. The difficulty is that, when we get beyond mammals and birds, the scientific name is sometimes the only way to refer to the creature. All too often, there simply are no English names. It didn't seem to make sense to start using scientific names halfway through the book, so I opted to clutch the nettle tightly and include them all the way through.

Scientific names can be daunting to

Kea, *Nestor notabilis*, male.

beginners, but they need not be. My advice, for what it's worth, is to ignore all the mystique, and think of them simply as bar codes or telephone numbers. It is possible that telephone numbers have some deep, arcane significance to telephone engineers. Does anybody care? All that matters to the rest of us is, you take the numbers specified and punch them into that little gizmo thing and, presto! You're talking to the person you wanted to talk to.

The function of scientific names is little different. If you feel you would like to know more about some animal mentioned in this book, the simplest way of going about it is to carefully note down its scientific name, just as you would a telephone number. You then walk into the nearest library, grab another book on New Zealand animals, and look for that name in its index, and keep going with other books until you feel you've learned all that pleases you for the moment. (Alternatively, of course, you can simply log onto the Internet.) You will be led repeatedly to exactly the same animal with the minimum of bother and fuss.

The other difficulty is one of format. Organising the material in any book like this under a series of headings for each animal, such as 'identification', 'voice', 'eggs', and so on, has so many obvious advantages in clarity, brevity and convenience that the device has long since become almost *de rigeur* in modern wildlife publishing. But it does have its disadvantages. Often, the significant details of a particular animal simply cannot be made to fit any array of categories laid down in advance. Occasionally the arrangement might tempt an unwary reader away from the realisation that sometimes an entire group of animals does a certain thing in exactly the same way — in itself a phenomenon well worth talking about. (There's always one that does it differently!) More importantly to me, the most fascinating things to be said about animals very often lie entirely outside the scope of such categories.

My own solution to this impasse has been to accept the categories, but to treat them as though made of rubber. Occasionally they have been shuffled, in cases where it was possible to

maintain an interesting storyline by so doing. And sometimes a category has been tossed overboard altogether if I felt that to be the only way of making space to enlarge upon something more interesting. This is not a handbook, and the intent is merely to offer you some help in pinning a name to some of the more common or interesting creatures you might encounter on your travels around New Zealand, and to sketch for you some of the key elements of the usually fascinating and sometimes fantastic ways they organise their lives.

Please don't put this book on your bookshelf. Put it in the glovebox of your car (or, if you're like me, toss it on the floor on the passenger's side — then you know where it is). Perhaps I can share with you something of my own passionate concern that a world without kea and kaka, kiwi and weta, simply isn't worth inhabiting, no matter what its comforts. If uniqueness were a quality that could somehow be cubed, then the result could legitimately be applied to New Zealand's wildlife. But it has received a most fearful battering over the past century or two, and is now greatly in need of some tender loving care. Every little bit helps.

Black robin, *Petroica traversi*, rescue team transferring robins (in pack) off Little Mangere Island, Chathams group.

The animal kingdom

The world of living things is so intricate that some system of organising the data becomes imperative. This book is organised roughly in standard taxonomic sequence, conforming to the hierarchical system by which biologists classify all living things, reflecting what is known of the pathways by which living things evolved.

All living things are grouped first into kingdoms, of which fungi, plants and animals are examples. All animals are grouped into phyla (singular phylum), of which three familiar examples are: Arthropoda (insects, spiders, crabs and several other groups which wear their 'skeletons' on the outside and have what many humans consider to be far, far too many legs); Mollusca (snails, slugs, oysters and squids — which, you might almost say, basically do without any skeletons at all); and Chordata (mammals, birds, fish and others that have internal skeletons and — mostly — carry their brains around in a bony box called a skull). In turn, phyla consist of one or more classes: mammals, birds and reptiles are distinct classes.

Classes consist of one or more orders: meat-eating mammals are grouped in the order Carnivora. Orders are made up of families: dogs (including wolves, foxes and jackals) and cats (including lions, tigers and leopards as well as domestic) differ in the way they go about their meat-eating — one group are solitary stalkers, the other sociable chasers. They are isolated in two different families (Canidae and Felidae). Among the dog family, the names wolves and foxes (loosely) correspond to the next category down, the genus (plural genera): *Canis* and *Vulpes*. All genera consist of one or more species: *Vulpes vulpes* is the scientific name of the particular species of fox, but there are others in the same genus. The species (singular or plural) is the fundamental unit of the entire system.

All animals can be divided into two categories: those with articulated backbones, skulls and four limbs, and everything else. The first group, which contains humans, are termed vertebrates; the second group, which includes insects, are termed invertebrates.

Tuatara, *Sphenodon punctatus*, adult female sharing a burrow with a fairy prion, Stephens Island.

The structure of the New Zealand fauna

Of the world's total land area, about 0.17 per cent lies under the New Zealand flag. The country has, roughly speaking, around one per cent of all known land animals, made up of around 10,000 species of insects, 2000 spiders, nearly 300 snails, and perhaps a further couple of thousand of all other groups combined. Zoologically, it is part of the Australasian region, its fauna having many obvious links with those of Australia, New Guinea, Melanesia and Polynesia, even though most of its species are endemic.

Comparisons are difficult to draw because there are no island groups elsewhere in the world comparable to New Zealand in size, latitude, climate and isolation. Great Britain, for example, comes close in size but its isolation is virtually nil and it is much further from the equator. Even so, in total number of species New Zealand seems little different from what might reasonably be expected of such an island group based on estimates elsewhere in the world.

But the constitution of those species is very different. The degree and extent of New Zealand's isolation is such that much of its fauna and flora is 'skewed' with respect to the rest of the world. For example, among flowering plants about 6 per cent are annuals, compared to around 13 percent botanists generally accept as 'standard' elsewhere in the world. Among species of insects, bee, wasp and butterfly numbers are low but those of aquatic insects are high.

Part of New Zealand's uniqueness lies in the fact that standard niches are often occupied by decidedly non-standard animals, as in the 'mouse-weta' mentioned elsewhere (page 16). But there are many other oddities in New Zealand's fauna. Elsewhere in the world, grasshoppers are creatures of arid grasslands, but in New Zealand most are alpine endemics. Similarly, with only 16 species, New Zealand is deficient in butterflies — so many moths have commandeered the vacant niches and New Zealand is crowded with colourful, conspicuous moths that fly by day and do several other things just not done by moths elsewhere.

Golden brown jumping spider, *Trite auricoma*, male.

New Zealand wildlife habitats

This book deals with seabirds, whales and seals, but oceanic habitats are otherwise ignored. Even coasts get scant mention, except for some small animals in which New Zealand is highly unusual: sand and shingle beaches have several skinks, spiders, beetles, earwigs and other small creatures found nowhere else.

Native forests

When Maori first came to New Zealand they found a land largely covered in forest, consisting of two broad types: beech forests are various combinations of four species of the genus *Nothofagus*, and podocarp forests are extremely variable in composition but typically dominated by native conifers, especially kauri and trees of the genus *Podocarpus*. Broadly speaking, beech forests predominate in the South Island, podocarp forests in the North Island.

Both kinds are vital reservoirs of native animals: the vast majority of New Zealand's snails and spiders, for example, are forest inhabitants. But these forests differ in many ways, with far-reaching consequences even for such mobile creatures as birds. Kaka, yellowheads, and yellow-crowned parakeets, for example, are especially strongly associated with beech forest. Conversely, New Zealand pigeons and the various honeyeaters are much scarcer in beech forest than in the more floristically complex podocarp forests. Even among fish, the question of whether a stream flows through beech or podocarp forest is one of several important parameters governing the distributions of several of the kokopu species.

Ferns, flax and scrublands

Flaxes, ferns and scrub form a low and sometimes almost impenetrable habitat, harbouring a distinctive wildlife community of its own. It often forms a band along the highest mountains just above the highest limit of true forest. In lowlands especially these plant communities also play a vital role as 'nurseries', sheltering the delicate seedlings of various forest giants during their first few years of growth.

Silver beech, *Nothofagus menziesii*.

Copper tussock, *Chionochloa rubra cuprea*.

Typical inhabitants include the green tree geckos, the fernbird, skinks, snails and insects.

Grasslands

New Zealand's indigenous grasslands are of the type known as 'tussock', where the plants grow in tight bunches rather than an even sward. Like the forests, they can be broadly subdivided into two major types: 'short-tussock' tends to be dominated by species of *Poa* and *Festuca* and is characteristic of the low-rainfall regions of the eastern South Island; 'tall-tussock' is dominated by various species of snowgrass, *Chionochloa*, and is typical of montane or high-rainfall regions. A few native birds, such as the New Zealand falcon and the takahe, are characteristic of grasslands, and such areas are the home of the day-active skinks and insects such as the grass-grub beetle and its relatives. On the other hand, the spider fauna has been almost entirely replaced by introduced species.

Alpine regions

High above the timberline at around 1200 m or more, especially in the South Island, lies a veritable wonderland where almost every living thing, plant or animal, is unique. For example, there are 24 species of endemic flowering plants restricted to scree slopes alone. Several birds are confined to high altitudes, notably the rock wren and the kea — the world's only truly alpine parrot. Few reptiles penetrate to really high altitudes, but their scarcity is outweighed by a host of unusual insects: most of the endemic grasshoppers, for example, are confined to alpine regions, and there are many unique moths and butterflies, weta and beetles.

Farmland and croplands

With one or two conspicuous exceptions (grass-grub and porina moth), New Zealand native animals have so far proved unable to extend their distributions into environments heavily modified and used by humans, whether for residential, recreational or agricultural purposes.

Farmland, Otago Peninsula.

The result is that the ordinary rural 'countryside' in New Zealand tends to be dominated by introduced birds such as starlings, sparrows and chaffinches, and even the insects and spiders are mostly alien. One prominent exception is the half-million or so hectares given over to *Pinus radiata* plantations. These often now support a rich flora of ground-dwelling plants, which in turn has allowed renewed immigration by many native insects, skinks, geckos and similar small creatures. Even such birds as kiwi, tomtit and morepork have locally adapted to these exotic forests.

Offshore islands

New Zealand is unusually well endowed with small islands dotted along most parts of the coastline. These constitute a significant extension of New Zealand environments because many harbour their own unique species of animals. The Three Kings are a typical example: a skink and several insects, spiders and harvestmen are entirely endemic here, and even several of the group's marine and seashore

Little Mangere Island, Chatham group.

unusually rich and diverse fauna of aquatic insects.

The fauna of lakes, especially at higher altitudes and particularly those with rocky shores, is also relatively sparse, often limited to a few freshwater snails, sponges, planarians and the larvae of aquatic insects. Coastal lakes and lagoons, especially those with more aquatic vegetation, tend to be far richer, with various fish, koura, and a wealth of waterbirds such as herons and ducks.

The descent along the eastern front of the Southern Alps is so abrupt that vast quantities of rock, pebbles and shingle are dumped by cascading waters where they reach the flat expanse of the Canterbury Plains. This leads to a distinctive geographical feature, 'braided river' systems, where the discharge is erratic and narrow, multiple channels tend to flow through broad fields of shingle. Such rivers support an unusually diverse fauna of endemic spiders, aquatic insects and similar small creatures, and they also serve as important nesting grounds for several birds, including black-billed gull, black-fronted tern, wrybill and black stilt.

creatures also occur nowhere else. This is even more true of the distant, outlying groups, some of them seldom visited by humans: the Kermadecs, Chathams, Campbell, Auckland, and Antipodes groups. Each of these remote island groups harbours many endemic animals — often insects but sometimes other groups: the Antipodes Island parakeet, for example, occurs nowhere else in the world.

Wetlands

The northern parts of the North Island have extensive stretches of mangroves, and parts of the coast have salt lagoons, marshes and tidal mudflats where migratory wading birds congregate. However, freshwater swamps and marshes tend to be relatively scarce (and severely threatened by development). The high profile of New Zealand means that rivers and streams reach the sea very quickly from their sources high among glaciers and snowfields, a pace that offers little opportunity for picking up nutrients. Aquatic vegetation is therefore relatively sparse, but alpine streams support an

Waimakiriri River, Canterbury.

Where did New Zealand animals come from?

Any animal (or plant) inhabiting New Zealand today was either already a part of the Gondwana fauna before the breakup of that ancient continent around 100 million years ago, or its ancestors flew, swam, or were carried here since. Except for the tuatara, New Zealand reptiles belong to two groups, geckos and skinks, well known for their colonising ability. Both groups are common across the Pacific.

Wherever there are forests, great trees fall into broad rivers, carrying with them quantities of foliage and debris, and the whole mass is swept downstream and out to sea. Such a tree might easily be cast up on a beach on a neighbouring island or landmass. But any tree is a veritable zoo, harbouring insects, snails, frogs, geckos and other small animals — perhaps even birds or bats roosting in its cavities, many of which are taken along for the ride.

Some survive long enough to land with the tree, and establish new populations — a worldwide colonising process known as rafting. Birds, mammals and frogs cannot survive long without food and fresh water, but reptiles and many other creatures can, so frogs rarely spread by rafting, but geckos and snails commonly do. Ocean currents between New Caledonia and New Zealand are favourable to rafting. Many

New Zealand animals, including several snails, harvestmen and spiders, have their closest relatives in New Caledonia *and* belong to groups physiologically best able to survive ocean crossings.

When birds grew wings they gained mastery of geographical barriers and their mobility became effectively limitless. Given luck and favourable winds, birds of many species are capable of crossing the Tasman Sea. Some do it routinely, twice annually. Some moths and butterflies are capable of the crossing, and many New Zealand birds and butterflies have their closest relatives in eastern Australia.

The yellow admiral butterfly, for example, has not been here long — but the monarch butterfly and at least three species of moths have established themselves within the period of European occupation. Similarly, some birds arrived long ago but others have established themselves recently — in at least one case, that of the silvereye, European observers witnessed the arrival. Perhaps many other Australian birds survived the crossing but, until recently, were unable to establish themselves in a land clad mostly in forest. Clearing for agriculture may have provided opportunities for many birds that were previously lacking. For example, the population of the masked lapwing has only recently exploded, yet it seems unlikely that its immediate ancestors were the first ever to land on New Zealand shores.

On the other hand, several of New Zealand's extraordinary creatures must have been here a very long time indeed. There is simply nothing like a kiwi, a tuatara, or a moa anywhere else in the world today — and in these cases it seems most reasonable to suppose that their ancestors were already occupants of that particular section of Gondwana when it first broke away and ultimately became New Zealand.

Black-fronted tern, *Sterna albostriata.*

The natural world of the Maori

The Maori world view is essentially inclusive. People, animals, birds, sea creatures, plants and all natural phenomena are inter-related within a complex universal family or community order.

To Maori, the forest, sea and other ecosystems were an integral part of their lives, identity and culture. Each ecosystem had its own mauri or vital principle, protecting and sustaining the safety and livelihood of its inhabitants. The principle of guardianship, a reciprocal arrangement between the gods (represented by nature) and humans, was at the heart of cultural practices of interacting with the environment to ensure an inheritance for future generations

For Tuhoe the forest of Te Urewera, for example, is called Te Waonui a Tane, the great forest of Tane. Tane was the offspring of Ranginui, the Sky Father and Papatuanuku, the Earth Mother, who heaved his parents apart to let in light so life could flourish on earth. Tane was the primogenitor of trees, shrubs, birds, insects and people. The forest is the cloak woven by Tane to cover Earth Mother, and is Tane's sacred shrine as the nursery for young plants and the pharmacy and food store for the tribe. For Tuhoe, a tree represents many things, it can be Tane; it can be a totara, as well as an ancestor or guardian with special properties and powers, and a shelter for birds, animals and insects.

The traditional Maori view of the natural world believed in the kinship of all things. This kinship, an integral part of Maori mythology and genealogy (whakapapa), clearly shows the source of all things to be the primal parents of Ranginui and Papatuanuku. Through whakapapa the lines of descent from a particular ancestor could be traced to a descendant. No matter how far removed individuals were from one another, whakapapa was an important device for tracing and linking them and their lines of descent, not only to human relations but also to non-human descendants.

The descent of insects, small creatures, birds and plants can be traced through the children of Ranginui and Papatuanuku. Tane became the primogenitor of humans through his liaison with Hineahuone (the woman made from earth). Caterpillars, phosphorescent creatures, forest grubs and lice came into being through his liaison with Hinetuamaunga (the mountain woman). Tane's brother, Tangaroa, the father of fish and sea plants, through his liaison with Punga became the father of spiders, centipedes and millipedes, parasitic and predatory insects, lizards and skinks.

By the beginning of the 20th century social, economic, political and cultural changes were occurring in tribal structures. These changes were due to the introduction of European cultural systems, technological innovations and introduced fauna and flora. While the enormous impact of these introduced animals, plants and technology upon Maori cannot be denied, the ability of traditional Maori culture to absorb and adapt to foreign changes, concepts and practices should not be underestimated.

Precedents in challenging and extending cultural boundaries to accommodate change were established in mythological times by the gods themselves. Tane, for example, established the practice of adoption in Maori society by taking on the fatherly duties of fostering his older brother's offspring, the birds of prey. Traditional Maori cultural frameworks were similarly flexible at including and adopting European concepts, systems, technologies, fauna and flora within its conceptual universal family and community network. All introduced fish and birds became the adopted offspring of Tangaroa and Tane respectively. However, domesticated animals posed a problem for Maori methodology. The solution was to include them conceptually as members of the farmer's extended family, thus finding a niche for them in the social system.

The impact of introduced species

For aeons 'exotic' animals large and small have been making their own way to New Zealand, using one means of transport or another, and almost always making a successful landfall by sheer chance alone and at purely random intervals. But the past few centuries have seen a flood of new animals added to the New Zealand fauna from an entirely new source — carried here, wittingly or unwittingly, by humans. Maori brought the kiore but Europeans brought almost all the rest, including many mammals and birds and a huge array of insects and spiders. Some prospered and became agricultural pests — provoking Europeans into fetching yet more species into the country in an unhappily imperative attempt to control them. This process shows little sign of abating, despite the best attempts of quarantine regulations and customs inspectors.

New Zealand's long isolation has had a profound effect on its wildlife. Until recently New Zealand had no land mammals of any kind, save two species of bats. But no niche remains vacant forever. Sooner or later, some creature evolves whatever equipment is needed to exploit the vacancy, moves in and makes it its own. Everywhere in the world, small mouse-sized creatures inhabit the forest floor, harvesting the 'rain' of nuts, seeds, berries and other plant parts that falls steadily from the foliage far above. Elsewhere, such creatures are indeed mice, but these small mammals were lacking in New Zealand for aeons, and several entirely different creatures evolved 'mousy' characteristics and moved to fill the empty niche. These included weta, bush wrens, and even one of the two bats. However, all proved in the end mere understudies, to be ruthlessly swept aside as amateurs when the 'professional' mice — the genuine mice — were finally brought here by Europeans. Mice and rats now dominate the forest floor, with devastating repercussions for a host of small ground-dwelling birds, insects, snails and other creatures.

The impact of introduced species on New Zealand's native wildlife has been so intricate

Feral cat, *Felis catus*, female about to feed on her kill, a little blue penguin.

and far-reaching it is nearly impossible to summarise. Endemic skinks and geckos, for example, once had very few natural enemies (only the kingfisher takes many), but now rats and mice exert significant predation pressure, a fact easily demonstrated by comparing their abundance on small offshore islands lacking mice and rats with their scarcity on rodent-infested islands. Similarly, many endemic snails now have an important predator — the hedgehog — where once there was none. And the tree-climbing ship rat, in particular, has proved repeatedly capable of decimating entire populations of songbirds by its relentless predation on eggs and chicks.

The impact of exotic animals can be direct or indirect and there is no simple answer to the question of which is worse, in the end. Stoats, weasels and cats are predators let loose in a land that never knew mammal predators, and the effect has been rather similar to letting a gang of small boys loose in a sweet shop. On the other hand, goats, rabbits and deer are grazing and browsing animals that have had a somewhat similar effect on New Zealand's endemic plants, on which native animals in turn depend. The overall effects may be additive, cumulative or compounded, but always complex. They may even tend to cancel out: ferrets, for example, prey largely on rabbits, another introduced animal, so that — when all is said and done — ferrets probably exert a relatively minor influence on New Zealand's native fauna. But many other effects have proved almost catastrophic. Red deer, for example, have severely damaged New Zealand beech forests — and if the forest is degraded, then all the other animals and plants that inhabit beech forests are also adversely affected. Even the deer's damage, however, pales into insignificance beside the wholesale devastation of entire forest ecosystems caused by the introduced brushtail possum. It is difficult to overstate the seriousness of the present situation; some effective way of controlling this foreigner has simply got to be

Southern tokoeka adult female killed by a stray dog.

found. To select just one example, in a stretch of incomparable totara and kaikawaka forest preserved in the Hihitahi Forest Sanctuary in the central North Island, more than 90 per cent of the mature trees are now standing dead, killed by possums. The reserve remains, but the forest it was designed to protect has already gone, perhaps forever.

New Zealand's national symbol, the kiwi, is a nocturnal bird that is hard to see, but its shrill whistling calls are an evocative part of forest nightlife. Kiwi remain common on several offshore islands, but mainland forests are now mostly silent at night. Kiwi have shown themselves to be very versatile in their choice of habitat, pottering happily about at night even in many exotic pine forests; but many are killed by traffic, and dogs (whether feral or domestic) have wiped out many a local population. Kiwi are being successfully bred in captivity at several New Zealand wildlife facilities, but unless or until their native habitat can be somehow rendered safe from predators there is little hope of widespread reintroduction into the wild.

Conservation in New Zealand

One of the most encouraging things about conservation in New Zealand is the dedication, commitment and expertise already demonstrated by community and government authorities alike, resulting in some spectacular successes. The story of the black robin might well serve as case study representing a much wider range of examples. By the mid-1970s, the black robin was reduced to nine individuals confined to a pathetic remnant of native akeake scrub perched on the very summit of a volcanic plug called Little Mangere in the Chatham Islands — a patch of scrub shared, incidentally, with several hundred thousand nesting sooty shearwaters, which surely can't have helped matters.

Clearly, there were already as many black robins in the world as its minute habitat could possibly hold, and its cause seemed hopeless. Nevertheless, a plan was devised to clear nearby Mangere Island (which had at one time been cleared for sheep farming), first of all feral animals, then to replant the entire island

(laboriously by hand) with flax, the flax to serve as 'nursery' cover to protect regenerating akeake seedlings (also to be hand-planted). After a few years, it was hoped, the akeake scrub would again cover Mangare as it once did, providing a suitable additional home for a much larger population of black robins. If only the handful of black robins on their precarious toehold on Little Mangere could just be helped somehow to hang in there for a few more years while their new home (actually their former natural home) was rehabilitated …

To cut a long story short, it worked. A helicopter and a team of wildlife experts were used to capture the surviving seven black robins on Little Mangere and transport them a few thousand metres across the intervening channel. The robins decided they liked their new home and set about rebuilding their numbers with enthusiasm. Now, 25 years later, there seems good reason to hope that black robins will once again thrive on their ancestral islands — if only, that is, the black rats and feral cats can

The release of a relocated male black robin.

somehow be kept away, a task that will require eternal vigilance.

A number of small, predator-free, offshore islands are serving a vital role in saving endangered species. These include Codfish Island off Stewart Island, Stephens Island in Cook Strait, Kapiti Island off the North Island's west coast and Little Barrier Island.

For some animals this strategy cannot be made to work. A conservation technique called a 'captive breeding programme' is being used for several bird species, notably the takahe, kakapo and black stilt. By this technique, birds or their eggs are brought from the wild into captivity and artificially reared. When they reach independence, the general idea is to release them back into the wild to boost the natural population. This seems a brilliantly simple technique in theory but proves enormously difficult in practice. The main difficulty is that, unless elaborate precautions are taken to prevent it, youngsters become dependent on human care during the rearing process, and prove unable to survive, find mates, and actually breed themselves once released into the wild.

Often, an animal becomes critically endangered, not because of any marked degradation of its general environment but because a particular key resource becomes compromised in some way. A typical example is the current predicament of the yellow-eyed penguin, now perhaps the rarest penguin in the world. Studies have failed to uncover any marked deterioration in its environment *per se*, but the bird is unable to breed normally because widespread clearing for agriculture has removed most of the coastal thickets it needs for secure nesting sites. In such cases sophisticated expertise isn't necessary: extensive community support can itself work wonders. On present knowledge, it seems reasonable to hope that, if enough coastal landowners can be persuaded to replant or allow regeneration of small coastal thickets and provide suitable nest sites — not in itself an enormously difficult or expensive task,

Don Merton with a kakapo, *Strigops habroptilus*, Pearl Island.

and one well suited to appropriately motivated local community groups — then the penguin's currently desperate problem should just quietly go away.

Human domination is now so all-pervasive that even such apparently secure treasures as the remote and uninhabited outposts of the Auckland, Campbell and Antipodes groups require vigilance if they are to remain pristine. There are two main concerns: one is the possibility of introduction, accidental or deliberate, of either the ship rat or the feral cat in particular. The other is more subtle: when a human steps ashore on such an island, who knows what plant seeds, spores, insect eggs or similar fragments of life lie buried in the mud on his or her boots, or lurking in the seams of clothing? Such minutiae have already ruined many a tiny island, and it is not for nothing that all visitors to subantarctic islands are now required to scrub their boots before disembarking, and the number and frequency of human visitation needs to be very carefully controlled.

How to look for wildlife

Watching animals need not be a highly disciplined activity requiring years of training. Keeping in mind a few elementary rules can certainly make an enormous difference to your success.

In noticing animals, silence is golden. Especially when in groups, we humans are instinctively so gregarious and sociable that on any outing in the bush we all tend to spend a great deal more time gossiping than in actually looking or listening for wildlife. If some 'quality time' together is the reason we're there in the first place, then that's good too. But if finding an animal to look at is paramount, then it helps to bear in mind that, not only are your own 'detection systems' temporarily turned off while you gossip, but any creature that may happen to be in the vicinity certainly has the gain on its own 'detection systems' turned up just as high as it will go. It stops whatever else it was doing while it attempts to decide whether the disturbance constitutes a threat or not. Not surprisingly, a large number of perfectly obvious animals get themselves entirely overlooked by this combination of effects.

Neither is sneaking and stalking generally a good idea. From your target's perspective, if you sneak and stalk and hide, whatever you're up to is probably dangerous. For ordinary nature-watching simply saunter quietly along with your eyes and ears wide open, doing nothing vigorous or conspicuous. The desirable state, if you can achieve it, is simple acceptance — obvious, but just part of the scenery.

It also helps to borrow a few simple hunting techniques. Stay downwind if you can. If the sun is behind you, then you can see your quarry much more clearly than it can see you. Resist the impulse to get too close, even if the animal proves unusually tame. Not only does this reduce any stress for the animal in the encounter but the further away you are, the more likely the animal is to behave naturally and the more likely you are to learn something of its habits.

For much the same reasons, 'bush-bashing' is often not a good idea. There are a number of animals for which there is no alternative but to 'go in after them', but much of the time it's unnecessary, it pointlessly damages the environment, and you often make so much noise you can't effectively use your ears and eyes. Sticking to a trail, you can be much less obtrusive and at the same time allow your senses a little elbowroom in which to function optimally.

Animals are everywhere, and there is almost always something to see in any habitat and at any hour of the day or night. Even so, a stroll in the forest at dusk or just after dawn is much more likely to be productive than at other times — these are the natural 'rush hours' of the bush, when overall activity is greatest and most animals are either hurrying home to bed or doing the animal equivalent of catching the bus to go to work. Numbers and species also tend to

An inquisitive kea, *Nestor notabilis*, juvenile, Fiordland.

be highest along ecotones, which is an ecological term for the junction or interface between any two different habitats. For example, if the road ahead of you forks, and there is forest on both sides of the track along one but the other has forest on one hand and meadow on the other, then pick the latter. It's following an ecotone and so your chances of seeing something worthwhile are generally just that little bit better.

Try to be precise in your observations. Browsing through photographs in a book to find the closest match to the creature you saw will often get you there in the end, but learning the precise features you need to look for is much more efficient. If you can say of a bird, for instance, 'it was black with a white rump' rather than 'I think there was a bit of white on it', then your chances of reaching a decisive identification are vastly improved.

Nature-watching needs no exotic equipment. A good pair of binoculars is almost essential for watching birds and mammals (you're likely to find something between 7x35 and 10x40 just

right — ask the salesperson in the camera store what the numbers mean), but you need little else. A notebook and pencil are handy; a small pocket magnifying glass is almost indispensable for insects and similar small creatures; and it's a good idea to have a small pocket torch with you at all times, with which to explore any tree cavity or rock crevice you might come across.

For an entirely different perspective on wildlife, try exploring your surroundings at night. With a little patience and practice, an extraordinary variety of animals can be observed quite easily at night, both by listening for their calls and using a torch to pick up eyeshine. A handy gadget is a small headlamp (the kind of strap-on device that cavers use, obtainable at outdoor, sports or camping stores). This leaves your hands free to deal with a more powerful torch or spotlight you use to actually look at your animal. The trick in spotting an animal's eyeshine is to look as nearly as you can precisely along the beam, not above or off to one side of it, holding the torch up to your face, not down at your side.

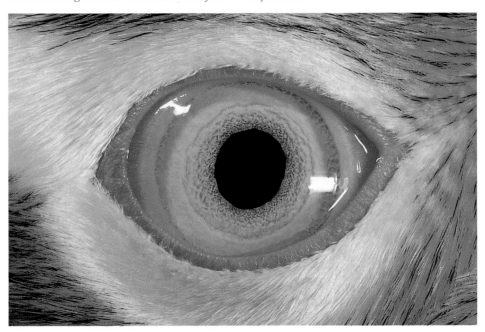

The eye of a yellow-eyed penguin, *Megadyptes antipodes*.

Brown Kiwi

Recognition Very often, just a single glimpse is all that is necessary to identify New Zealand's national symbol, the kiwi. Seeming 'all bill and drumsticks' it presents a most un-bird-like silhouette, and its odd loping trot is also very distinctive. The eyes are minute, the tail non-existent, the tiny wings hidden in feathers, the bill long and slender, and the powerful legs make up about a third of the total body weight. The plumage has an unusually loose and shaggy look. Brown kiwi are about 40 cm long and weigh about 3.5 kg.

Distribution Once widespread on New Zealand's North Island, South Island and Stewart Island, the brown kiwi population has been much reduced by habitat destruction and other factors, until it now seems to be effectively confined to Stewart Island, Fiordland and Westland in the South Island, and north of the Manawatu Gorge in the North Island. In 1910 brown kiwi were released on Little Barrier Island and in 1940 on Kapiti Island. In both these instances, the introductions were successful, but especially so on Little Barrier, where kiwi are now abundant and can be easily observed.

Habits Kiwi are most common in native forests, but they also occur in scrub, sand dunes, tussock grassland, and even pine plantations. Brown kiwi often feed in daylight, especially on Stewart Island, but for the most part kiwi are nocturnal. The most characteristic of the calls they make is a shrill, strident whistle, which is repeated in series; the female's version is briefer and hoarser than the male's. Kiwi also make loud snuffling noises as they forage, blowing hard to clear their nostrils of mud and soil.

Food Kiwi are omnivorous, eating fruit and seeds as well as a very wide range of small ground-dwelling animals, including earthworms, insects, slugs and snails.

Breeding In the North island the male is responsible for the domestic arrangements, assisted only casually by his mate. She lays (usually) two large eggs, often several weeks apart, but he prepares the nest, incubates the eggs until they hatch at around 80 days, and broods and guards the chicks. They are largely independent within a month of hatching.

Order • Apterygiformes	**Species** • *Apteryx australis*
Status • endemic; uncommon; resident	**Maori name** • kiwi, tokoeka

Great Spotted Kiwi

45 cm

Recognition Slightly larger than the brown kiwi, but the pale brown feathers are marked and mottled with black, giving the plumage a brindled or finely banded — not streaked — appearance. More reliably, the calls differ from those of the brown kiwi: the male's call has been described as a 'high-pitched rolling whistle', and the female has a low harsh *churr*. Like brown kiwi, great spotted kiwi forage mainly at night, prey largely on earthworms, beetle larvae and similar small invertebrates, and are most common in undisturbed beech forests.

ORDER • Apterygiformes
SPECIES • *Apteryx haastii*
STATUS • endemic; rare; resident
MAORI NAME • roa

Distribution Much the least known of the three kiwi, the great spotted has apparently always had a limited range in the mountains of the north-western South Island, south to about Franz Josef Glacier. It seems to be most frequently reported in the Tasman and Paparoa Ranges.

Little Spotted Kiwi

30 cm

Recognition The little spotted kiwi is substantially smaller than the other two species — about 30 cm long — but it shares the great spotted kiwi's finely barred appearance. Like its larger cousins, it lives mainly in native forests and is active mainly at night. The male's strident trill differs from the brown kiwi's whistle, and the female utters a low *churr*.

ORDER • Apterygiformes
SPECIES • *Apteryx owenii*
STATUS • endemic; rare; resident
MAORI NAME • kiwi-pukupuku

Distribution When first discovered by Europeans, this kiwi was common on the western side of the South Island, from Fiordland to Nelson, extending north-eastwards into the Marlborough Sounds, and on Mount Hector in the North Island. However, its smaller size makes it especially vulnerable to predation from feral dogs and stoats, and it is already extinct in its natural range. A thriving population remains on Kapiti Island, where it was successfully introduced in 1913.

Great Crested Grebe

50 cm

Recognition   Unmistakable — look for the long slender neck, normally carried almost vertically. Grebes loosely resemble ducks except for their generally spike-like bills and lack of any obvious tail. They dive for their food and are so aquatic that they almost never come ashore. They seldom fly, and then usually only at night. The diet includes small underwater animals of all kinds.

ORDER • Podicipediformes
SPECIES • *Podiceps cristatus*
STATUS • native; rare; resident
MAORI NAME • puteketeke

Distribution   The great crested grebe is widespread in Africa, Eurasia and Australia, but in New Zealand it is confined to the South Island, mainly Fiordland, Westland and the Canterbury high country.

Breeding   This grebe is notable for its spectacular mutual courtship displays, which involve a great deal of graceful posturing and mad, churning chases across the water.

New Zealand Dabchick

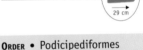

29 cm

Recognition   The dabchick is easily told from the great crested grebe by its small size and dumpy silhouette, but it is not easy to distinguish from two occasional visitors from Australia, the Australasian grebe and the hoary-headed grebe, unless in breeding plumage — a blackish body and a deep chestnut throat. The sexes are alike, and winter birds and immatures are drab grey. The downy chicks are fluffy white, intricately marked and spotted with black. They often ride about on the back of one or other of their parents on the water, occasionally clinging on as the adult dives.

ORDER • Podicipediformes
SPECIES • *Poliocephalus rufopectus*
STATUS • endemic; uncommon; resident
MAORI NAME • weweia

Distribution   Though once much more widespread, the dabchick is now confined to the North Island, where its stronghold appears to be the Rotorua and Taupo lakes district. Its total population is probably little more than 500 breeding pairs.

Royal Albatross

Habits Among the largest of all flying birds, the great albatrosses — the royal albatross of New Zealand and the somewhat more widespread wandering albatross — are the most spectacular of a group of seabirds known as 'tubenoses' (referring to the tube-like nostrils on the upper bill, which help cope with a high salt intake). These birds are unfamiliar to many people because their home is the open ocean, far beyond sight of land, and they come ashore only to breed. Once common, both species are now in severe decline.

Recognition The royal albatross is roughly the size of a domestic goose, but with enormously long, slender wings, giving it the greatest wingspan of any bird (well over 3 m). It is easily distinguishable from the several species of mollymawks in New Zealand by its larger size and white back (mollymawks are dark between the wings), but the only certain feature distinguishing it from the wandering albatross is a narrow black line along the cutting edge of the bill — which is often very hard to see.

Distribution It breeds only in New Zealand, but its colonies are on remote islands such as Auckland and Campbell — with one exception: there is a small nesting colony at Taiaroa Head near Dunedin, which gives Dunedin the enviable distinction of being the only city in the world where you can easily watch nesting albatrosses. This colony is very small — only a few pairs — and entry is severely restricted to avoid disturbance to the birds, but they can be watched from an observation hide erected some distance from the nests.

Breeding The royal albatross is so large that — unlike most birds — it takes more than a single summer to rear a chick, and 8 months or so to reach full independence. This means successful parents can nest (at best) only every alternate year. Unsuccessful parents sometimes try again the following year. Only one egg is laid, which the birds incubate in shifts until it hatches after about 80 days. The chick is brooded constantly for about five weeks but then abandoned by both parents, who visit only to feed it.

Order • Procellariiformes	**Species** • *Diomedea epomophora*
Status • native; restricted; migrant	**Maori name** • toroa

Sooty Shearwater

46 cm

Recognition   Length 40–46 cm; wingspan about 100 cm. This is one of many all-black or very dark brown shearwaters that are extremely difficult to distinguish at sea. The sooty shearwater is the only one of these with pure white underwings — but at sea this feature is surprisingly deceptive and difficult to see.

Distribution   Some sooty shearwaters breed on various islands in southern Chile, near Cape Horn, and on the Falkland Islands, and a few more on islands off the coast of south-eastern Australia, but the majority breed in New Zealand. Here they nest on numerous small islands off the coast of the three main islands (but especially Stewart Island), and also on the Chatham, Auckland, Campbell, Antipodes, and Snares Islands. All populations cross the equator twice annually to spend the austral winter in the North Pacific.

Habits   This may well be New Zealand's most abundant bird. It is nearly impossible to estimate the vast numbers nesting on many offshore islands, but the grand national total is certainly many millions of pairs. The sooty shearwater is strongly gregarious, often nesting, feeding and travelling in very large flocks, but it is also frequently encountered at sea alone. Most birds form permanent pairs, returning to the same nest burrow year after year, but the 'divorce' rate is about 16 per cent per year.

Food   The diet includes squid and small fish — mostly obtained by shallow dives from the surface — but the main summer food is krill.

Breeding   Nesting colonies are usually on tussock slopes near the sea and occupied from late September to early May. Most colonies are visited only at night. Laid in late November, and incubated in alternate shifts lasting up to 12 days, the single egg takes about 53 days to hatch. Chicks fledge at about 97 days, but they are abandoned by their parents two or three weeks earlier; the adults are already well on their way north before, driven by hunger, the chicks finally go to sea alone.

ORDER • Procellariiformes	**SPECIES** • *Puffinus griseus*
STATUS • native; common; migrant	**MAORI NAME** • titi

Other Shearwaters

to 46 cm

Hutton's shearwater

Buller's shearwater

The cold waters of the Southern Ocean teem with krill, supporting the largest community of oceanic birds in the world. With its many offshore and outlying island groups, New Zealand represents, from the seabirds' perspective, very desirable real estate for rearing young. No less than 41 species of 'tubenoses' (shearwaters and allies) breed within New Zealand's territorial boundaries — many of them nowhere else. Those that breed only in New Zealand include the following:

The fluttering shearwater breeds on numerous small islands off the coasts of the North Island and in Cook Strait. One of the smaller shearwaters, it is especially vulnerable to predation from feral cats and ship rats, which have wiped out many mainland colonies.

Hutton's shearwater nests only amid the snow at high altitudes in the Seaward Kaikoura Range in the South Island. Hutton's shearwater is dark above, pale below, with dusky underwings, but it is very difficult to distinguish at sea from the fluttering shearwater. Youngsters of both Hutton's and fluttering shearwaters spend their early years circumnavigating Australia before returning to their natal colonies to breed for the first time.

The only known colonies of Buller's shearwater are all on the Poor Knights Islands, where a total of about two million pairs nest. Buller's shearwater has a slow, lazy flight, and is easily identified by its grey upper parts, white underparts, and a prominent dusky 'M' band across the upperwings. It winters in the North Pacific, but little is known of its ocean journeys.

Other, more widespread shearwaters that also breed in the New Zealand region include the wedge-tailed shearwater, which very much resembles an all-dark-brown Buller's shearwater, the aptly named little shearwater on the Kermadecs, and the unusually big and burly flesh-footed shearwater on islands surrounding the North Island. Other shearwaters that visit — but do not breed — in New Zealand waters from time to time include the short-tailed shearwater, Manx shearwater, Christmas Island shearwater, and the North Atlantic shearwater.

Grey-faced Petrel

41 cm

Recognition   Length about 41 cm, wingspan about 110 cm. Also called the great-winged petrel or northern muttonbird, this bird is easily distinguished from other common New Zealand petrels as an entirely dark seabird with a grey face — detectable over a surprising distance at sea — and featureless underwings. To the very experienced eye, it has a distinctive towering, impetuous flight style.

Distribution   The grey-faced petrel breeds on many islands in the southern Atlantic and Indian Oceans and on a few off the coast of south-western Australia. In the New Zealand region it breeds in numerous colonies on headlands and small offshore islands around the North Island — notably Mokohinau, Aldermen, and the Hen and Chickens. Although mostly sedentary, its distribution at sea virtually encircles the southern hemisphere in warm temperate waters (approximately 25°–50° S).

Habits   Adults are non-migratory, but juvenile birds disperse widely. Although they nest in loose colonies, they are solitary at sea. Graphic evidence of their deep-ocean habits emerges from banding returns: in studies spanning several decades, more than 10,000 grey-faced petrels have been banded (fitted with a lightweight, numbered metal band around one leg), but only one has ever been recovered away from the colonies.

Food   Feeding is mainly at night, squid and luminescent zooplankton making up the bulk of the diet. New Zealand birds forage mainly about 100–600 km east of the North Island.

Breeding   Grey-faced petrels breed in winter and colonies are reoccupied in late February. A few birds nest on the surface, but most lay in burrows. The birds court, mate, and prepare the nest site, then the colony is largely abandoned in a 'honeymoon' exodus at sea lasting about two months, while the female forms her single egg and both fatten up in preparation for the lengthy incubation shifts (about 17 days each). Most egg-laying occurs in the first week of July.

Order • Procellariiformes	**Species** • *Pterodroma macroptera*
Status • native; common; migrant	**Maori name** • oi

Other Petrels

to
41 cm

Mottled
petrel

Confusingly, several different groups of seabirds are called petrels, but the abundant grey-faced petrel is typical of the largest and most widespread group, sometimes referred to as gadfly-petrels to distinguish them — although keen seabird watchers simply use the scientific name, *Pterodroma*. The two prominent characteristics of gadfly-petrels that distinguish them sharply from shearwaters (page 27) are that they are solitary at sea, and they are, like albatrosses, the 'real' seabirds — they inhabit the vast empty spaces between the continents, remaining far beyond sight of land except when visiting their nests. Many species of gadfly-petrels inhabit the Pacific Ocean and ten of them breed within New Zealand's territorial boundaries — the following five of them nowhere else:

Most of the mottled petrels in the world breed on the small islands surrounding Stewart Island, and on the Snares; the rest breed on a few islands off the coast of Fiordland and Southland. The species is now very rarely encountered at sea in New Zealand waters, but beach-wrecked specimens are found with some frequency, especially in the North Island in the summer months.

The group also includes the almost legendary taiko, which was collected during Captain James Cook's voyages but not again encountered for nearly two centuries, when the mystery bird was finally tracked down in the 1970s to its sole nesting grounds on the Chatham Islands.

Rangatira Island in the Chatham group is also the only known nesting place of the Chatham Island petrel. There are probably about 100 pairs in existence, but only a handful have ever been seen at sea.

Pycroft's petrel nests only on the Poor Knights Islands, the Hen and Chickens, and a handful of other islands off the eastern coast of the North Island; its oceanic distribution remains unknown. The total population is less than 1500 pairs.

Virtually all of the world's Cook's petrels — about 50,000 pairs — breed on Little Barrier Island; the rest — less than 200 pairs — nest on nearby Great Barrier Island, and on Codfish Island near Stewart Island. Small, with plain white underwings, Cook's petrel and Pycroft's petrel are nearly impossible to distinguish at sea. Gadfly-petrels breeding in New Zealand and elsewhere include the grey-faced petrel, Kermadec petrel and black-winged petrel.

Yellow-eyed Penguin

65 cm

Recognition About 65 cm in total length, this is the only penguin with yellow eyes — but the pale yellow plumage encircling the eye and extending backwards to the nape is equally distinctive and much more obvious.

Distribution The yellow-eyed penguin is entirely confined to New Zealand, breeding on Auckland and Campbell Islands as well as Stewart Island and the Canterbury, Otago and Southland coasts. The populations on Auckland and Campbell Islands seem reasonably secure, but Stewart and South Island populations are severely reduced due to destruction of nesting habitat. Recent estimates place the total population at around 1000 breeding pairs — probably the world's rarest penguin.

Habits Perhaps the most solitary of its tribe, the yellow-eyed penguin only occasionally forms loose and temporary groups, and even mated pairs spend time together only at the nest. They seldom wander far from their breeding sites, even outside the nesting season.

Food Mostly fish — especially red cod and mullet — and squid.

Breeding Yellow-eyed penguin mothers are extremely fussy about where they raise their young. The question of neighbours seems especially important — neighbouring pairs should be out of sight but within hearing distance. Dense shrubbery is also vital to shelter both chicks and brooding adults. Since European settlement, such habitat is now in very short supply.

The season begins in early September, when clutches of two faintly greenish eggs are laid. Incubated by both parents in alternate shifts lasting up to a week, these hatch in about 40–50 days. Chicks are brooded constantly for the first two weeks, but later they are visited only to be fed; they go to sea alone at about 106 days. The parents remain together at the nest while they moult — an unusually stressful process for penguins because they cannot go to sea and therefore cannot feed until their new coat of feathers is complete.

Order • Spheniciformes	**Species** • *Megadyptes antipodes*
Status • endemic; rare; resident	**Maori name** • takaraka, hoiho

Crested Penguins

60 cm

More than half of the world's penguins occur in the New Zealand region. In particular, New Zealand is the headquarters of a group called the crested penguins, rather large, long-tailed, stout-billed penguins that are not at all easy to tell apart. They make up the genus *Eudyptes*. All have long, bushy, bright yellow-orange plumes or tassels sweeping backwards from just above the eye.

As its name implies, the Fiordland crested penguin is found only in the quiet sounds and bays of Fiordland and Stewart Island, although vagrants occasionally wander north to Cook Strait. The most useful distinguishing feature of this species is that the tassels *droop* noticeably at the tips. This is an uncommon, very local, elusive penguin whose total numbers are probably something under 2500 pairs. Fiordland penguins are difficult to find because they are not markedly gregarious, nest in caves or under logs in deep forest and seldom loaf conspicuously along the shoreline.

With a total population of about 25,000 pairs, the Snares penguin breeds only on the Snares Islands, although the population on the Chatham Islands, now long extinct, may have belonged to this species. It is especially difficult to identify away from its breeding colonies, but is relatively short and squat in build, with more black on the underside of the flippers than other crested penguins. Its tassels are exceptionally bushy at the tips.

The erect-crested penguin closely resembles the last two species, except that its tassels sweep distinctly *upwards* at the tips. It breeds abundantly on Bounty and Antipodes Islands, in lesser numbers on Auckland and (until recently) Campbell Islands.

Immediately identifiable by its white face and throat, the royal penguin breeds in vast colonies on Macquarie Island. Its close relative the macaroni penguin, with a black throat, breeds

Erect-crested penguin

on South Georgia, South Shetland, and other nearby islands, but has been recorded as a straggler at Campbell and Snares Islands.

The rockhopper penguin breeds on Marion, Heard, Macquarie, Campbell, Antipodes and Auckland Islands in the Southern Ocean, and also at Tristan da Cunha and the Falkland Islands in the Atlantic. Its hairstyle is distinctly punk, its tassels standing out in all directions, and where other penguins walk, rockhoppers bound from boulder to boulder like humans in a sack race.

All of these penguins (except the macaroni penguin) occur on the shores of New Zealand's main islands — some species frequently, others only very rarely, and very often in search of a quiet and secluded beach on which to undergo the annual moult.

Blue Penguin

Recognition Also known (in Australia) as the little penguin or fairy penguin, the blue penguin is the smallest of all penguins; adults average about 40 cm in length and weigh around 1 kg. Easy to identify, they are plain steely blue above and satiny white below. The sexes are nearly identical, and young birds differ only in being markedly dingier in appearance.

Distribution Blue penguins frequent the cool temperate coastal waters of New Zealand and southern Australia (approximately from Brisbane to Perth). They are common around the coasts of all three main islands of New Zealand, as well as the Chatham Islands.

Habits Blue penguins are mainly solitary at sea but breed in colonies, usually on offshore islands, and also locally along mainland coasts. Fully mature birds that have successfully bred at least once tend to be sedentary, never moving very far from their nesting colonies, and form lifelong partnerships, returning to the same site year after year. Younger birds are much less attached to either site or partner, and may swap mates several times, or wander several hundred kilometres from their natal colony. Blue penguins sometimes call at sea — like a puppy barking — but they are most noisy at their breeding colonies, where the characteristic call is a long breathy moan followed by a brief upward wail.

Food Usually forages in shallow coastal waters, capturing mostly small fish such as anchovies.

Breeding Visited only at night, colonies vary in size from a few pairs to several hundred. Blue penguins commonly nest in burrows, but they sometimes select crevices between boulders, under jetties, or even the foundations of beach-side holiday baches. They usually breed near the shore, but nests may sometimes be several hundred metres inland. Two eggs form the usual clutch (normally laid about 3 days apart), and incubation takes about 36 days. Chicks are brooded constantly for their first 20 days, then visited only to be fed; they go to sea at about 56 days. Blue penguins commonly return to their colonies — and sometimes to the nest-site itself — to undergo their annual moult once their chicks have fledged, and after a few weeks at sea fattening up in preparation. Young birds return to their colonies to breed for the first time at two or three years of age.

Order • Sphenisciformes		**Species** • *Eudyptula minor*	
Status • native; common; resident		**Maori name** • korora	

Australasian Gannet

91 cm

Recognition Length about 85–91 cm, wingspan about 180 cm; sexes similar. Adults are easy to identify — look for pure white body, yellow head, black trailing edge to the wings and long, pointed, mainly black tail.

Distribution The Australasian gannet has nesting colonies in south-eastern Australia and New Zealand, mostly on small offshore islands around the North Island and in Cook Strait. There are, however, several mainland colonies, including an especially famous one at Cape Kidnappers. The total population is around 60,000 pairs, of which about 10,000 pairs are Australian; a few pairs nest also on Norfolk Island. Outside the breeding season, gannets are widespread throughout the region, including the Campbell, Auckland and Chatham Islands.

Habits Gannets are exclusively marine, but they usually forage over inshore waters within sight of land. They mate for life. Mature adults tend to be sedentary, but younger birds are migratory; many New Zealand-bred birds cross the Tasman Sea to spend several years in Australian waters, returning when they are old enough to breed themselves.

Food Almost exclusively small fish. Gannets catch most of their prey by plunge-diving from a height of 30 m or so. Spearing down bill-first on steeply back-angled wings, and sending up a dramatic plume of spray as they enter, they snatch their fish from below as they float back up to the surface. When a big school of fish is located near the surface, gannets often congregate in large numbers, hurling into the sea in salvo after salvo.

Breeding Colonies are reoccupied in July and egg-laying begins in late September, peaking through October. Colonies are generally large and crowded, and nests are typically about 1 m apart. One egg forms the clutch, and incubation lasts about 44 days. The chick leaves the colony as soon as it can fly, at about 100–110 days, and colonies are largely deserted throughout the non-breeding season.

Order • Pelecaniformes
Status • native; common; migrant

Species • *Morus serrator*
Maori name • takapu

Black Shag

Recognition Length about 80–85 cm; sexes alike. The black shag is easily recognised by its large size and almost entirely black plumage, with a conspicuous yellowish throat. When breeding it has white thighs, white cheeks and wiry white filaments on the neck. Gregarious but not social, it forages — apparently indiscriminately — alone, in small parties, or in large flocks, without any apparent preference for salt or fresh water.

ORDER • Pelecaniformes
SPECIES • *Phalacrocorax carbo*
STATUS • native; common; resident
MAORI NAME • kawau-tua-whenua

Distribution Also widely known as the great cormorant, this bird is widespread across much of North America, Europe, Africa, Asia, Australia, and New Zealand, where it is common in coastal waters and on interior wetlands of all kinds throughout all three main islands, as well as the Chatham Islands. Stragglers reach the Campbell Islands and the Snares Islands from time to time.

Little Shag

Recognition Length about 58 cm; sexes similar. A small, stocky shag, with a *stubby yellowish* bill. Black above, variably white below — in New Zealand often only the face and upper breast is white, and juveniles may be entirely black.

ORDER • Pelecaniformes
SPECIES • *Phalacrocorax melanoleucos*
STATUS • native; common; resident
MAORI NAME • kawaupaka

Distribution Otherwise known as the little pied cormorant or white-throated shag, the little shag is widespread from Malaysia through Indonesia and Australia to the Solomon Islands, New Caledonia and New Zealand, where it is common throughout all three main islands, straggling occasionally to Campbell Island. It visits farm dams more frequently than other shags. It tends to forage alone rather than in flocks, favours both fresh water and salt, and koura and aquatic insects tend to figure more prominently in the diet than is the case with the other three shags, which feed largely on fish.

Little Black Shag

60 cm

Recognition Length about 60 cm; sexes similar. In plumage the little black shag much resembles the black shag, but is appreciably smaller, less solidly built, with a relatively longer tail. Also note the much more slender bill. In breeding plumage it has inconspicuous white filaments on the neck.

ORDER • Pelecaniformes
SPECIES • *Phalacrocorax sulcirostris*
STATUS • native; uncommon; resident
MAORI NAME • kawaupaka

Distribution The little black shag's range extends from central Indonesia southward across Australia and eastward to New Caledonia and New Zealand, where it occurs on both main islands, but is much more common in the North Island. It tends to avoid marine waters and, though it often frequents coastal estuaries and sheltered inlets, shows an obvious preference for inland freshwaters of various kinds. It sometimes forms flocks — occasionally mixed with other shags — but it also often forages alone.

Pied Shag

82 cm

Recognition Length about 80–82 cm; sexes similar. About the size of a black shag, but with white underparts. Note blackish feet, pale slender bill, and small yellow patch in front of the eye. Like all shags, the pied shag often perches on rocks or in trees with wings outspread, and is usually silent, except in the vicinity of its nest.

ORDER • Pelecaniformes
SPECIES • *Phalacrocorax varius*
STATUS • native; common; resident
MAORI NAME • karuhiruhi

Distribution Confined to Australia and New Zealand, the pied shag is widespread in the North Island, South Island and Stewart Island, as well as some of the closer offshore groups; stragglers occasionally visit the Snares. Unlike the little shag, it favours extensive wetlands, and is usually encountered on harbours and sheltered inlets on the coast, and large lakes and broad rivers inland. Estimates place the total New Zealand population of pied shag at around 10,000 birds.

Stewart Island Shag

Auckland Island shag

Stewart Island shag

Recognition Length about 68 cm, weight about 2.3 kg; sexes alike. Easily recognised by its pink feet, the Stewart Island shag is variable in plumage. Most birds are black above, white below, with conspicuous white shoulder patches, but some birds also have a white rump, and many others are entirely bronze-black in colour.

Distribution This shag is confined to Stewart Island and the southern coasts of the South Island where it is a common sight loafing in small groups on low rocky headlands.

Habits The Stewart Island shag is exclusively marine, but seldom forages at any great distance out to sea, preferring to dive for its food in

shallow seas up to 15 km from land. Although often seen alone, it usually occurs in small groups except when congregated at its breeding colonies. Strongly sedentary, it belongs to a group of marine cormorants (usually called shags elsewhere) that is especially characteristic of subantarctic islands in the Southern Ocean, including those in the New Zealand region. New Zealand has six species, including two on the main islands (King shag and Stewart Island shag) and several confined to the island groups indicated by their names: Chatham Island shag; Campbell Island shag; Bounty Island shag; and Auckland Island shag.

Food Mostly fish, but the Stewart Island shag also takes crabs, squid, octopus, polychaete worms and similar small marine invertebrates.

Breeding The Stewart Island shag breeds in colonies mostly containing up to about 50–60 pairs. Two or three eggs make up the usual clutch, and the chicks, like those of other shags, are black-skinned and naked on hatching. Few other details are known.

ORDER • Pelecaniformes	**SPECIES**	• *Leucocarbo chalconotus*
STATUS • endemic; common; resident	**MAORI NAME**	• mapua

Spotted Shag

73 cm

Recognition   Length about 73 cm; sexes alike. The spotted shag is much more slender and more elegant than other shags or cormorants, with a narrow bill and yellowish feet. In breeding plumage it is unmistakable — bronze-grey above with bold black spots; black throat; jade green face; broad white eyebrow stripe; and two jaunty crests (arranged fore and aft). The more dingy winter plumage — whitish underparts, drab grey head — is, however, worn for much of the year.

Distribution   The spotted shag is confined to the three main islands of New Zealand, where it is is common on rocky shores, headlands and offshore islands. The total population is probably around 50,000 pairs.

Habits   Unlike ducks and other waterbirds, cormorants and shags lack waterproof plumage. Waterlogged plumage reduces buoyancy, thus reducing the energy required to chase fish under water as well as the time spent beneath the surface. One of the most distinctive behavioural characteristics of cormorants and shags is their habit of coming ashore after foraging to stand, often in groups, for an hour or so with their wings outstretched in heraldic pose, giving their plumage time to dry. Spotted shags also have the habit of swallowing small pebbles — it is not known why —perhaps to reduce buoyancy still further. Almost exclusively marine, they usually forage a kilometre or so out to sea, but frequently enter sheltered coastal waters such as estuaries, harbours and inlets, to loaf and preen on stacks, rocky headlands, or human-built structures such as buoys or channel markers. Gregarious but not social, they fish either alone or in flocks.

Food   Mainly fish and small crustaceans, captured — as with other cormorants and shags — by diving from the surface.

Breeding   Spotted shags nest in colonies, usually on coastal cliffs or stacks. The breeding season is very variable, both from year to year and colony to colony. The nest is an untidy heap of grass, seaweed, ice plant and similar vegetation. Three eggs form the normal clutch. The parents incubate in alternate shifts, and the chicks hatch in about 30 days, fledging about 55 days later.

ORDER • Pelecaniformes
STATUS • endemic; common; resident

SPECIES • *Stictocarbo punctatus*
MAORI NAME • parekareka

White-faced Heron

68 cm

Recognition   Length about 66–68 cm; sexes similar. The most abundant heron in New Zealand, the white-faced heron is easily recognised by its plain bluish-grey plumage and white face.

Distribution   The species is widespread from eastern Indonesia south throughout Australia and eastward to the Solomon Islands, New Guinea, New Caledonia and New Zealand. Although now common virtually throughout New Zealand, including the Chatham, Campbell and Kermadec Islands, it was formerly known only as a rare straggler until a pair was found breeding in 1941. Its present abundance is the result of an early 1960s population explosion.

Habits   The white-faced heron's success in New Zealand is probably largely attributable to its ability to find food in almost any wetland environment, from roadside ditches to the margins of large lakes, and even marine habitats such as beaches and tide pools. In summer it usually forages alone, sometimes defending discrete foraging territories, at least under some circumstances, but in winter it roosts communally and often feeds in flocks. It is mostly sedentary, but there is some evidence of movement from harsher climates and higher altitudes in autumn in the South Island. It is rather silent, except at the nest, but it sometimes utters a guttural croaking note in flight.

Food   Although small fish such as bullies are often taken, the bulk of the diet consists of aquatic insects and their larvae, koura, molluscs, tadpoles, frogs and small reptiles.

Breeding   The breeding season varies widely with locality but mainly peaks in October to December. The nesting site, often shared with several other pairs, is typically a small and isolated grove of tall trees, not necessarily near water. The nest is a loose untidy pile of sticks, and three to five eggs make up the normal clutch. Incubation, by both parents, lasts about 24–25 days. Chicks remain in the nest until they fledge at 38–42 days.

Order • Ciconiiformes
Status • native; common; resident

Species • *Ardea novaehollandiae*
Maori name • matuku

Reef Heron

66 cm

Recognition   Length about 61–66 cm; sexes similar. Entirely slate-grey (though in the tropics many individuals are pure white). The only heron-like bird commonly seen on the ocean shore. Occasionally white-faced herons and white herons spend an hour or so fishing on the shore (and habitually forage on estuarine mudflats) but the well-named reef heron feeds nowhere else.

Distribution   The reef heron is widespread from Burma through the Philippines, New Guinea and Australia eastward to Japan, New Zealand and the islands of the south-western Pacific. In New Zealand it occurs around the coasts of all three main islands, as well as the Kermadecs and the Chatham Islands, but it is much more common in the North Island than elsewhere. Vagrants have been recorded at the Auckland Islands.

Habits   This heron is especially characteristic of coral reefs, but it also commonly frequents rocky coasts, headlands and sometimes visits beaches and even estuarine mudflats. When foraging it is strictly solitary and will not tolerate neighbours, but it often roosts or loafs between tides, in small flocks. There is some evidence of a population decline in recent decades. It is usually silent away from the nest.

Food   Mostly small fish, captured in tide pools and similar places. Much of its prey is captured by stalking in a distinctively hunched, stealthy, arthritic posture. Because foraging is dictated by tides, it hunts indiscriminately by night or day.

Breeding   The breeding cycle begins in late September. Nesting is usually in solitary pairs and the nest, sometimes reused and added to over several years, is an untidy structure of sticks and debris placed in a tree, under a bush, or in a cave or rock crevice. The clutch is two or three eggs, which hatch in 25–28 days. The chicks fledge at about 42 days and scatter from the territory very soon afterwards. Both parents cooperate fully in nest building, incubation and rearing the young.

ORDER • Ciconiiformes
STATUS • native; uncommon; resident

SPECIES • *Egretta sacra*
MAORI NAME • matuku-moana

White Heron

Recognition Length about 90 cm; sexes alike. Plumage entirely white. Very long slender neck, with obvious midway kink. The white heron is usually solitary and is a prominent exponent of the 'stand-and-wait' hunting tactic, much less likely to stalk or chase prey than the smaller herons. The diet includes small aquatic creatures of all kinds, from fish to frogs and koura.

ORDER • Ciconiiformes
SPECIES • *Ardea alba*
STATUS • native; uncommon; migrant
MAORI NAME • kotuku

Distribution The white heron's range is virtually worldwide in tropical and warm temperate regions. In New Zealand it has only one breeding colony, near Okarito in south Westland, but outside the breeding season it scatters to all parts of New Zealand, sometimes wandering as far afield as the Auckland Islands and the Chathams. White herons frequent shallow wetlands of all kinds, including estuarine mudflats.

Royal Spoonbill

Recognition Length about 76–80 cm; sexes similar. Identity immediately obvious by the extraordinary black, flattened, spoon-shaped bill. Plumage entirely white, with a shock of long white plumes on the back of the head in summer. In flight, herons tuck their heads well back between their shoulders, but spoonbills fly with neck fully extended. Spoonbill foraging is also very distinctive — the bird wades in shallow water, sweeping its bill from side to side in steady, rhythmical arcs to filter out minute snails, crustaceans and similar aquatic animals.

ORDER • Ciconiiformes
SPECIES • *Platalea regia*
STATUS • native; uncommon; resident
MAORI NAME • kotuku-ngutupapa

Distribution The royal spoonbill occurs across much of Indonesia, New Guinea and Australia. Only a few hundred spoonbills inhabit New Zealand, but these scatter widely after breeding to many of the broad river estuaries, especially in the North Island (notably the estuary of the Manawatu River).

Cattle Egret

Recognition   Length about 51 cm; sexes alike. Easily identifiable as a small, stocky, short-necked heron with a rather stout, bright yellow bill — although the bird often gives away its identity instantly by riding on a cow's back. Unlike other herons and egrets, cattle egrets seldom forage in shallow water, and are usually seen in close association with cows, sheep or other domestic livestock. The plumage is entirely white except during the breeding season, when the head and breast are strongly suffused with rich rusty orange.

Distribution   Cattle egrets visiting from Australia were first recorded in New Zealand in 1963. Noted alone or in pairs at first, by the early 1970s the pairs had become dozens, and by the early 1980s the dozens had grown to hundreds. Now the cattle egret visits New Zealand in large numbers every winter, and banding studies have confirmed a regular, two-way, trans-Tasman passage.

Habits   Cattle egrets are gregarious birds that roost, travel, forage and nest in flocks, often very large. Occasionally they visit marshes and swamps to forage with other herons, but mainly they are grassland birds with no particular attachment to water. They forage by snatching at grasshoppers and similar prey flushed from long grass by the movement of cattle. Originally confined to Africa and southern Asia, cattle egrets underwent a spectacular range expansion between about 1900 and 1940. Unaided by humans, they crossed the Atlantic to colonise both North and South America, meanwhile also moving north into Europe and eastward to Australia. Today the cattle egret's range is virtually global, wherever cattle are grazed.

Food   Small animals of all kinds, including earthworms, spiders, ticks, frogs, mice and ground-dwelling insects such as crickets, flies, and grasshoppers.

Breeding   Cattle egrets nest in colonies, usually in trees overhanging water, and very often in company with other species of herons and egrets. Built by the male, the nest is a rough platform of sticks in a tree-fork, usually at least 3 m from the ground. Both sexes incubate the five or six eggs, which take about 22–23 days to hatch. Not known to breed in New Zealand.

ORDER • Ciconiiformes	**SPECIES**	• *Bubulcus ibis*
STATUS • native; common; migrant	**MAORI NAME**	• none

Black Swan

1.5 m

Recognition Unmistakable, as the world's only all-black swan (but in flight it reveals white wingtips). Black swans average about 1.5 m in length, with a wingspan of nearly 2 m, and they weigh around 6 kg. The sexes are nearly identical in appearance but males are a little larger than females and have slightly longer, more slender necks. Chicks are dull grey.

Distribution Originally confined to Australia, the black swan has been widely introduced elsewhere in the world. It was brought to New Zealand as a game bird in the 1860s and is now widespread on wetlands of all kinds throughout the country, including the Chatham Islands.

Food Almost entirely vegetarian in diet, black swans usually feed in shallow water, using their long necks to explore the bottom for aquatic plants. In slightly deeper water they freely 'up-end', tail in the air, like ducks. Occasionally they forage on land, grazing like geese.

Habits Black swans are nomadic and strongly gregarious when not breeding; they form large flocks and travel freely from one lake to another, sometimes by day but more often at night. Like other wildfowl, black swans moult all of their flight feathers at once, and are therefore flightless for several weeks while the new feathers grow. During this vulnerable period, swans congregate far out in the centre of large shallow lakes and coastal lagoons.

Breeding Domestic arrangements among black swans are flexible. Nesting may be solitary or colonial and initiated at almost any time. Older birds generally pair for life but divorce is common among younger birds, and nesting trios and even same-sex pairs are not unknown. The nest is a large untidy heap of reeds and grasses, often moored in shallow water and savagely defended against trespass by neighbouring pairs. The usual clutch consists of five or six eggs and takes 35–45 days to hatch. Led to water immediately after hatching, the chicks fledge at about 160 days, but remain with their parents for many weeks thereafter.

Order • Anseriformes	**Species** • *Cygnus atratus*
Status • introduced; common; resident	**Maori name** • wani

Canada Goose

Recognition   Dull brown body and black head and neck, contrasting with white chin and cheek, arranged like a broad chin strap. The sexes are alike, although females are slightly smaller than males. Young birds are noticeably dingier and fluffy, newly-hatched goslings are mainly brown above, bright yellow below.

Distribution   A native of North America, the Canada goose was brought to New Zealand as a game bird in 1905 and again in 1920. Although it quickly built up and maintains a large population (a peak annual total of about 20,000 birds), it has shown little propensity to spread far beyond the first introduction sites. Most assemble at Lake Ellesmere and nearby Lake Forsyth, and almost all nest in the headwaters of major Canterbury rivers, such as the Clarence and the Rangitata. Except for a few that breed in the North Island, Canada geese visit only casually elsewhere in New Zealand.

Food   Canada geese are terrestrial grazing birds; grasses, clovers, cereals and similar plants make up most of their diet. However, they also sometimes forage, swan-like, in shallow water. Culling has sometimes been necessary to control damage to pasture.

Habits   Mature birds often form permanent pairs that remain together even outside the breeding season, and young birds form family units with their parents until they are chased off at the start of the next breeding season. Such family units spend much of the year with others, combined in large flocks that feed and travel together but disperse to nest. When travelling any significant distance, Canada geese usually fly in V-formation. The annual moult takes place on the wintering grounds. Calls include hisses in alarm or threat and a characteristic loud, trumpeted honking note.

Breeding   In New Zealand the season begins around the third week of September. Often far from water, nests are built of grasses and lined with down from the female's breast. The male guards his mate while she alone incubates her clutch of, usually, five or six white eggs. They hatch at about 30 days and the chicks are led from the nest when all have hatched and are dry. Geese guard their chicks solicitously, but do not feed them.

Order • Anseriformes
Status • introduced; common; resident

Species • *Branta canadensis*
Maori name • kuihi

Paradise Shelduck

62 cm

Habits An abundant and conspicuous species, the paradise shelduck is most numerous where livestock are grazed, but it is also common on grassy river flats, the margins of lakes, and it occasionally visits estuarine mudflats. Forming lifelong pair-bonds, it is usually encountered in pairs or family parties, but youngsters and non-breeding birds form flocks. Young birds are nomadic but adults seldom stray far from their territories, except for about two months during the annual moult, which is communal. Flocks are extremely noisy, both in flight and on land, but the most characteristic call is the male's goose-like honk, which has been transcribed as *zonk-zonk*, and the female's high-pitched, piercing *zeek-zeek*. Shelduck are widely hunted, making up around 10 per cent of the total waterfowl harvest and the population is closely monitored.

Food Although they feed on small animals such as insects and earthworms as opportunity offers, paradise shelducks are largely vegetarian: they graze open turf, like geese, sometimes causing damage to grain and cereal crops, and take the seeds of a wide range of aquatic plants.

Recognition Length about 62 cm. Males and females differ strikingly: the male looks mostly blackish at any distance, whereas the female is chestnut, with a white head. A large white patch on each upper wing is obvious even at a considerable distance.

Distribution Confined to New Zealand, the paradise shelduck is widespread on the three main islands, including many of the larger offshore groups, such as Kapiti, Great Barrier Island and Little Barrier Island. Formerly resident on the Chatham Islands, it now appears to be merely a rare vagrant there.

Breeding Egg-laying peaks in October. Shelducks resemble geese in nesting as a family unit, with both parents participating fully — though the female alone incubates while the male stands guard. The nest site, usually under cover of some kind, is variable; it may be on the ground, or up to 20 m high in a tree. The nest is a rough bowl of plant material densely lined with down. The clutch consists of 8–12 eggs and incubation takes about 30 days. The chicks are led to water by both parents the day after they hatch, and they can fly at about 55 days.

ORDER • Anseriformes	**SPECIES** • *Tadorna variegata*
STATUS • endemic; common; resident	**MAORI NAME** • putangitangi

Blue Duck

53 cm

Recognition Difficult to confuse with anything else in its restricted habitat, the blue duck is easily identified as a plain, slate-blue duck with a whitish bill. The sexes are alike in plumage, and young birds are similar but duller.

Distribution One of the most highly specialised of all the world's waterfowl, the blue duck is confined to New Zealand's rushing mountain torrents. Although uncommon to rare, it remains widespread in alpine regions of both North and South Islands, wherever suitable habitat exists.

Food Mostly aquatic insects, occasionally taken by diving, up-ending, or snatched from the surface, but most characteristically by nibbling systematically over the downstream faces of boulders in shallow white water, wading with only the head and neck under the surface.

Habits Rather secretive in behaviour, the blue duck feeds largely at dawn and dusk, spending most of the day hidden against shaded banks or among log jams, where it can be very hard to see. It is extremely territorial and pairs regularly patrol their 'patch' — usually about 1 km of stream — to prevent the incursion of trespassers. Except in very hard winters, blue ducks seldom leave their territories, and even young birds, newly evicted from their parents' territory, seem unwilling to wander far. The male's characteristic call — often the best way of locating the bird — is a high-pitched, wheezy whistle, which sounds much like its Maori name 'whio'; the female has several low-pitched, grating notes.

Breeding The breeding season is variable, but usually begins in August. Placed in almost any convenient streamside shelter, nests are little more than piles of twigs and debris raked together, with very little down. The clutch varies from four to nine. As in all ducks, the female incubates alone, but the period remains uncertain (about 31 days in artificial incubators). Escorted constantly (but not fed) by their parents, chicks fledge at about 75 days.

ORDER • Anseriformes
STATUS • endemic; uncommon; resident

SPECIES • *Hymenolaimus malacorhynchus*
MAORI NAME • whio

Mallard

60 cm

Recognition Length about 58–60 cm. The male mallard, or drake, is easily recognised by its iridescent green head, mahogany breast and narrow white collar. Females are plain and brown, very easily mistaken for grey ducks except for their drab faces.

Distribution The mallard is native to North America, Eurasia, and north-western Africa. Introduced into New Zealand for sport in the 1930s, it is now widespread on all three main islands, and vastly outnumbers the indigenous but very closely related grey duck (estimated national population about five million, versus the grey duck's half million).

Habits Strongly gregarious, mallard inhabit a wide range of wetlands but they are uncommon on the coast and rare along remote rivers and streams. They do best in farming country with abundant water in the form of stock dams, lagoons and meandering rivers. Where unpersecuted — as on ornamental ponds in city parks — mallard are among the tamest of

wildfowl, and often join pigeons to be fed picnic scraps. Their status in New Zealand as the most abundant dabbling duck is in dramatic contrast to the situation in Australia, where — despite early introduction in the 1860s — mallard remain largely confined to urban and suburban habitats. The most common call is the female's well-known, raucous *quaak-quaak-quaak* — familiar as the quack of the ordinary domestic duck.

Food Mallard are omnivorous. Much of their food consists of the fruits and seeds of aquatic and other plants — often grain — but it also takes a wide range of small aquatic animals, including insects, pond snails and tadpoles. Although it often forages ashore, it usually feeds in shallow water, by dabbling and up-ending.

Breeding The nest is a simple bowl of vegetation on the ground, usually hidden in thick grass or under a bush. Peak laying is in October, and 8–14 eggs make up the clutch. Incubation takes about 27 days.

Order • Anseriformes	**Species** • *Anas platyrhynchos*
Status • introduced; common; resident	**Maori name** • rakiraki

Grey Duck

Recognition   Length about 55 cm; sexes alike. One of the distinctive features of wildfowl is a large rectangular patch of metallic colour, called the speculum, on the trailing edge of the upper side of the inner wing. In the grey duck the speculum is bright iridescent green, conspicuous on the otherwise entirely dark-brown upperwing. At rest, pure-bred grey ducks are easily distinguished by their 'zebra-stripe' faces, complicated to describe but quickly recognised. They frequently interbreed with the introduced mallard (opposite).

ORDER •	Anseriformes
SPECIES •	*Anas superciliosa*
STATUS •	native; common; resident
MAORI NAME •	parera

Distribution   Known elsewhere as the Pacific black duck, this species is widespread from Indonesia and Australia eastward to New Zealand and much of Polynesia. In New Zealand it is widespread, but generally favours the more remote interior wetlands. The estimated national population is about 500,000.

Grey Teal

Recognition   Length about 43 cm; sexes similar. Among the smallest of New Zealand wildfowl, grey teal are best identified on the water by the abrupt contrast between dark brown cap and pale face, cheeks and throat; in flight, look for a conspicuous white triangle on the upper wing. Like mallards, grey teal are members of the 'dabbling ducks', distinguished by their habit of 'nibbling' for minute particles of food on the surface of mud and water.

ORDER •	Anseriformes
SPECIES •	*Anas gracilis*
STATUS •	native; common; migrant
MAORI NAME •	tete

Distribution   This species extends from Indonesia through Australia to the Solomon Islands, New Caledonia and New Zealand, where it is widespread but scattered on all three main islands, most numerous in the North Island and Otago. It is highly mobile, and its numbers are boosted substantially by immigrants in times of severe drought in Australia.

New Zealand Shoveler

53 cm

Recognition   Length 45–53 cm. The male's white flanks are a conspicuous field-mark even when considerable distance renders all other colours indistinguishable; with practice, shovelers can also be identified even as a distant silhouette — they ride much lower in the water than other dabbling ducks, and the head is appreciably bigger, the neck shorter, and the bill long and wedge-shaped. At close range, the male is unmistakable, with grey-blue head, mahogany sides, a vertical crescent of white just before the eye — as well as the unique, broad, shovel-shaped bill. Females are drab brown, and best identified by shape. Even in flight the shoveler is distinctive, much swifter and more agile in the air, and with a large, diagnostic powder-blue patch on the upper wing.

Distribution   The New Zealand shoveler is confined to south-western and south-eastern Australia and New Zealand, where it is widespread on the main islands although nowhere numerous (the national population is probably about 150,000 birds).

Habits   Shovelers prefer extensive, shallow, raupo-fringed freshwater marshes in the lowlands, of the kind most threatened in New Zealand because they are highly fertile and under constant pressure for drainage and reclamation as valuable agricultural land. Extremely wary, shovelers usually remain well away from wetland margins, mingling inconspicuously with other ducks. They are highly mobile, given to wandering far and seldom remaining long in one place.

Food   The large spatulate bill is fringed with small comb-like projections (called lamellae) which function like a sieve to filter small creatures from the water; the diet is almost entirely animal, supplemented occasionally by small seeds. Most feeding is at night.

Breeding   Shovelers build well-hidden nests on the ground near water. The clutch consists of 8–10 eggs, which hatch in about 25 days. The male occasionally helps guard the ducklings but for the most part is little involved in nesting.

ORDER • Anseriformes
STATUS • native; common; resident

SPECIES • *Anas rhynchotis*
MAORI NAME • kuru whengi

New Zealand Scaup

Recognition   Length about 40 cm. Easily identified as the only diving duck in New Zealand, and by its rich, dark, glossy plumage, especially on the head. Females resemble males but are paler and browner, with a band of white surrounding the base of the bill. In flight, scaup show a broad white bar on an otherwise dark upper wing, and are difficult to distinguish from the closely related hardhead. Once common in the North Island, hardhead were extinct by 1900, but are still reported occasionally as vagrants from Australia. Hardheads are warm brown, where scaup are black, a distinction obvious at close hand but deceptive at any distance. More reliable is the hardhead's white under-tail and distinctive 'two-tone' bill.

Distribution   Confined to New Zealand, this scaup is widespread on both main islands, but it is most common on high country lakes of both the North and South Islands.

Habits   Scaup favour large, deep bodies of freshwater, such as lakes and reservoirs. They generally shun both running water and marine environments and, on the whole, they tend to leave shallow, marshy wetlands to the dabbling ducks — though they often visit briefly. They are strongly gregarious, and usually travel, loaf and forage in small groups or large flocks — on occasion they even nest in dispersed colonies. Pair bonds last only one season. Like most ducks, they tend to feed most actively in the evening and early morning, or even at night, and they often doze through the hours around midday. Underwater, both steering and propulsion are supplied by the broad, splayed feet, the wings remaining closed. The total population is probably about 20,000 birds.

Food   Little is known of the diet, beyond that it includes both the seeds and shoots of submerged plants, and such small aquatic animals as insect larvae, tadpoles and freshwater crustaceans.

Breeding   Nesting peaks in October and November. Usually on the ground, well hidden in waterside vegetation, nests are rough, down-lined piles of reeds or coarse grass. Clutches contain five to eight eggs and incubation takes about 28–30 days. The male plays no part in incubation, but he remains on guard close by, and joins his mate to help rear the ducklings once they have hatched.

ORDER • Anseriformes	**SPECIES**	• *Aythya novaeseelandiae*
STATUS • endemic; common; resident	**MAORI NAME**	• papango

Australasian Harrier

58 cm

Recognition Length 50–58 cm; sexes similar. Mainly brown, with a distinctive white rump. Most easily identified by its characteristic flight: broad-winged and long-tailed, its aerodynamics allow an extremely low airspeed without stalling which gives the bird ample time to minutely scan the ground below for small, well-hidden prey in dense grass. A hunting harrier systematically quarters reed beds or crops at a height of 6–8 m, in brief flurries of wingbeats interspersed with long glides on upswept wings, often rocking slightly from side to side in the breeze, and pouncing when anything is detected.

Distribution The Australasian harrier occurs in New Guinea, Australia, New Zealand, New Caledonia, Fiji and many other islands of the south-western Pacific region. In New Zealand it is widespread on all three main islands — including many offshore islands — as well as the Kermadecs and Chatham Islands. It is a fairly frequent visitor to Campbell and Auckland Islands.

Habits The harrier inhabits open, treeless, lowland country of all kinds. It usually hunts alone, but at evening it gathers at communal roosts — small in summer, much larger in winter — to spend the night. During the breeding season, pairs mutually defend territories — typically about 30 ha in extent — but they hunt over a much wider area of up to 8 or 9 sq km. Often seen on roads as it feeds off carrion. The most common call is a faint, plaintive *kee-aa*, but harriers are usually silent away from the nest.

Breeding Egg-laying peaks in October, but this follows many weeks of residence on the territory and frequent flight displays in courtship. Nests are built on the ground with three or four eggs forming the usual clutch. The incubation period is 32–34 days and the young can fly at about 40–50 days. The female builds and broods alone while the male supplies her food; he may also bring food for the chicks, but he often loses interest in his family after the first week or two.

ORDER • Falconiformes
STATUS • native; common; resident

SPECIES • *Circus approximans*
MAORI NAME • kahu

New Zealand Falcon

47 cm

Recognition Falcons are hawk-like, but with narrow, pointed wings, slender tails and a dashing, impetuous flight style. Only two species occur in New Zealand: the nankeen kestrel, a rare straggler from Australia, is very small, pale rust above, and habitually hovers — something the second species, the endemic and dark-backed New Zealand falcon, very seldom does.

Distribution The New Zealand falcon is uncommon and local but widespread in rugged, mountainous country on all three main islands and the Auckland Islands. It has been recorded as a rare straggler to Campbell Island. Strongholds include the Nelson Lakes region and the Mackenzie district but, subject to human persecution and unusually vulnerable to the residual effects of pesticides, it is probably declining steadily in number. Its total population is estimated at under 5000 pairs.

Food This is a powerful, relentless and versatile predator, using a wide repertoire of tactics to overpower mainly birds up to the size of grey ducks and herons, but also other small animals ranging from skinks to hares and rabbits. Falcons frequently raid the nests of other birds, and catch dragonflies and beetles in midair — sometimes, apparently, just for fun.

Habits Although birds sometimes wander in winter when food is scarce, for the most part the New Zealand falcon is sedentary. Birds apparently mate for life and jointly defend permanent territories, but are usually solitary when hunting. Calls include chittering notes in courtship and squeals during disputes, but the most distinctive and frequent call is a sharp, stuttering *kek-kek-kek-kek-kek*.

Breeding Falcons generally do not build nests, usually laying their eggs on the bare rock of a sheltered ledge on a cliff, although New Zealand falcons occasionally nest on the ground or in dead trees. Three eggs make up the normal clutch. Shared by both parents, incubation takes 30–33 days, and the young can fly about 35 days after hatching.

Order • Falconiformes	**Species** • *Falco novaeseelandiae*
Status • endemic; uncommon; resident	**Maori name** • karearea

California Quail

24 cm

Recognition Length about 24 cm. Easily
recognised as a small bluish grey gamebird with
a black face and a black, forward-curving crest
or topknot on the forehead. The sexes are
similar, except that the female is slightly smaller
and duller, and her face is grey, not black.
California quail mostly live in family parties in
summer, larger flocks or coveys in winter. They
live mostly on the ground, but often perch on
fence posts or fallen timber.

ORDER • Galliformes
SPECIES • *Lophortyx californica*
STATUS • introduced; common; resident
MAORI NAME • kuera

Distribution A native of western North
America from Vancouver Island to Mexico, the
California quail has been widely introduced
elsewhere, including New Zealand in 1862.
Widespread in the North Island and northern
and eastern parts of the South Island, it is most
common in open scrub and mixed farmland,
especially where the average yearly rainfall is
between 500 and 1500 mm.

Brown Quail

18 cm

Recognition Length about 18 cm; sexes
similar. A very small, round-bodied, chicken-
like bird with a negligible tail and intricately
marked brown plumage. Usually they are
difficult to see unless accidentally flushed, when
they whirr away on short round wings, low and
swift, for 100 m or so before pitching back into
dense grass. Fond of dust-bathing, they can
sometimes be found along quiet dirt roads or
tracks. They live entirely on the ground, usually
in coveys of half a dozen or so birds.

ORDER • Galliformes
SPECIES • *Coturnix ypsilophora*
STATUS • introduced; common; resident
MAORI NAME • kuera

Distribution The brown quail is widespread
in Indonesia, New Guinea and Australia and has
been introduced to Fiji and New Zealand. It was
released numerous times and in many places
from about 1860 on, but it failed to establish in
the South Island and is common only in parts of
the North Island. It favours rough, often
swampy grassland.

Ring-necked Pheasant

90 cm

Recognition   Length 60–90 cm. Unmistakable — a large, chicken-like bird with a very long, pointed tail. Males are copper-coloured, with bottle-green heads, red cheeks and a narrow white collar; females are substantially smaller, shorter-tailed, and sober brown in colour.

Distribution   Originally widespread across Asia, the ring-necked pheasant was introduced into Europe centuries ago, and from there to other parts of the world. First brought to New Zealand in 1842, the pheasant now occurs across much of the North Island and parts of the eastern coastal strip of the South Island.

Habits   Pheasants are common in rough or mixed farming country, especially where there are scattered thickets, copses, hedgerows or scrub-filled gullies for cover. They live alone for much of the year, normally seen in groups only in hard weather. Strongly sedentary, they seldom wander far from their home ranges. They spend much of their time in dense cover, often to be seen only when inadvertently flushed, when

they rocket up on noisy wings, uttering a loud *korrrk* of alarm, fly swift and low for a few hundred metres, then pitch back into cover. They usually roost in trees. Seed-eating songbirds, such as finches, owe their success to their efficient seed-cracking bills, but gamebirds, such as pheasants, habitually swallow fine grit or gravel to achieve the same result internally, in the muscular gizzard.

Food   The diet is extremely varied, and includes green leaves and shoots, seeds, berries, and insects.

Breeding   The pheasant is polygamous. Each successful male mates with several females, no pair bond is formed, and the male plays no part in nesting. The nest is a mere depression in the ground, lined with grass and usually well hidden in a thicket. Nine eggs make up a typical clutch. Incubation takes about 24 days, and the fluffy chicks follow their mother away as soon as they are dry. They can fly short distances by their twelfth day.

ORDER • Galliformes
STATUS • introduced; common; resident

SPECIES • *Phasianus colchicus*
MAORI NAME • peihana

Australasian Bittern

76 cm

Distribution This bittern inhabits south-eastern and far south-western Australia (including Tasmania), New Zealand, New Caledonia and the Loyalty Islands. In New Zealand it occurs in suitable habitat on all three main islands (including several of the larger and closer offshore islands), but it appears to be extinct on the Chatham Islands.

Habits The bittern is fairly rigidly confined to extensive, shallow, permanent, freshwater wetlands with large stands of dense reeds. Solitary, sedentary and elusive, it seldom leaves the cover of dense vegetation except to forage, and even then mainly at night or at dawn or dusk. The male's distinctive territorial calls are a prominent feature of suitable wetlands at dusk — a low, hollow, booming note. The total New Zealand population is probably less than 1000 birds. The bittern is probably a 'lynchpin' species in New Zealand wetlands, the essence of the concept being that, if a given swamp can be conserved and managed in such a way that its bittern population remains intact, then the chances are very good that all other inhabitants of the marsh are doing well also.

Recognition Length about 66–76 cm; sexes similar. The bittern is a typical heron in everything but its brown, intricately marbled, mottled and streaked plumage, and in its extraordinarily secretive habits. Once glimpsed, however, its identity is obvious. When disturbed, it is most likely to face the threat and freeze, bill pointed at the sky — its streaked breast is then all but impossible to distinguish from surrounding reeds, and the bird may even sway gently from side to side to mimic a light breeze. It is usually encountered only when accidentally flushed at close range, when it lumbers clumsily into the air, flies low for 50 m or so, then plunges back into deep cover.

Food The diet consists largely of frogs, reptiles, aquatic insects, koura and small fish, mostly obtained by slow, stealthy stalking.

Breeding Breeding is in solitary pairs, but little is known of the pair bond — it appears to last only through a single breeding cycle and males are not known to assist nesting in any way. The nest is a saucer of trampled reeds, well hidden in dense cover. Four or five eggs make up the clutch. Incubation lasts about 25 days, and chicks take about 50 days to fledge.

ORDER • Ciconiiformes		**SPECIES** • *Botaurus poiciloptilus*	
STATUS • native; uncommon; resident		**MAORI NAME** • matuku-hurepo	

Banded Rail

31 cm

Recognition About 31 cm in total length, the banded rail looks very like a miniature weka in shape and proportions, but with an intricate plumage pattern that includes narrowly barred black and white underparts, a band of warm buff across the breast and a conspicuous white streak above the eye. Fed, brooded and guarded by both parents, the fluffy chicks are plain soot black. Extremely secretive, but not especially shy, it is best located by its most common call which resembles the screech of a very rusty gate.

ORDER • Gruiformes
SPECIES • *Gallirallus philippensis*
STATUS • native; uncommon; resident
MAORI NAME • moho-pereru

Distribution Widespread throughout much of Australasia, from Australia to Indonesia, the Philippines, and islands of the south-west Pacific. Reported on all three main islands of New Zealand and many offshore groups, most frequently from Auckland northwards, where it is most common in mangrove swamps.

Crakes

19 cm

Crakes constitute a worldwide group of species, all of which rather resemble a minute pukeko in all but colour, and the fact that they are intensely secretive, seldom leave the shelter of dense marsh vegetation, and are extremely difficult to see. Two species occur in New Zealand: marsh crake and spotless crake.

ORDER • Gruiformes
SPECIES • *Porzana* spp.
STATUS • native; uncommon; resident
MAORI NAME • puweto, koitareke

The marsh crake can be identified by its greenish legs, barred flanks, and streaked upperparts. Widespread from Australia to Europe, little is known of either distribution or behaviour in New Zealand, beyond that reports are scattered, sporadic, and possibly more frequent in the South Island than elsewhere.

The spotless crake is a little larger than the marsh crake, with plain brown upperparts, solid grey head, breast and flanks, and red legs. Widespread from Australia to Oceania, in New Zealand it seems to be most common in the North Island.

Spotless crake

Weka

53 cm

Recognition Length about 53 cm; sexes similar. Unmistakable. Flightless. The plumage colour is extremely variable, ranging from strongly rufous through various shades of brown to buff and greyish.

Distribution Confined to the three main islands of New Zealand (and introduced on the Chathams), the weka is now rare in many areas where it was formerly common. Once widespread, it suffered a devastating population crash around 1915 — cause unknown, but possibly a disease epidemic of some kind — and its subsequent recovery has been extremely slow, faltering, and local. It is still uncommon in the North Island, but common in parts of Nelson, Westland, Fiordland and Stewart Island.

Habits It inhabits most kinds of forest and scrub, wherever dense shrubbery offers suitable cover, and it will forage in open areas of all kinds, from alpine meadows to ocean beaches. Adults mate for life and usually occupy joint territories vigorously defended at all seasons.

Young birds wander widely — one marked bird on record, transported from Gisborne to Hawke's Bay, later turned up again at Gisborne, having walked the 130 km home! Where it remains common it is not at all difficult to observe — it is, for example, a common uninvited guest at many a South Island forest picnic, fearlessly approaching humans to beg for food scraps. The most distinctive call is a rapid series of strident whistled shrieks.

Food Mostly seeds, fruit and insects, taken on the ground, but the weka is a versatile omnivore and will eat almost anything available. Weka often kill mice, rats and young rabbits, with birds' eggs or chicks a favourite food in season.

Breeding Nests are substantial bowls of vegetation, well hidden, and lined with hair or feathers. Five or six eggs make up a typical clutch and incubation takes about 26 days. A couple of days after hatching, the fluffy black chicks are led away and remain with their parents for several months.

ORDER • Gruiformes
STATUS • endemic; uncommon; resident

SPECIES • *Gallirallus australis*
MAORI NAME • weka

Eurasian Coot

39 cm

Recognition Length about 32–39 cm; sexes similar. The coot is every inch a rail except in one respect — it is entirely aquatic and dives for much of its food. Easily identified as a small, slate-grey, duck-like bird with a white bill and forehead shield, it is usually seen afloat.

Distribution The coot has a vast range across much of Africa, Europe, Asia, and Australasia, and closely related species occur throughout North and South America. In New Zealand it is common over much of the North Island, but confined to Otago and Canterbury in the South Island. It is one of several Australian birds — others include the white-faced heron and royal spoonbill — that established themselves as New Zealand residents in the 1940s and 50s. Coots were first found breeding at Lake Hayes, Otago, in 1958 and have since increased slowly but steadily in number.

Habits Coots prefer large, deep, permanent lakes, lagoons and swamps fringed with extensive beds of reeds or rushes. Here they spend much of their time in flocks, well away from shore (although they occasionally come ashore to forage) and on some ornamental ponds in city parks where they join ducks accosting passers-by for breadcrumbs. Occasionally they visit rivers and other flowing waterways or marine environments and estuaries but seldom stay long. Ashore, their distinctive lobed (not webbed) toes are easily visible. Like ducks, they moult all their flight feathers at once, and spend their annual period of flightlessness in dense rafts far out on broad waters. Little is known of movements in New Zealand but elsewhere coots are strongly nomadic. Calls are loud, harsh, and strident.

Food Largely aquatic plants growing in deep water, obtained by diving.

Breeding Breeding peaks in October and November, and nesting pairs are vigorously territorial. The nest is a bulky platform of reed stems, often with an entrance ramp, often with a sheltering woven hood, and often under a tree. The usual clutch is five or six eggs, which hatch in 22 to 26 days. Both parents incubate and help rear the fluffy chicks, which leave the nest almost immediately but are led back to be fed and brooded for several weeks.

Order • Gruiformes	**Species** • *Fulica atra*
Status • native; common; resident	**Maori name** • none

Pukeko

48 cm

Recognition   Length 44–48 cm; sexes alike. Easily identified as a chicken-sized marsh bird with rich purple-blue underparts, bulky red bill, and white under the tail. Pukeko often forage in the open where they stalk about, persistently flicking their tails, and dashing for cover when disturbed. Parrot-like, they often hold food in one claw while using the bill to break it apart.

Distribution   Widespread in the lowlands of the North and South Islands, the pukeko (elsewhere called the purple swamphen) also occurs on many Pacific islands, in Australia and across southern Asia to Europe and Africa.

Habits   Pukeko inhabit the margins of well-vegetated lagoons and swamps of all kinds, especially those adjacent to cultivated land. Around ornamental ponds in city parks they are often so tame they can be handfed. They are sociable birds that live in permanent groups with an intricate social structure that includes a hierarchical system of ranking — birds low on the 'pecking order' seldom breed and are usually

confined to marginal habitat. Strongly sedentary, they seldom move unless forced by food shortages or changing water levels. Most groups contain fewer than a dozen birds, but much larger flocks occasionally form in winter. Most calls are loud, strident and monosyllabic; the most distinctive is a ringing, raucous screech.

Food   Mainly vegetarian: mostly seeds, shoots and corms of aquatic plants, sometimes damaging crops; its varied diet also includes aquatic insects, frogs, carrion, stranded fish and, occasionally, eggs and chicks of other birds.

Breeding   Breeding may extend from August to February but peak activity is from September to December. The nest is a deep bowl of woven marsh vegetation well hidden in reeds, and five or six eggs make up a typical clutch. Incubation takes 23–24 days, and the chicks take about 85 days to fledge. Both parents build, incubate and rear the chicks, often assisted by other adults and youngsters from an earlier brood. Usually several broods are reared in a season.

ORDER • Gruiformes
STATUS • native; common; resident

SPECIES • *Porphyrio porphyrio*
MAORI NAME • pukeko

Takahe

Recognition Length 63 cm; sexes similar. Unmistakable — like a giant pukeko on steroids; flightless, with deeper bill and shorter, stouter legs.

Distribution Subfossil remains show a wide distribution in both North and South Islands a few centuries ago, but the takahe was known from only four specimens (all from Fiordland) throughout the nineteenth century, and none at all in the twentieth until it was dramatically rediscovered in 1948. A population of about 200 pairs was located in the Murchison and Stuart Mountains near Te Anau. Today just over 100 birds remain in the wild.

Habits Strongly sedentary, takahe form persistent, possibly lifelong, pair bonds. Deep snow and foul weather compels some movement as they search for food in winter but pairs return to the same territories in summer. Surviving takahe live in high-altitude hanging valleys, but it seems unlikely these represent optimum habitat. Its desperately precarious status is not helped by red deer, which compete with it for food and degrade its habitat.

Food Strictly vegetarian, takahe live mainly on tussock seeds, leaves and shoots in summer, but move into adjacent forest in winter to feed on fern rhizomes.

Breeding Egg-laying begins in mid-October, two eggs form the clutch and the incubation period is about 30 days. Chicks remain at least partly dependent on their parents for food for many weeks after they have fledged. Takahe do not breed until at least three years of age and chick mortality is very high — reinforcing the hypothesis that the existing habitat is marginal at best. The fact that two eggs are laid but normally only one survives prompts a recovery tactic that has been used successfully with several endangered birds worldwide: the superfluous egg is removed shortly after laying, taken to a captive-breeding establishment, and placed in an incubator to be artificially raised and later released.

Order • Gruiformes	**Species** • *Porphyrio mantelli*
Status • endemic; rare; resident	**Maori name** • takahe, moho

South Island Pied Oystercatcher

46 cm

Recognition   Length 46 cm; sexes similar. A large black-and-white shorebird with pink legs and a long, straight, orange-red bill. There is a crisp, clean-cut border between black breast and white underparts, and the white spills up and around the bend of the folded wing to form neat white 'shoulder tabs'. In flight, a bold white band extends almost the entire length of the upper wing.

Distribution   The South Island pied oystercatcher breeds only on the South Island, mainly along the broad, shingle river systems flowing eastwards from the Southern Alps, but a few breed on the west coast. Many cross Cook Strait in autumn to spend the winter on beaches in the North Island.

Habits   Called sipo by local bird-watchers, the South Island pied oystercatcher is a noisy, wary, excitable and conspicuous shorebird with high-pitched, piercing calls. It lives in permanent pairs which are strongly territorial in summer but congregate in dense flocks of hundreds in winter. It was once hunted for food, but its numbers increased dramatically after receiving protection in 1940 — an increase that may be continuing. Courtship involves 'piping ceremonies' in which birds chase each other, bodies hunched forward, bills pointing straight down, uttering hysterical streams of shrill, piping notes.

Food   The diet is mainly bivalves such as pipi and cockles, but the bird also takes worms, crustaceans and other small marine invertebrates. It also frequently forages on cultivated fields for grubs and insects.

Breeding   Both sexes participate fully in territory defence, nest building, incubation and care of the young. The nest is a sparsely lined scrape in the ground, usually with a clear view all about. Egg-laying peaks in September, three eggs form the normal clutch and incubation takes about 28 days. The chicks can fly about 42 days after hatching but the family usually remains together through the following winter.

ORDER • Charadriiformes
STATUS • endemic; common; resident

SPECIES • *Haematopus finschi*
MAORI NAME • torea

Variable Oystercatcher

46 cm

Recognition   Length about 46 cm; sexes alike. The bird gets its name from its variable plumage: some individuals are pied, some are black, and some are intermediate. The black form is obvious by its completely black plumage, but others are very difficult to distinguish from South Island pied oystercatchers. Key points to note: the margin between the black breast and white belly is blurred and smudgy in 'pied' variable oystercatchers; and there is no small white patch above the bend of the folded wing.

Distribution   Confined to New Zealand, the variable oystercatcher occurs almost everywhere along the coastline of all three main islands. The total population is about 4000 birds.

Habits   Around the world, oystercatchers come in two styles: black or pied. The relationship is puzzling but broadly true everywhere: pied birds live on beaches, black birds on rocky coasts. In the South Island, where most birds live among rocks, the black form predominates,

but in the North Island, where many oyster-catchers live on beaches, most birds are pied or intermediate. New Zealand oystercatchers share much the same lifestyle: they live in lifelong pairs that return year after year to the same stretch of coast to breed. However, the two species normally feed in different ways: South Island pied oystercatchers probe in sand or mud for prey, but variable oystercatchers use their somewhat stouter bills as hammers or chisels to batter their prey free from rocks.

Food   Almost entirely molluscs such as chitons, mussels, and limpets; variable oystercatchers also occasionally visit coastal farmland seeking insects, grubs and earthworms.

Breeding   Egg-laying begins in October but peaks in December. Nest sites vary: on a sandy ridge, atop a boulder, a cliff ledge, or under a cast-up log. Three eggs form the usual clutch, and both parents incubate in alternate shifts averaging about 90 minutes. Incubation lasts about 28 days; chicks can fly at about 40 days.

ORDER • Charadriiformes	**SPECIES** • *Haematopus unicolor*
STATUS • endemic; common; resident	**MAORI NAME** • torea-pango

Pied Stilt

35 cm

Recognition Unmistakable — black and white, with extremely long bright pink legs; it is often the most conspicuous bird on any shallow marsh, lagoon or tidal mud flat. Mobs react vigorously to any disturbance or human intruder in their territory, flying about overhead and yapping like hysterical puppies. Length about 35 cm; sexes similar.

ORDER • Charadriiformes
SPECIES • *Himantopus leucocephalus*
STATUS • native; common; resident
MAORI NAME • poaka

Habits The pied stilt is widespread from Indonesia and the Philippines to Australia and New Zealand where it is common on the North and South Islands, less so on Stewart Island and the Chathams, and a visitor to several other island groups. It is strongly gregarious, foraging in loose flocks and usually nesting in colonies. It feeds on minute aquatic animals, including insects, molluscs and crustaceans, probing with its long slender bill in shallow water — or sometimes in waterlogged marsh grass.

Black Stilt

40 cm

Recognition Adults are all but identical to the pied stilt except for their entirely black plumage; hybrids of the two species — smudged irregularly with white — are not uncommon — in fact frequency of hybridisation may well be the chief impediment to its future survival prospects. Youngsters, however, are white below and sooty black above, until they don adult plumage some six or seven months after fledging.

ORDER • Charadriiformes
SPECIES • *Himantopus novaezelandiae*
STATUS • endemic; rare; resident
MAORI NAME • kaki

Distribution As a breeding bird the black stilt is confined to tarns, lakes and shingle riverbeds in Otago and Canterbury, but a few birds migrate annually to the Firth of Thames and Kawhia in the North Island. One of the world's most critically endangered birds, this elegant wader has a total population of no more than 50–60 birds in the wild and in captive breeding pairs.

Wrybill

Recognition Length about 20 cm; sexes similar. This small dotterel is best identified by its plain, pale greyish upperparts; the narrow black band on its upper breast, distinctive in summer, is generally lost in winter. At close range, note its extraordinary bill, unique among all birds: the tip bends to the right some 15 to 20 degrees. The bent bill is used to good effect for probing for aquatic insects in crevices between and under pebbles on its breeding grounds, but in winter the wrybill forages mainly on mud flats.

ORDER • Charadriiformes
SPECIES • *Anarhynchus frontalis*
STATUS • endemic; uncommon; migrant
MAORI NAME • ngutu-parore

Distribution Wrybills nest along the broad shingle riverbeds of Canterbury and Otago. Most migrate to the North Island to spend the winter, mainly at the Firth of Thames, Manukau Harbour, Tauranga, Whangarei and a few other places. Pairs stay together from year to year but congregate in large flocks in winter.

Ruddy Turnstone

Recognition Length about 23 cm. The ruddy turnstone has lengthy, intricate moults as it alternates between very different breeding and winter plumages; it often seems that each bird in a flock differs at least slightly from every other bird. Nevertheless, it is probably the easiest of all migratory waders to identify — look for tubby build, a short stout bill, short orange legs, and a black or smudgy grey breast cut off abruptly from white underparts. In flight it reveals a white rump and bold white wing bars.

ORDER • Charadriiformes
SPECIES • *Arenaria interpres*
STATUS • native; common; migrant
MAORI NAME • none

Distribution It breeds on tundra along the entire Arctic Ocean coastline but winters in the southern hemisphere. About 5000 birds winter in New Zealand, arriving mainly in September and departing in March, although a few very old or sick birds will not attempt the journey and remain all year. It usually avoids marshes and favours rock pools and beaches over mud flats.

Banded Dotterel

Recognition   Most members of this worldwide group have at least one band across the upper breast in breeding plumage (mainly lost in winter), but this bird, elsewhere called the double-banded plover, is distinguished by having two, the upper (and narrower) one black, the other chestnut. Identification is much more difficult in winter, but usually at least some faint vestige of the two bars remains.

ORDER • Charadriiformes
SPECIES • *Charadrius bicinctus*
STATUS • native; common; migrant
MAORI NAME • pohowera, tuturiwhatu

Distribution   Abundant and widespread throughout New Zealand, including several offshore islands, as well as the Chatham Islands, nesting on beaches, ploughed fields, alpine meadows and similar open spaces. As a breeding bird it is confined entirely to New Zealand, but most migrate across the Tasman to winter in south-eastern Australia; stragglers visit Fiji, Vanuatu, New Caledonia and several other islands with some frequency.

New Zealand Dotterel

Recognition   Length about 27 cm; sexes similar. Substantially larger than other dotterels, the New Zealand dotterel is easily identified in summer by its rich rufous breast and warm brown upper parts — though the extent and saturation of rufous varies widely. Much faded in winter, the bird is best identified by size, and its comparatively long, stout bill. When not breeding it lives on dunes and sand and shingle beaches, but sometimes visits pasture.

ORDER • Charadriiformes
SPECIES • *Charadrius obscurus*
STATUS • endemic; uncommon; resident
MAORI NAME • tuturiwhatu-pukunui,
            paturiwhata

Distribution   Confined entirely to New Zealand, this plover has two separate populations. About 20 pairs nest on bleak hilltop moors on Stewart Island and spend the winter along the coast — and a few in nearby Southland. At the other end of the country some 1400 birds nest on sand and shingle beaches from the Bay of Plenty and Kawhia northwards.

Black-fronted Dotterel

Recognition Smaller than the banded dotterel (about 17 cm), this dotterel is easily recognised by the bold black V on its white breast; note also the bright red eye-ring and, in flight, large white patches in the rather blunt wings. The most common call is a distinctive, quiet *kik-kik-kik*.

ORDER • Charadriiformes
SPECIES • *Edithyornis melanops*
STATUS • native; uncommon; resident
MAORI NAME • none

Distribution Formerly confined to Australia, it was unknown in New Zealand before 1954, when numbers apparently crossed the Tasman to establish a breeding nucleus in the North Island; it is now widespread on both main islands. Normally sedentary, and almost exclusively a freshwater bird, it nests along the banks of many rivers, wherever there are shallow mud or gravel margins on which to forage. Especially in winter, it sometimes feeds along roadside ditches or farm stock dams.

Shore Plover

Recognition Similar in size to the banded dotterel, in flight the shore plover calls to mind a turnstone, but at rest it is easily recognised by its dull brown crown, white eyebrow, and black face. The sexes are similar, except that females are noticeably duller and less boldly patterned than males. The shore plover usually forages on flat rock platforms.

ORDER • Charadriiformes
SPECIES • *Thinornis novaeseelandiae*
STATUS • endemic; restricted; resident
MAORI NAME • kukuruatu

Distribution One of the rarest of the world's shorebirds, this species is entirely confined to the tiny island of Rangatira in the Chatham Islands, where its total population is about 120 birds. It was once widespread on the main islands of New Zealand but the reasons for its catastrophic decline remain unclear. So far, all attempts to transfer some birds even to nearby islets have failed and it remains extremely vulnerable to the possibility of ship rats getting ashore on the island.

Lesser Knot

Recognition In breeding plumage the lesser knot is easily identified by its reddish breast, but in winter plumage — largely pale grey above, white below — it looks bewilderingly like most migratory shorebirds. In general proportions the lesser knot suggests a large (about 25 cm) stint; it has a distinct pale eyebrow, nearly uniform mid-grey crown, and greyish — not white — rump. Extremely gregarious, it often feeds, flies and roosts in dense packs of thousands.

ORDER • Charadriiformes
SPECIES • *Calidris canutus*
STATUS • native; common; migrant
MAORI NAME • huahou

Distribution Also called the eastern knot or red knot, the lesser knot breeds around the shores of the Arctic Ocean in Alaska, Canada, Greenland and Russia. At other seasons it is widespread in the southern hemisphere. Though the total fluctuates from year to year, many thousands winter in New Zealand, where it is almost exclusively coastal in distribution.

Red-necked Stint

Recognition Not much bigger than a sparrow, the red-necked stint is a small and tubby shorebird with a comparatively short, straight black bill. In breeding plumage it is easily identified by the strong tinge of rufous about the head and neck, but winter birds are nondescript, grey-brown above and white below. Like other migratory shorebirds, it forms dense packs with other species at high tide roosts, then scatters to feed as the receding tide exposes adjacent mud flats.

ORDER • Charadriiformes
SPECIES • *Calidris ruficollis*
STATUS • native; common; migrant
MAORI NAME • none

Distribution The red-necked stint breeds in northern Siberia and Alaska. Its main wintering grounds are along Australia's far north-western coastline where flocks exceeding 100,000 birds are often seen. A total of about 500 birds winter annually in New Zealand, widely scattered in small groups around the coast. Occasionally they visit freshwater lagoons and marshes.

Bar-tailed Godwit

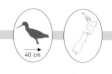

Recognition Length 40 cm. Godwits can be identified as large shorebirds with long, slender, faintly upturned bills. In turn, the bar-tailed godwit is most easily recognised by its relatively featureless upper parts, immediately apparent in flight (other godwits have a white rump and very obvious white wing bars). The underparts are mostly rufous in breeding plumage.

ORDER • Charadriiformes
SPECIES • *Limosa lapponica*
STATUS • native; common; migrant
MAORI NAME • kuaka

Distribution The bar-tailed godwit breeds from Scandinavia across northern Asia to Alaska and winters across Africa and southern Asia to Australia and New Zealand. In New Zealand it is perhaps the most numerous migratory wader. At any one time, about 10,000 birds are resident — mostly birds that are very old, ill, injured or otherwise indisposed to attempt the journey — their numbers boosted to about 100,000 in summer by birds arriving from their breeding grounds.

Eastern Curlew

Recognition By far the largest migratory wader to be seen in New Zealand (about 60 cm long), the eastern curlew is easily recognisable by its size and its extraordinarily long, strongly down-curved bill (about 18 cm long). Wary, aloof and deliberate, it stalks the mud flats, probing deeply for worms, molluscs, and especially small crabs. Often shunning other company, it is much less likely than other migratory waders to join mixed species roosts at high tide. The eastern curlew's most distinctive call is a loud, ringing, desolate *koo-lee*.

ORDER • Charadriiformes
SPECIES • *Numenius madagascariensis*
STATUS • native; uncommon; migrant
MAORI NAME • none

Distribution The eastern curlew nests in eastern Siberia and migrates twice annually across the equator to winter mainly in Australia. The total population is estimated at about 6000 birds, but perhaps 100 of these regularly winter along New Zealand coasts in small, widely scattered groups; a few remain all year.

Masked Lapwing

39 cm

common throughout the three main islands of New Zealand, as well as several of the nearer offshore groups. It is now common on the Chatham Islands through vigorous colonisation through the 1980s, and has wandered to Campbell Island.

Habits Widely known as the spur-winged plover (an unhappy choice, because lapwings differ from plovers in many obvious ways, and wing spurs are typical of the group), the masked lapwing is excitable, noisy and conspicuous. It favours broad, cropped grasslands near water — golf courses, playing fields and highway median strips are often a perfectly acceptable substitute for the real thing — but it occurs also on lagoon margins, coastal mud flats, and other wide, flat, empty places. Though mainly sedentary, small parties may wander widely, especially in winter. While nesting it lives in pairs which defend territories with conspicuous aggression, but at other times it is strongly gregarious. The most common call is a sort of loud, shrill, grating rattle; it often calls and travels at night.

Recognition Length 35–39 cm; sexes similar. Easily recognised by its plain brown upper parts, white underparts, and — at closer range — prominent, fleshy, bright yellow wattles between eye and bill.

Distribution The masked lapwing is widespread in Indonesia, southern New Guinea, and Australia. The first New Zealand record was of two birds at Invercargill in 1932; the two became five in 1934, and 100 in 1951. By 1965 they were nesting throughout Otago and Southland and in 1980 the first North Island nesting was reported. Today the species is

Food Mainly small invertebrates of all kinds — spiders, grubs, earthworms, water snails, aquatic crustaceans, and so on — captured in grass or by wading in shallow water.

Breeding Egg-laying often begins in June. The nest is a simple depression in the ground (usually on sparse, dry grassland), lined with a few wisps of grass. The normal clutch consists of three or four eggs. Incubation lasts 30–31 days, and fledging takes about 56 days. Both parents are involved at all stages of the nesting cycle, and the family unit usually remains intact until the following spring.

ORDER • Charadriiformes		**SPECIES** • *Vanellus miles*	
STATUS • native; common; resident		**MAORI NAME** • none	

Caspian Tern

52 cm

Recognition   Largest of all terns (length about 52 cm), the Caspian tern is easily recognised by its long, stout, bright red bill. The shaggy black cap turns mainly white in winter. The sexes are similar and young birds differ only in being substantially greyer, duller and more mottled.

Distribution   The species has a broad but discontinuous distribution across much of North America, Eurasia, Africa and Australasia. In New Zealand it breeds in both the North and South Islands, but in greatest numbers in the northern half of the North Island. The total New Zealand population is probably about 3500 birds.

Habits   The Caspian tern favours extensive wetlands, fresh or salt, such as lakes, broad rivers, coastal lagoons or ocean beaches. Much less gregarious than most terns, it usually forages alone, but small parties may join other terns to preen, loaf or roost. It is partly migratory with many South Island breeding birds moving to the North Island to spend the

winter. The most distinctive call is a deep, gruff *karrr-kaa*.

Food   Almost entirely small fish such as mullet and piper, captured by diving from a cruising flight of up to 10 m above the surface.

Breeding   Caspian terns usually nest in colonies of up to 100 pairs or so, usually on sand or shingle beaches, with a preference for small offshore islets. The season begins with birds revisiting the site in early September and the first eggs are laid a few weeks later. The nest is a mere scrape in the sand, occasionally lined with a few wisps of grass. Two eggs make up the clutch and incubation takes about 21 days. Both parents incubate and rear the chicks. Clad in sandy grey down, the young chicks are guarded constantly at the nest for the first week or so by at least one of their parents. The chicks are then led away to a more sheltered site and are thereafter visited only to be fed. They fledge about 30 days later. They are fed on small fish, presented whole.

ORDER • Charadriiformes
STATUS • native; uncommon; resident

SPECIES • *Hydroprogne caspia*
MAORI NAME • taranui

White-fronted Tern

43 cm

three main islands, and in the Chatham and Auckland Islands. Mature adults are resident, but juvenile birds and many young adults migrate across the Tasman Sea to winter in south-eastern Australia (mainly between Sydney and Adelaide). Vagrants wander from time to time to Campbell and Snares Islands.

Habits This is probably New Zealand's most abundant tern. Exclusively marine at all seasons, it inhabits beaches, harbours, estuaries, reefs, and shallow coastal waters. It often forages alone but lives otherwise in flocks that mingle freely with other terns and gulls at high-tide roosts. Sometimes it joins 'feeding frenzies' of gannets and other seabirds attacking large shoals of fish near the surface. The most common calls include a sharp, rolling *krrrik*.

Food Mainly small fish, captured by plunge-diving from hovering flight a few metres above the surface of the sea.

Breeding White-fronted terns breed in small colonies on sand, shingle or rock shelves, often within metres of the surf, and often with fewer than 50 pairs. Pair bonds persist for several years, possibly for life, but colonies are not necessarily consistently occupied from one year to the next, and may even be abandoned for several seasons. Nesting occurs mainly between October and February, and most young are on the wing by late December. Two eggs make up the normal clutch. Incubation, by both parents, takes about 23 days, and the young fledge at 29 to 35 days. Very young birds resemble winter adults except for strong brownish scallops on the back — largely lost within a few weeks of leaving the colony.

Recognition Length: 40–43 cm, wingspan about 80 cm; sexes similar. Easily identified in summer by its black cap, white forehead, and jet-black bill, the white-fronted tern is buoyant in flight and elegant at rest, with cleanly white underparts, pearl-grey upper parts and deeply forked tail. As in most terns, the black cap moults largely to white in autumn, except for a dusky-grey nape. It can easily be confused with the black-fronted tern, with which it sometimes associates, but is noticeably larger, whiter and has a jet black bill.

Distribution The white-fronted tern nests in colonies scattered along the coastlines of all

ORDER • Charadriiformes		**SPECIES** • *Sterna striata*	
STATUS • native; common; migrant		**MAORI NAME** • tara	

Black-fronted Tern

30 cm

Recognition   Length 30 cm; sexes similar. In flight most terns look crisply white but the black-fronted tern looks distinctly grey, its white rump conspicuous by contrast. The yellow-orange bill is also a useful identifying feature. The solid black cap of the breeding plumage turns mainly white in winter, except for a broad smudged band around the nape.

Distribution   Confined to New Zealand, the black-fronted tern breeds in the South Island, mainly along the braided shingle rivers flowing eastward from the Southern Alps. It may once have bred in the North Island but there have been no confirmed reports in 50 years or more. A few may remain at their colonies all winter but most migrate to the coast and disperse along the shores of all three main islands. Vagrants have been recorded at the Chathams and Snares.

Habits   Mainly a bird of inland rivers and lakes in summer, sometimes foraging over ploughed fields or flooded meadows, but in winter its main habitat is estuaries and river mouths

where flocks roost on sandbanks and mud flats and hunt over coastal shallows. Its most common call, a sharp *kit* or *kit-kit*, is not conspicuously different from that of other small terns.

Food   Aquatic insects are the main food in summer, mostly obtained in flight by 'dipping' rather than plunging — that is, the bird remains in flight and only the bill actually enters the water. In winter they plunge-dive for small fish.

Breeding   The black-fronted tern breeds in small colonies, typically about a dozen pairs and occasionally in the company of black-billed gulls. The nest is a twig-lined scrape in sand or light shingle and most laying occurs from mid-October through November. Two eggs form the normal clutch, incubated for about 23 days by both parents in alternate shifts. Chicks leave the nest a few days after hatching and wander about the colony being fed by their parents several times an hour, until they fledge at about 30 days.

Order • Charadriiformes	**Species** • *Sterna albostriata*
Status • endemic; uncommon; migrant	**Maori name** • tarapiroe

Southern Skua

Recognition   Big, burly, and aggressive, the southern skua is difficult to mistake for any other common seabird — the lumbering flight, massive build, dark brown plumage, and the large white flash in each wing are all obvious even at a considerable distance. On its breeding grounds it preys heavily on other seabirds, but in winter it lives on fish, squid, carrion, and whatever it can bully from other seabirds.

ORDER • Charadriiformes
SPECIES • *Catharacta lonnbergi*
STATUS • native; common; migrant
MAORI NAME • hakoakoa

Distribution   The southern skua is a common breeding bird on most of the outlying island groups in the New Zealand region, including Snares, Campbell, Auckland, Antipodes, and Chatham Islands, as well as Stewart Island and parts of Fiordland. Elsewhere it breeds at Heard, Macquarie, and various other subantarctic islands. Most spend the winter at sea when they can sometimes be seen from the main islands, especially after storms.

Arctic Jaeger

Recognition   Closely related to skuas but much smaller and more dashing, the three jaeger species are often extremely difficult to tell apart. All three have white wing flashes. The one most common in the New Zealand region is the Arctic jaeger, which is much more likely than the other two (the pomarine and long-tailed jaegers) to enter estuaries and harbours. About the size of a red-billed gull, it can be reliably identified by two moderately long spike-like feathers projecting beyond the tail — but these are often broken off or moulting. On their tundra nesting grounds, jaegers prey mainly on lemmings, while at sea they live as pirates, bullying other birds into giving up their catch.

ORDER • Charadriiformes
SPECIES • *Stercorarius parasiticus*
STATUS • native; common; migrant
MAORI NAME • none

Distribution   All three jaegers breed around the shores of the Arctic Ocean and winter at sea in the southern hemisphere.

Southern Black-backed Gull

59 cm

Recognition Length: 53–59 cm; sexes similar. Often called the kelp or Dominican gull, the black-backed gull is best identified by its large size and very dark grey — nearly black — upper parts. Young birds are much mottled with brown, assuming full adult plumage only in their fourth year.

Distribution The black-backed gull is widespread in cool temperate parts of the southern hemisphere, including most subantarctic islands. It is common everywhere along New Zealand coasts, as well as outlying groups such as the Antipodes and Chatham Islands, and it sometimes wanders to the Kermadec Islands. Unknown in Australia before about 1940, it is now well established in Tasmania and the south-eastern mainland.

Habits Although most common along the coast, this large gull also visits lowland farming country and can sometimes be encountered on alpine tarns. Like many other gull species it has multiplied substantially during the twentieth

century, an increase that can be attributed in part to a plentiful food supply brought about by human activities of all kinds.

Food Gulls owe much of their success to their flexible feeding habits, and black-backed gulls can thrive on almost anything organic. They flock to garbage dumps, at fur seal colonies they scavenge afterbirth and dead pups, at sea they follow fishing vessels for offal and dumped bycatch — and they are even sufficiently enterprising to carry seaside molluscs to a height and drop them on rocks below to smash the shells.

Breeding Occasionally black-backed gulls nest in isolated pairs, but mostly they breed in colonies. These are occupied from about July, but most egg-laying is from mid-October to January. The nest is little more than a rough mound of grass and other local vegetation. Two or three eggs form the usual clutch and incubation takes about 29 days; chicks fly at about 50 days.

ORDER • Charadriiformes	**SPECIES** • *Larus dominicanus*
STATUS • native; common; resident	**MAORI NAME** • karoro

Red-billed Gull

38 cm

Recognition Length about 37–38 cm; sexes similar. Where the two species occur together, the differences between this species and the black-billed gull (opposite page) are far from obvious. The bright red bill is immediately diagnostic — but many young red-billed gulls have black bills, especially in winter. The two species are best distinguished in flight. The two outermost primaries (flight-feathers) are mainly white in the black-billed gull, but mostly black with a distinct white splash near the tips, in the red-billed gull.

Distribution The red-billed gull occurs in Australia, New Zealand and New Caledonia; a very closely related species inhabits South Africa. It is abundant and nearly ubiquitous around the coasts of all three main islands of New Zealand, including the offshore island groups, as well as Snares, Campbell, Auckland, and Chatham Islands in lower numbers.

Habits Like the black-backed gull, it is largely a coastal bird, but often frequents inland lakes and rivers in small numbers. Noisy, conspicuous and quarrelsome, it usually forages, travels and roosts in flocks — occasionally in thousands. Adult red-billed gulls are mainly sedentary, but young birds may wander far from their natal colonies.

Food During the nesting season, red-billed gulls rely heavily on small marine crustaceans gathered a few kilometres out to sea; at other seasons they are nearly omnivorous. Large numbers congregate at garbage dumps, they sometimes follow tractors at ploughing time, they frequently steal food from other birds, and they scavenge food scraps at holiday beaches.

Breeding Colonies are occupied from late July to late January, and egg-laying begins in early October. The nest is a rough saucer of seaweed, sticks and other debris. Two eggs make up the usual clutch and they take about 26 days to hatch. Both parents participate in nest-building, incubation, and rearing the chicks, which may be attacked by neighbours if they stray.

Order • Charadriiformes	**Species** • *Larus novaehollandiae*
Status • native; common; resident	**Maori name** • tarapunga, akiaki

Black-billed Gull

37 cm

Recognition Length 37 cm; sexes similar. The pattern of black and white at the wing tips differs considerably between the black-billed gull and the very closely related red-billed gull (opposite page) but otherwise the two birds are very similar in appearance. Even its calls resemble those of the red-billed gull, though slightly more strident and more highly pitched.

Distribution An endemic New Zealander, the black-billed gull is mainly confined to the South Island where it nests on inland lakes and — especially — along braided shingle riverbeds in Southland, Canterbury and Otago. A few colonies exist in the North Island. Most birds remain in the South Island, wintering along the coast, but some cross to the southern coasts of the North Island. Strays have been recorded on Stewart Island and at the Snares.

Habits Like most gulls it is strongly gregarious, and usually forages, travels, nests, and roosts in flocks. Very much an inland species, it tends to avoid coastal environments except in winter.

Food Small freshwater fish and aquatic insects make up the bulk of the diet in summer, though the birds also follow ploughs for grubs and earthworms. In some places, such as Te Anau, they cadge handouts from picnickers, but they are far less enterprising as scavengers than red-billed gulls.

Breeding Colonies are normally occupied from mid-September until January, and nest building begins in early October. Nests are deep, neatly constructed saucers of small sticks, lined with grass. Two eggs form the clutch. Incubation lasts about 22 days, and chicks have normally grown their flight feathers about 26 days after hatching. Both parents participate at all stages. The chicks are led away almost immediately on hatching and the nest abandoned. As they grow, chicks congregate in crèches guarded by a few adults, which releases both parents to forage away from the colony at the same time. This effectively doubles the net rate of food delivery to the chicks, which reduces their period of dependency, improving survival prospects.

Order • Charadriiformes		**Species** • *Larus bulleri*	
Status • endemic; common; migrant		**Maori name** • tarapunga	

New Zealand Pigeon

51 cm

European settlement: for example, it often feeds — and even nests — in urban parks and gardens. It is mostly sedentary except for local movements in search of flowering trees. Not at all gregarious, it usually feeds and roosts alone.

Food   Almost entirely fruit, especially miro, matai, karaka and tawa but also a very wide range of other species, both native and exotic. Most fruit is gathered in trees, rarely on the ground. When fruit supplies fail, as in winter, pigeons survive on flowers and leaves; in some areas, by late winter, leaves may be almost the sole food. Most fruit it swallows whole, and the seed is later voided undamaged: in terms of the ecological machinery of the forest, this reduces to much the same thing as saying the plant bribes the bird with food to act as courier for its seeds, and many native forest trees are almost totally dependent on the New Zealand pigeon for dispersal.

Recognition   Length about 51 cm; sexes similar. Unmistakable. Even when completely hidden by foliage, the 'rustle-and-swish' sounds produced by pigeons as they feed in tree foliage is itself a distinctive field-mark.

Distribution   Common almost throughout the three main islands of New Zealand and many of the closest and largest offshore groups; also the Chatham Islands.

Habits   Although it reaches its greatest numbers in mature podocarp forest, the New Zealand pigeon has proven itself well able to cope with the habitat disruptions that followed

Breeding   Pigeons are notorious for building flimsy nests and the New Zealand pigeon is no exception. Nests lack lining, and are little more than a few twigs criss-crossed to form a platform — it is not unusual to be able to count the eggs from the ground below. Nests are usually within 2–6 m of the ground, occasionally much higher, and they are usually well screened by dense foliage. Normally only one egg forms the clutch; incubation takes 29–30 days, and the chick fledges about 45 days after hatching. Both parents participate fully. Breeding has been recorded in all months, but peak activity is between October and January. Breeding is strongly influenced by food supply, and in years of poor fruit crops in the forest, may even be suspended altogether.

Order • Columbiformes	**Species** • *Hemiphaga novaeseelandiae*
Status • endemic; common; resident	**Maori name** • kereru, kuku, kukupa

Rock Pigeon

33 cm

Recognition Length about 33 cm; sexes alike. Unmistakable. The ancestral rock pigeon is mainly dark blue-grey, shot with iridescent green and violet on the sides of the neck, and with a grey rump and two very dark grey wing bars. But 4000 years of domestication has resulted in a multitude of carefully bred strains and plumages — some entirely white, some nearly black, some nearly rufous, and others banded and chequered in various ways. The situation in most cities today, where no two pigeons seem exactly alike, results from a random mixture of all such breeds and types.

Distribution The rock pigeon probably originated in the mountains of the Middle East, but it has accompanied humans as a domesticated animal ever since Roman times and feral populations are now common in cities almost worldwide. It almost certainly accompanied the first European settlers to New Zealand and has been reimported many times since. It is now abundant in towns and farmland throughout New Zealand.

Habits Gregarious but not social, rock pigeons live in pairs that are territorial only in the immediate confines of the permanent nest site, and they usually travel and forage in company with other pairs. Mostly sedentary, they usually commute no further than necessary to reach suitable forage; when they travel, they fly in swift, tight flocks. In a display familiar to most urbanites, courting males trot briskly after a female, attempting to circle round her, with neck arched and upper breast inflated.

Food Largely seeds and similar plant items, supplemented by snails, insects and other arthropods and, around human habitation, food scraps and spilt grain.

Breeding There is no distinct nesting season. Females can lay fertile eggs within six months of hatching, and often rear broods more or less continuously throughout the year. The nest is a rough platform of sticks in a crevice — usually in a building but sometimes in a cliff — and two white eggs form the clutch.

ORDER • Columbiformes	**SPECIES**	• *Columba livia*
STATUS • introduced; common; resident	**MAORI NAME**	• none

Kea

46 cm

where flocks of double that number may be common; such larger flocks consist largely of males. Solitary kea often fly high, and they may even wheel and soar in updraughts, like a hawk. Kea often preen each other (called alloopreening), and young birds especially may tumble together on the ground like puppies. Despised as sheep killers for many years, thousands of kea were once killed for bounty, until receiving full protection in 1986. Today the playful and inquisitive kea is a great attraction at tourist centres, although they are less popular when their curiosity leads them to damage cars and camp sites. The strong beaks that can dig out roots and grubs can also tear the rubber seals from car windows, undo zip-fasteners on packs, and even let air out of car tyres!

Food   Mostly roots, leaves, berries, nectar, insects and carrion — but keas are inventive and enterprising scavengers that constantly explore their surroundings for anything edible. They scavenge at refuse dumps, ski resort car parks and mountain huts. Some have learnt how to dig into shearwater burrows to raid eggs and chicks, and a few even attack high country sheep. Landing on a woolly back, they use their beaks to dig through skin and feed on the layer of fat above the kidneys.

Recognition   Length about 46 cm; sexes similar. Mostly dark olive-green, with scarlet underwings. The kea might easily be mistaken for the kaka (page 79) at any distance, but note the much slenderer bill and the lack of a pale cap. The most distinctive call is a loud, ringing *kee-ah*, uttered mainly in flight.

Habits   The only alpine parrot in the world, the kea ranges from the upper fringes of beech forest to the highest peaks. In winter it may visit forests at lower altitude when compelled by hard weather. It is usually encountered in pairs or small parties of up to ten or so, except at garbage dumps, ski resorts or picnic grounds

Breeding   Kea build nests — a trait unusual among parrots, which mostly lay their eggs in bare tree-hollows — and may continue their construction over several years: one nest on record lay unused but added to for seven years. The female incubates her clutch of two or three eggs alone for about 24 days, but her mate — and sometimes other adults — help rear the chicks, which fly at about 100 days.

ORDER • Psittaciformes	SPECIES • *Nestor notabilis*
STATUS • endemic; uncommon; resident	MAORI NAME • kea

Kaka

46 cm

Recognition The kaka resembles the kea in size, appearance, calls, and much of its behaviour, but at close range the dark plumage resolves to reddish brown rather than green, and it has an obvious silvery cap. The sexes differ little in appearance.

Distribution Endemic to New Zealand, the kaka was formerly abundant throughout all three main islands, including the nearest and largest offshore islands. It is now rare in most areas and is effectively confined to old-growth beech and podocarp forests. It may once have occurred on the Chatham Islands.

Habits The kaka prefers old-growth, lowland and mid-mountain forest, but it extends up to the treeline in alpine country where it may occur together with its close relative, the kea (page 78). Although it often forages in flocks, it is not especially sociable. It is generally sedentary or locally nomadic, but may wander further afield in winter, when it sometimes turns up in city parks. The calls of the two species are

distinct but not dissimilar, and the kaka often calls, like the kea, in flight high overhead.

Food Beech-mast is prominent in the diet, but kaka also eat a wide range of insects, seeds, flowers and fruits such as miro and puriri. It uses its powerful bill to tear apart rotten wood for grubs, and its brush-tipped tongue to take nectar from flowers. Kaka usually feed silently high in the canopy where they can be easily overlooked, but will frequently forage on the ground.

Breeding The breeding season is long and its timing strongly influenced by the prevailing food supply. Most egg-laying occurs between September and March. The nest is usually a deep cavity at least 3 m up in a tree and the normal clutch contains four eggs. Incubation takes about 24 days and chicks leave the nest about 70 days after hatching. As with other parrots, the male takes care of the family food supply while his mate incubates and broods the chicks.

ORDER • Psittaciformes
STATUS • endemic; rare; resident

SPECIES • *Nestor meridionalis*
MAORI NAME • kaka

Kakapo

63 cm

Recognition   Length about 63 cm; weight up to 3.4 kg. Unmistakable — big, bulky, camouflage green, with owl-like facial disks. Reckoned by weight, this strange bird is by far the largest parrot anywhere.

Distribution   Once widespread and abundant in both main islands, the kakapo is now perilously close to extinction. Less than 70 birds remain on Codfish Island, off Stewart Island, and Maud Island in the Marlborough Sounds. It became extinct in Fiordland in the 1980s.

Habits   Almost everything about the kakapo is extraordinary. Almost all of the world's 300-odd parrot species are active by day — but kakapo are nocturnal. Swift and agile flight is a prominent feature of all parrots — but kakapo are flightless. Parrots are noisy and conspicuous birds — but kakapo are so secretive it requires a specially trained dog to locate one. Parrots form affectionate and permanent partnerships — but male kakapo gather on 'arenas' or 'leks' to compete with each other for the right to mate

with any female who happens by. Several of its oddities are compounded: for example, it is the only New Zealand bird, and the only flightless bird anywhere, with a lek mating system. It is one of only a handful of birds that actually constructs its lek: each member of the lek digs one or more saucer-shaped depressions or 'bowls' in the ground, linked with other bowls by a network of tracks. The bowls function as amplifiers to enhance projection of the male's very deep, resonant booming notes, used in courtship to attract females.

Food   Kakapo eat a variety of leaves, fruits, stems and roots, grinding fibrous foods to extract juices. They often leave dry, fibrous material attached to the plant.

Breeding   Males play no part in nesting. Nests are in crevices on the ground — among the roots of a storm-thrown tree is a typical site — and the usual clutch consists of three eggs, but details of incubation and chick rearing remain unknown.

ORDER • Psittaciformes
STATUS • endemic; rare; resident

SPECIES • *Strigops habroptilus*
MAORI NAME • kakapo, tarapo, tarepo

Eastern Rosella

32 cm

Recognition   Length 30–32 cm. Easily identified by its bright red head and breast, yellow underparts and white cheeks; the distinctive apple-green rump is very obvious in flight. Females and immatures resemble adult males except in being much duller. The closely related crimson rosella (also introduced from Australia) is deep crimson above and below, with blue cheeks; immatures are dark green.

Distribution   The eastern rosella is a native of south-eastern Australia and was originally introduced to New Zealand as a cage bird in the late nineteenth century; escapees gradually became established across much of the North Island. A small population was established at Dunedin when a shipment of birds was refused entry in 1910 and the disgruntled owner liberated them from his ship in the harbour rather than take the birds back to Australia.

Habits   Eastern rosellas inhabit most kinds of lightly wooded country, including orchards, urban parks and gardens. Both eastern and crimson rosellas sometimes occur together but, on the whole, crimson rosellas prefer taller forest in high rainfall areas. Both species are gregarious, spending much of the year in family parties that often coalesce into larger flocks in winter. They are mostly sedentary. The most common call is a loud, ringing *kwink*, uttered usually in flight.

Food   Mostly vegetarian: seeds, fruits, flowers, buds and shoots, occasionally supplemented with insects such as case moths. They forage with almost equal frequency on the ground or in trees. Rosellas sometimes cause damage to tomatoes, apples, citrus and other orchard fruit.

Breeding   Rosellas nest in tree cavities. The usual clutch is five or six plain white eggs which hatch in about 19 days. Only the female incubates but her mate brings her food, and both parents rear the chicks. Youngsters leave the nest about 35 days from hatching, the family normally remaining together at least until the following breeding season.

ORDER • Psittaciformes
STATUS • introduced; common; resident

SPECIES • *Platycercus eximius*
MAORI NAME • none

Red-crowned Parakeet

28 cm

Recognition Length about 28 cm; sexes similar. A small, bright green parrot with a red cap and a narrow red band extending behind each eye.

Distribution This bird was formerly very common in the North and South Islands where it is now extremely rare, but it remains common on numerous offshore islands such as Kapiti, Little Barrier and Stewart Islands, as well as the Kermadecs, Auckland, Chatham and Antipodes Islands. Elsewhere the species occurs in New Caledonia and on Norfolk Island; it once inhabited Lord Howe and even distant Macquarie Island.

Habits Often a coastal bird, the red-crowned parakeet inhabits most kinds of forest and scrub. It lives in permanent pairs that frequently join with other pairs, together with their young, to form flocks in winter. The most distinctive call is a brisk chattering note, *ki-ki-ki-ki-ki*. Aside from the yellow-crowned parakeet (opposite page) there are two other members of

this mainly New Zealand group of parrots. The orange-fronted parakeet of the South Island high country has always been so rare that very little is known of it, and it has not even been firmly established that it is indeed a distinct species. The Antipodes Island parakeet is a distinct all-green species entirely confined to the Antipodes Island group.

Food Red-crowned parrots eat a wide variety of plant seeds, berries, buds, shoots and flowers, as well as nectar and small insects. Much of their food is taken on the ground or in low shrubbery, seeds tending to predominate in winter, buds and shoots in summer.

Breeding Kakariki — as these birds are commonly known — normally nest in cavities in trees, living or dead. The normal clutch consists of five eggs, incubated by the female alone for about 20 days. Both parents feed the chicks which leave the nest at about 40 days — although they normally remain with their parents through the following winter.

ORDER • Psittaciformes
STATUS • native; uncommon; resident

SPECIES • *Cyanoramphus novaezelandiae*
MAORI NAME • kakariki

Yellow-crowned Parakeet

25 cm

Recognition   Length about 25 cm; sexes similar. The yellow-crowned parakeet is very similar to the red-crowned parakeet except for its yellow cap. Note also that a band of red extends backward from the eye in the red-crowned species, a feature lacking in the yellow-crowned species.

Distribution   Entirely confined to New Zealand, it inhabits all three main islands and many of the closer offshore islands such as Kapiti and Little Barrier Island, as well as the Auckland Islands and the Chathams — although new evidence suggests the Chatham Island population (called Forbes' parakeet) is more closely related to the red-crowned parakeet, and may indeed be a distinct species.

Habits   More rigidly a forest bird than the red-crowned parakeet, this species is largely confined to old-growth beech and podocarp forests. It has declined markedly since European settlement, mainly through loss of habitat and the depredations of introduced predators such as stoats and ship rats (the Chatham Island population, in particular, has all but vanished). More recently, however, there have been encouraging signs that it may be slowly recovering lost ground. It lives in sedentary pairs in summer but forms small wandering parties in winter. Especially in winter, it often forms mixed flocks with red-crowned parakeets, or with the very rare and little-known orange-fronted parakeet. Its characteristic rapid chattering call is fainter and slightly higher pitched than that of the red-crowned parakeet.

Food   Beech-mast is important in the diet but these parrots also eat a very wide range of plant

foods, including tender buds, flowers, seeds and small insects. Much of its food is gathered high in the trees and, where introduced predators are absent, it sometimes forages on the ground.

Breeding   Nesting normally begins in October and ends in December, but the season is heavily influenced in timing, duration and intensity by the current year's beech-mast harvest. The nest is usually a cavity in a living or dead tree, and the clutch varies from five to nine eggs. Incubation lasts about 20 days, the chicks fledge and leave the nest at about 40 days. Fed by her mate, the female incubates alone but both parents feed the chicks.

ORDER • Psittaciformes	**SPECIES** • *Cyanoramphus auriceps*
STATUS • endemic; uncommon; resident	**MAORI NAME** • kakariki

Shining Cuckoo

18 cm

Recognition Length: 17–18 cm; sexes similar. The shining cuckoo is easily recognised by its barred black-and-white (actually dark bronze-green at very close range) underparts and glossy, metallic green upper parts.

Distribution The species has a broad distribution in eastern Indonesia, Australia, New Guinea, New Caledonia and Vanuatu as well as New Zealand. In New Zealand it occurs on all three main islands and the Chatham Islands, and it has also been recorded on the Snares and the Kermadecs. A few birds remain for the winter, especially in the North Island, but in autumn most migrate north to winter in the Bismarck Archipelago and the Solomon Islands, returning in late September.

Habits It is common in most wooded environments, native or exotic, and often occurs in city parks and gardens. It is usually solitary, although it often forms 'parliaments' — noisy, excited temporary gatherings whose function is still uncertain — in spring, and sometimes small flocks in autumn, prior to departure. The distinctive call or song is a series of up-slurred, silvery whistles.

Food Mostly insects and their larvae, with a strong preference for hairy caterpillars which few other birds eat. Typically, the bird gathers three or four in its bill, then sits at its perch for some time, visibly munching, as it separates and swallows the flesh, leaving the empty skins, with their toxic hairs, dangling from its bill. It then drops the debris and goes back for more.

Breeding Like many other cuckoos, the shining cuckoo is a host parasite — that is, it does not rear its own young but lays its eggs in the nest of some other bird. The 'host' is usually a small songbird which takes on the role of foster parents to rear the young cuckoo in its stead. Details of the shining cuckoo's breeding are scanty, but the incubation period is only 15 days, which gives the young cuckoo several days' head start over any of the hosts' own chicks sharing the nest. Grey warblers (or, in the Chatham Islands, the locally endemic Chatham Island warbler) are the favoured hosts of this particular cuckoo. How the cuckoo inserts her egg into the much smaller warbler's domed nest without damaging it remains a minor mystery.

ORDER • Cuculiformes	**SPECIES** • *Chrysococcyx lucidus*
STATUS • native; common; migrant	**MAORI NAME** • pipiwharauroa

Long-tailed Cuckoo

40 cm

Recognition   Length about 40 cm; sexes alike. Easily identified as a lean, long-tailed bird with yellowish white underparts heavily streaked with dark brown. The dark brown upper parts are liberally spotted with white and barred with dull rufous. Very young birds have mottled, dull reddish underparts.

Distribution   The long-tailed cuckoo breeds only in New Zealand, including all three main islands and the Auckland, Chatham and Kermadec Islands. After breeding it migrates to Polynesia, where it is widespread from the Solomon Islands through Fiji to the Tuamotu Archipelago. Some of the flights on its island-hopping travels into the south-western Pacific involve non-stop, over-water crossings of several thousand kilometres.

Habits   Long-tailed cuckoos arrive in New Zealand in early October and leave again by March. Elusive and secretive in behaviour, it is much more often heard than seen. It is most common in native forest and scrub but it sometimes occurs in orchards, suburban parks, gardens and pine plantations. It forages mostly at night and calls most vigorously at dawn and dusk. It is usually solitary, though frequently mobbed vigorously by small birds — which is sometimes the best way of finding it. Its most distinctive call is a harsh rising screech, uttered by day or by night, often in flight, and often in series.

Food   The long-tailed cuckoo's diet consists mainly of large insects such as weta and stick insects, skinks, frogs and small birds. It is also known to raid the nests of other small birds for eggs and chicks.

Breeding   The long-tailed cuckoo is a host parasite, playing no part in rearing its own young. Eggs are laid in the nests of other birds — mostly whitehead, yellowhead and brown creeper — and abandoned to the foster parents' care, but beyond this very little is known of the details of its reproductive behaviour. The female will often remove or damage one or more of the hosts' eggs before laying, or the young cuckoo chicks pushes its nest-mates out of the nest on hatching; in either case the young cuckoo is normally left alone in the nest to receive all the food its foster parents can deliver.

ORDER • Cuculiformes
STATUS • native; uncommon; migrant

SPECIES • *Eudynamys taitensis*
MAORI NAME • koekoea, kohoperoa

Morepork

29 cm

Habits   The distinctive territorial call may well be the most familiar night sound to most New Zealanders. Uttered by both sexes throughout the year, it sounds a bit like the name, 'morepork'. The pace may vary, from brisk to measured, but the second note is normally pitched lower than the first. Originally characteristic of dense native forests, the morepork has adapted well to European influence and is now often heard in city parks, pine plantations and other exotic woodlands. It is mainly sedentary, living in pairs that occupy permanent territories — usually with several daytime roosts, used in rotation for perhaps a week at a time. The morepork is strictly nocturnal, and only very rarely hunts in daylight. It is often mobbed, if discovered, by many small songbirds at its roost — sometimes providing the most effective means of locating it by day.

Food   Diet depends to some extent on availability, but beetles, moths and especially weta figure most prominently, supplemented by frogs, geckos, small birds and mice.

Recognition   Superficially resembling the little owl (opposite page), the morepork is noticeably bigger (about 29 cm long), darker and browner, and is the only owl to be seen in forest habitats (little owls inhabit open country). The sexes differ little in size or appearance.

Breeding   Mating normally begins in mid-August, the clutch of two eggs usually laid in October. The nest is most often in a tree cavity but sometimes hidden in dense foliage. Once begun, the female seldom leaves the nest throughout the nesting cycle, surviving herself and rearing her chicks largely on food brought by her mate. As is characteristic of carnivorous birds, eggs are laid several days apart but incubation begins with the first, so the chicks are unequal in size. Incubation takes about 30 days and fledging about 40 days. Chicks have two down coats; white then smoky brown.

Distribution   The morepork is common in wooded country throughout Australia (where it is usually called the boobook owl) as well as eastern Indonesia and New Guinea. In New Zealand it is widely distributed on all three main islands, including the closest offshore groups. It also inhabits Norfolk Island and has been introduced to Lord Howe Island.

ORDER • Strigiformes	**SPECIES** • *Ninox novaeseelandiae*
STATUS • native; common; resident	**MAORI NAME** • ruru

Little Owl

23 cm

Recognition Small, squat, and short-tailed, the little owl is about 23 cm long, and easy to confuse with the slightly larger morepork, especially at night. However, the little owl's greyish plumage is heavily spotted and streaked with white. Also, the little owl favours open country where the forest-loving morepork is unlikely to occur. The bouncing, undulating flight is also characteristic. The sexes are nearly identical in appearance and seasonal variation is negligible.

Distribution The species has a vast range across most of Asia, Europe and North Africa. Birds from Germany were released in Otago after 1906 and are common across most of the South Island east of the main divide, and occasionally seen in Westland and Fiordland.

Habits In the early days of New Zealand agriculture, farmers complained of serious damage to their crops by songbirds. The little owl was selected as a possible counter to the threat — an unhappy choice, because small birds don't figure prominently in this owl's otherwise comprehensive diet. Little owls are most likely to be seen in open country such as mixed farmland dotted with old buildings and scattered clumps of trees, where they are often seen perching on fence posts and telegraph poles. Not rigidly nocturnal, they sometimes hunt by day. The most common call is a high, clear *kieuw* or *kieuwik*.

Food Little owls prey on a broad range of small animals, from worms, snails and insects to frogs, skinks and mice, captured mostly on the ground (young birds are frequent victims of highway traffic). Prey is often carried to a

favourite perch to be dismembered, the indigestible fragments regurgitated as pellets.

Breeding Little owls form simple monogamous pairs that may last for life. The usual nesting site is a hole in a dead tree or a suitable cavity in an abandoned building. Three round white eggs, laid in October and hatching in 28 days, make up the normal clutch. The female incubates alone but both parents rear the chicks. These leave the nest about 40 days after hatching, often while still partly downy, but they remain dependent on their parents for about a month thereafter.

ORDER • Strigiformes		**SPECIES** • *Athene noctua*	
STATUS • introduced; common; resident		**MAORI NAME** • ruru waho	

Sacred Kingfisher

24 cm

occurs on all three main islands, as well as the Kermadecs, but it is much more common in the North Island than elsewhere.

Habits   Kingfishers occupy most kinds of open, lightly wooded habitats, not necessarily near water, from mangroves and coastal scrub to native and exotic forest — though they are usually rare in beech forest. Most live in resident, territorial pairs in summer, but many birds move to mangroves or open coastal farmlands in winter. Many Australian birds migrate to New Guinea and the Solomon Islands, but there is no clear evidence that New Zealand kingfishers ever leave the country. They seldom form flocks, but often several may be visible, spaced well apart, wherever hunting is especially profitable, such as coastal mudflats or mangroves. The most distinctive call is a deliberate, staccato *ek-ek-ek-ek*. Another characteristic call is a harsh descending screech, uttered mostly by females near the nest.

Food   Despite the bird's name, fish is not an especially prominent component of the diet, which includes a very wide range of small animals from earthworms, insects, skinks, mice and even small birds to tadpoles, crabs and eels.

Recognition   Length about 24 cm; sexes similar. The kingfisher is a large-billed, short-legged bird that frequently chooses prominent perches on dead trees, power lines, fences or utility poles, persistently raising and lowering its tail. It is generally blue-green above and buff or creamy white below, the white throat extending as a conspicuous band around the nape.

Breeding   The nest is a simple chamber, either in a deep cavity in a tree or at the end of a burrow dug by the birds in an earthen bank or similar site. The same burrow may be used for several years. There are five eggs in a typical clutch. Incubation lasts about 19 days, and the chicks leave the nest at about 26–28 days — though they remain largely dependent on their parents for another three or four weeks thereafter.

Distribution   The sacred kingfisher has an extensive distribution in Indonesia, New Guinea, Australia (including Norfolk and Lord Howe Islands), New Zealand and much of Melanesia and Polynesia. In New Zealand it

Order • Coraciiformes		**Species** • *Todiramphus sanctus*	
Status • native; common; resident		**Maori name** • kotare	

Welcome Swallow

15 cm

Recognition Length about 15 cm; sexes similar. Easily identified by its swift, swooping flight, glossy blue-black upper parts, rusty throat, and deeply forked tail. The closely related and similarly sized tree martin is a frequent straggler from Australia, but it has a square-tipped tail and a whitish rump.

Distribution Once confined to Australia, the welcome swallow colonised southern New Guinea and New Zealand during the 1950s. It spread rapidly from Northland, and is now widespread on all three main islands, as well as the Kermadec, Auckland and Chatham Islands.

Habits Swallows are highly specialised to exploit aerial 'plankton' — swarms of minute flying insects such as gnats and midges. And they do so with minimum expenditure of energy, a specialisation helped by their long pointed wings, streamlined shape and swift flight. Habitat matters little, so long as it's open. Swallows most often forage low over rivers, pastures, suburban playing fields, sand dunes

and similar places, and over the canopy of forests. Strongly gregarious, swallows usually feed in loose groups, and 'off-duty' birds gather in small twittering groups on fences and power lines. In winter they sometimes form large wandering flocks.

Food Almost exclusively small flying insects, captured in sustained flight which is usually low, swift, graceful and erratic over open country.

Breeding Swallow nests are distinctive, though shape and placement vary. Feather-lined and built of mud pellets and dry grass, they are deep and cup-shaped and most often plastered to a rough vertical surface — traditionally a rock face but now most often the inner wall of a barn or under a bridge. Sometimes the birds build on an exposed beam or under the eaves of a roof. Nesting extends from August until February and several broods are reared in a normal season. Three to five eggs make up the clutch. Incubation lasts about 18 days and chicks leave the nest at about 24 days.

ORDER • Passeriformes		**SPECIES**	• *Hirundo neoxena*
STATUS • native; common; resident		**MAORI NAME**	• warou

Rifleman

8 cm

Zealand (though not north of the Coromandel Peninsula) as well as some of the closer associated islands, such as Little Barrier Island.

Habits   In virgin beech forests the rifleman is sometimes the most numerous small bird. It sometimes extends into other forest types — even old pine plantations if the undergrowth is dense, it has also been recorded in gorse, scrub and hedgerows. Strongly sedentary, it seldom flies any significant distance. Most pair for life and defend permanent territories. Calls are mostly confined to a thin, high, abrupt *zeet*.

Food   Mostly small insects, occasionally supplemented with berries. Most of its foraging is on the trunks and major limbs of trees, diligently searching bark, moss and epiphytes for prey, and frequently relying on its strong, sharp-clawed feet to cling sideways or dangle upside down.

Recognition   Easily identified as a tiny (length about 8 cm, weight about 7 g), tail-less, almost frantically active bird. The rifleman constantly flits its wings in its ceaseless fidgeting, but it also frequently holds them outstretched, as though to display the clear yellow band along the centre of each wing. Male and female riflemen differ conspicuously in appearance: males have bright green backs, whereas females are brown and streaked. Young birds of both sexes resemble adult females.

Distribution   The rifleman remains common and widespread in old-growth forests almost throughout the North and South Islands of New

Breeding   Riflemen normally begin nesting in September and raise two successive broods. The nest is a loosely woven domed structure of small twigs, stems and similar plant materials, with an entrance tube several centimetres long, feather-lined and placed in a tree cavity. Riflemen willingly use suitable nest boxes. Often four or five nests are built before one is chosen for the brood. Four eggs make up the typical clutch. Incubation takes 20–21 days and the chicks leave the nest at about 28 days. Both parents participate in building, incubation and chick-feeding, but the male often takes over sole care of the first brood while his mate begins nest-building for the second. The young of the first brood have been noted helping rear young of the second.

Order • Passeriformes	**Species** • *Acanthisitta chloris*
Status • endemic; common; resident	**Maori name** • titipounamu

Rock Wren

9 cm

Recognition Length about 9 cm. Virtually unmistakable by its minute size, absurdly short tail and alpine habitat, the rock wren is greenish brown above and near-white below, with yellow flanks and a narrow white eyebrow stripe. The female is distinctly duller and browner than the male.

Distribution Confined to the South Island, the rock wren is reasonably common at high altitudes (mainly 900–2500 m) all along the Southern Alps from Nelson to Fiordland.

Habits The rock wren and its close relative the rifleman are the surviving members of an entire family of songbirds found only in New Zealand; a third member, the bush wren, may be extinct, while a fourth, the Stephens Island wren, was exterminated by a cat almost immediately on discovery. Subfossil remains suggest there may have been several other species that vanished before the arrival of Europeans. Largely restricted to alpine environments, the rock wren's preferred habitat consists of steep boulder screes, sometimes scrub-covered, where it scuttles mouse-like through the crevices, occasionally popping up to perch briefly, bobbing up and down on some large boulder to look about before resuming its almost subterranean foraging. It can fly strongly when pressed, but normally only flutters a few metres between boulders when foraging. Getting a good view usually calls for considerable patience, and the best way to locate it is to listen intently for its faint, shrill *zipt*. Rock wrens live in resident pairs, and spend the winter among the boulders, secure under a sheltering blanket of snow.

Food Seeds, berries and small insects.

Breeding September and October constitute the breeding season. Domed and bulky with a side entrance, the nest is woven of grass, lined with feathers and placed in a sheltered rock crevice. Two to five eggs make up the clutch, both parents rear the chicks, but few other details are known.

Order • Passeriformes	**Species** • *Xenicus gilviventris*
Status • endemic; uncommon; resident	**Maori name** • hurupounamu

Skylark

18 cm

Recognition Length about 18 cm; sexes similar. Small, brown, streaked and very ordinary-looking. On the ground the skylark is not easy to distinguish from the pipit (opposite page), except that the skylark is stockier and does not wag its tail; the pipit has a much more slender bill. However, the skylark's prolonged, rapturous song is unmistakable, usually delivered while the bird hovers 50 m or more from the ground and lasting several minutes. The bird begins singing during the nearly vertical, fluttering ascent, and continues the breathless, melodic jumble of notes without a break as it hovers and then throughout the abrupt downward swoop, finally stopping just before touching the ground. The usual contact call is a liquid *chirrup*.

Distribution Native to Eurasia and North Africa, the skylark has been introduced to western Canada, Australia and New Zealand where it is widespread on all three main islands and the Chatham Islands. Vagrants reach the Kermadecs, Snares and Auckland Islands with some frequency.

Habits Skylarks are common in most kinds of open country from sand dunes and rural pastures to alpine meadows. They sometimes perch on fences but almost never in trees. On the ground they walk, not hop. They seldom visit water but often dust bathe along country tracks. They live in territorial pairs in summer but frequently form flocks in winter.

Food Gathered entirely by foraging on the ground, the diet is made up of a wide range of seeds and insects.

Breeding Nesting begins in late September. The nest is a flimsy, shallow cup of dry grass built into a slight depression in the ground (a cow's hoof-print is a typical site) in the shade of tussock. Two to five eggs form the clutch. The incubation period is about 11 days, and the chicks leave the nest about ten days after hatching and about ten days before they can fly. Only the female builds and incubates but both parents rear the chicks. Skylarks often raise two or three broods in a season.

ORDER • Passeriformes
STATUS • introduced; common; resident

SPECIES • *Alauda arvensis*
MAORI NAME • hioi, whioi

New Zealand Pipit

18 cm

Recognition   Length: 16–18 cm; sexes similar. In its open country habitat the pipit is likely to be mistaken only for the skylark as both these birds are drab, brown, streaked and very similar. The best clues are behavioural: pipits frequently run — very nimbly — and they persistently flick their tails up and down. At close range, note the pipit's slender bill and smooth crown — the skylark has a stouter bill and a short shaggy crest. Both birds have white outer tail feathers, but the pipit's are more obvious.

Distribution   The New Zealand pipit has an enormous distribution across most of Africa, Asia and Australia, where it is sometimes called Richard's pipit, as well as New Zealand. It is common across all three main islands, most of the associated offshore groups, and the Auckland, Antipodes, Campbell and Chatham Islands. It has also been recorded as a vagrant at the Kermadecs and the Snares.

Habits   Pipits favour the barest and flattest land, and are widespread in open country of all kinds from ocean beaches to alpine meadows — golf courses are a favourite environment — but generally avoid lush pasture. The flight is quick and undulating; pipits may fly far but seldom high. Like the skylark, they live in territorial pairs in summer but often form loose flocks in winter. The pipit's song is a brief, unpretentious trill, with the most distinctive call a high, slurred *trr-eep*.

Food   The pipit's diet is mainly invertebrates, feeding on a wide range of small insects and seeds gathered almost entirely on the ground.

Breeding   Most nesting occurs between early September and late February, with pairs usually rearing two or three broods in a season. The nest is a deep, substantial cup of woven grass, well shaded and concealed under tussock or a small shrub. The clutch of three to five eggs is incubated for about 14 days and the chicks fledge about 15 days after hatching. The female builds and broods alone but both parents care for the chicks.

ORDER • Passeriformes	**SPECIES** • *Anthus novaeseelandiae*
STATUS • native; common; resident	**MAORI NAME** • pihoihoi

Hedge Sparrow

14 cm

Recognition   Length 14 cm; sexes similar. Often called the dunnock, the hedge sparrow is one of the most nondescript of New Zealand birds; mainly brown above and grey below, it lacks any distinctive plumage features. Look for the dark, *slender* bill — the finches and sparrows with which it is most likely to be confused have stout, conical bills.

Distribution   The hedge sparrow is one of the most ubiquitous small birds in its original home — Europe, from Iran and the Caucasus west to the British Isles. Introduced to New Zealand several times from 1867 it is now widespread throughout all three main islands as well as the Campbell, Auckland and Chatham Islands.

Habits   The hedge sparrow inhabits shrubbery of all kinds, natural or exotic, and it has become locally common in New Zealand gardens. It is mainly sedentary, and usually solitary, but sometimes forms small flocks with other small ground-feeding birds in winter, especially in bad weather or when food is scarce. Hedge sparrows

spend much of their time on the ground where they crouch low, resulting in a distinctive, oddly shuffling gait. They forage in a quiet, preoccupied manner, using their bills to flick aside dead leaves and other debris. The most distinctive call is a shrill *tseep*.

Food   Hedge sparrows eat mainly small insects, spiders and similar small ground-dwellers, but the diet also includes seeds and small fruits, especially in winter.

Breeding   The hedge sparrow has an unusually intricate and variable mating system. Both females and males may each have several partners; trios are common, and even multiple polygamy has been recorded, with several females simultaneously mated with several males. The nest, well hidden on the ground or close to it, is a hair-lined cup of twigs, stems and grass. Normally four eggs form the clutch. Incubation and fledging both take about 12–13 days; only the female builds and incubates, but both parents feed the young.

Order • Passeriformes		**Species** • *Prunella modularis*	
Status • introduced; common; resident		**Maori name** • none	

Blackbird

26 cm

Recognition Length 25–26 cm. The male blackbird is easily recognised as an all-black bird with a yellow bill, but females and young birds are more or less entirely dark brown.

Distribution The blackbird has a vast natural range across most of Europe and Asia as well as North Africa, and was introduced to Australia and New Zealand in the 1860s. In New Zealand it is abundant on all three main islands, and the Kermadec, Chatham and Auckland Islands.

Habits The blackbird rivals the starling as the most ubiquitous garden bird in New Zealand, and is considerably more conspicuous in appearance and behaviour. It feeds on open lawns, carols lustily from treetops and roosts in hedges and shrubbery where its distinctive, emphatic *chak* of alarm or warning is a common suburban sound. The song resembles that of the songthrush but is mellower. Like the chaffinch, it has also had considerable success in penetrating native forest where it tends to be more shy and elusive than in suburbia.

Blackbirds are mainly sedentary and live in territorial pairs in summer but they may form flocks in winter. Both sexes vigorously defend their territory and boundary scuffles may involve either males or females.

Food Earthworms, snails and slugs are prominent in the diet, which also includes ground-dwelling insects and spiders; fruit of almost any kind is eaten avidly when available — a frequent source of complaint from orchardists and market gardeners.

Breeding Territories are established in April and laying begins normally in late August. The nest is a sturdy grass-lined bowl of twigs, well hidden in a hedge or shrubbery several metres from the ground; a feature unusual among New Zealand bird-nests is that a good deal of mud is used to consolidate the structure. The female normally builds her nest and incubates her clutch of three or four eggs which hatch at about 14 days. Her mate joins in helping her rear the chicks.

ORDER • Passeriformes
STATUS • introduced; common; resident

SPECIES • *Turdus merula*
MAORI NAME • manu pango

Song Thrush

23 cm

Recognition   Length about 23 cm; sexes similar. The song thrush is easily identified by its white breast, boldly spotted with brown, and its plain, olive-brown upper parts. Chicks look like fluffy versions of their parents.

Distribution   The song thrush was introduced into New Zealand from its natural home in Europe and western Asia in the 1860s, and is now common throughout all three main islands. Migratory in its native range, it wanders frequently to most outlying groups, including the Kermadecs, Chathams and even Macquarie Island.

Habits   Like the blackbird, the song thrush is very common in most wooded habitats, especially parks and gardens, but it has not had the blackbird's success in adapting to native forests. It lives in pairs that are strongly territorial for much of the year and may form small wandering flocks in winter, especially in exceptionally hard weather. The famous song is mostly delivered between May and December,

occasionally at other times; loud, clear and rich, it consists of a long series of phrases, each repeated several times. The usual calls include a harsh scolding chatter and an abrupt *chip*.

Food   Mainly earthworms, slugs, snails and ground-dwelling insects, supplemented occasionally with fruit. Song thrushes have the distinctive habit of selecting an appropriate rock or similar convenient object within their territories and using it as an anvil, to which they bring snails and hammer them until the shell breaks and the animal can be swallowed.

Breeding   Nesting has been recorded in most months in New Zealand, but occurs mostly between August and December. The nest resembles that of a blackbird except for its distinctive mud lining; a typical site is 1–3 m up in a shrub or hedge. Three or four pale blue eggs make up the clutch. Incubation takes 12–13 days, fledging a day or two longer. The female builds and incubates alone, but both parents rear the chicks.

ORDER • Passeriformes
STATUS • introduced; common; resident

SPECIES • *Turdus philomelos*
MAORI NAME • tiutiu

Fernbird

18 cm

Recognition Best identified by its skulking behaviour, long ragged tail, rufous-tinged crown and the dense narrow streaks on both breast and upper parts. Total length about 18 cm; sexes similar.

Distribution Confined to New Zealand, the fernbird is uncommon and patchy in distribution but widespread on all three main islands and some of the closest of their associated offshore groups, as well as the Snares.

Habits It is intensely secretive, though inquisitive and quite tame, and can usually be coaxed into allowing an observer at least a glimpse of it by mimicking its terse, metallic calls, the most common of which sounds like *s'tik* or *tchik*. It is very reluctant to fly, preferring instead to slip stealthily through dense foliage. When it does take to the air, the flight is laboured, fluttering and brief, with its tail dangling downward behind. It occurs in most kinds of low, dense vegetation but especially favours sedge, rata, flax or pakihi swamp. It

lives mostly in pairs, which persist apparently for life and occupy permanent territories.

Food Almost entirely insects and other arthropods such as spiders and millipedes, generally obtained by thorough searching — digging in soft earth, sifting through leaf litter, or tugging at loose bark.

Breeding Nesting generally begins in mid-October, and often two broods are reared in succession. Nests are built mostly of woven rush stems or tussock blades and lined with feathers, usually within a metre of the ground; on sodden ground some nests are built on circular woven platforms, presumably to resist damp. Two to four eggs make up the clutch. Incubation takes about 16 days and fledging about 20 days, but the chicks — brooded constantly for their first four days after hatching — do not reach full independence until about five weeks after leaving the nest. Both parents participate fully in nest-building, incubation, and care of the chicks.

ORDER • Passeriformes
STATUS • endemic; uncommon; resident

SPECIES • *Bowdleria punctata*
MAORI NAME • matata

Brown Creeper

13 cm

Recognition   Length about 13 cm; the sexes are similar with young birds resembling adults. Plain dark smoky-brown above and reddish-buff below, it is best identified by the sharp contrast between its dark grey head and silvery-grey throat.

Distribution   The brown creeper is confined to the South Island, Stewart Island and a few of the closest small offshore island groups.

Habits   It inhabits most forest types, native and exotic, from coastal lowlands to alpine scrub, foraging most often in the canopy high overhead where it is difficult to observe. It lives mainly in sedentary, territorial pairs, but in winter it is often encountered in parties or small flocks, sometimes in company with other small forest birds such as yellowheads, warblers and fantails. Always on the move, the birds fossick actively in their ceaseless search for insects, rummaging in leafy tangles, dangling upside down from twigs and carefully searching crevices in bark. In spring the brown creeper's sprightly song is

distinctive, but its most characteristic call all year round is a rather husky *dee-dee-dee*.

Food   In summer the diet consists almost entirely of small insects, spiders and similar animals; forest fruits and berries are added in winter.

Breeding   Breeding usually begins in late September. The nest is a deep cup-shaped structure of small twigs, leaf stems, and bark fragments, bound with spider silk and lined with feathers and fine grass, and usually well hidden high in dense foliage. Two to four eggs form the clutch. Incubation lasts about 18–19 days and the chicks fledge and leave the nest at about 20 days. The female builds and broods alone with most of her food brought to her by her mate; both parents feed the chicks. Staying together as a family unit, the chicks remain at least partly dependent on their parents for up to eight weeks after fledging. The species is generally a favourite victim of the long-tailed cuckoo (page 85).

ORDER • Passeriformes
STATUS • endemic; common; resident

SPECIES • *Mohoua novaeseelandiae*
MAORI NAME • pipipi

Whitehead

Recognition About 15 cm in total length, the whitehead is easily recognised as a small, plain, very pale songbird — whitish at the front end and light yellowish brown at the other. The sexes are similar. Whiteheads are extremely social — even nesting is often a family affair, with several family members participating — and they are usually encountered in flocks high in the forest canopy where they bustle actively about as they scrutinise the bark and foliage for insects. Less frequently, they forage on tree trunks, on fallen timber and sometimes even on the ground. The diet occasionally includes fruit.

ORDER • Passeriformes
SPECIES • *Mohoua albicilla*
STATUS • endemic; uncommon; resident
MAORI NAME • popokatea

Distribution Entirely confined to the North Island and a few of the closer offshore islands, such as Kapiti and Little Barrier Island. Once abundant, it is now uncommon and rather patchily distributed, mainly in beech forest and manuka scrub.

Yellowhead

Recognition Length about 15 cm. Unmistakable — the bright, clear yellow head is diagnostic; females are similar but duller. The calls are varied but not especially distinctive. In behaviour the yellowhead closely resembles the whitehead of the North Island, yet there are some intriguing differences. For example, the yellowhead is much more rigidly confined to the upper canopy in its foraging and, while the whitehead normally builds its cup-shaped nest in foliage, the yellowhead almost invariably selects a hole in a tree.

ORDER • Passeriformes
SPECIES • *Mohoua ochrocephala*
STATUS • endemic; rare; resident
MAORI NAME • mohua

Distribution Confined to the South Island. Like the whitehead in the North Island, the yellowhead was once an abundant inhabitant of beech forests at all altitudes; now it is very local in distribution, common only in parts of Nelson, Westland and Fiordland.

Grey Warbler

10 cm

Recognition   Dull grey above, dingy white below, and only about 10 cm long, this tiny bird is possibly the most nondescript bird in New Zealand. Its distinctive bright red eye is apparent only at very close range, but the minute white flashes in the tail, visible in flight, are surprisingly easy to see, once you know what to look for. The sexes are nearly identical, and variation by age or season is negligible.

Distribution   One of the most abundant native birds, the grey warbler is widespread on all three main islands, as well as the closest of the outlying island groups. Vagrants have been recorded at the Snares. A closely related species, the Chatham Island warbler, is confined to the Chathams, where it is abundant in all undisturbed native scrub habitats.

Habits   Unlike many other native birds, the grey warbler has evidently been unaffected by European settlement and its attendant disruptions: it remains common wherever there are trees, including urban parks and gardens,

mangroves and plantations of exotic pines. It is extremely active and is usually encountered busily feeding in the upper foliage of trees or shrubbery. Grey warblers are sedentary, and pairs often persist in the same territories from year to year, though their boundaries are normally undefended in winter. Although the bird is often difficult to observe, the frail, melodic, wavering song is one of the evocative features of the New Zealand bush and — according to Maori folklore — a certain sign of spring.

Food   Small insects, mostly gleaned from foliage in trees.

Breeding   Intricately constructed of twigs, rootlets, moss, bark fragments and similar materials, the grey warbler's nest is an ovoid structure suspended from a tree branch with a neat circular entrance in the side and a long tail dangling below. The four eggs making up the typical clutch hatch in about 19 days and the chicks leave the nest about 16 days later.

ORDER • Passeriformes	**SPECIES** • *Gerygone igata*
STATUS • endemic; common; resident	**MAORI NAME** • riroriro

Fantail

16 cm

Recognition   Despite its sober colour pattern of greyish-brown and white, the fantail is instantly recognisable by its shape and behaviour. Almost constantly active, with drooping wings and broadly fanned tail, it flutters amid foliage or chases tiny insects in clearings with intricate and frenetic aerobatics. The total length is about 16 cm and the sexes are nearly identical. Birds in the South Island are sometimes sooty black.

Distribution   The grey fantail has an extensive range across much of Australasia. It is widespread in Australia (including Tasmania), as well as New Guinea, the Solomon Islands, Vanuatu, New Caledonia, Norfolk and Lord Howe Islands. It is very common virtually throughout New Zealand, including the Chatham Islands, and has recently colonised the Snares Islands.

Habits   Unusually tame, inquisitive and confiding, the fantail is probably the most familiar native bird, common almost anywhere

there are trees. It is partly migratory. Usually encountered alone or in pairs in summer, in winter it often forms flocks. Fond of water, it often bathes, either in shallow pools, or by performing its elaborate feeding manoeuvres in the spray of garden sprinklers. It is often the only bird active in drenching rain. Its vivacious, twittering song is high-pitched, thin and squeaky.

Food   Almost entirely small flying insects, usually captured in flight.

Breeding   The breeding season begins in very early spring and extends through mid-summer, during which three or even four broods are commonly reared. Securely anchored to the outer branches of a shrub or small tree, the nest is a compact, intricate structure of rootlets, moss, bark fragments and similar materials, tightly bound with spider silk, lined with hair and, usually, with a long untidy tail dangling below. Three or four eggs make up the clutch. Incubation takes about 14 days.

Order • Passeriformes	**Species** • *Rhipidura fuliginosa*
Status • native; common; resident	**Maori name** • piwakawaka

Tomtit

13 cm

Recognition Length about 13 cm. The various island populations of tomtits vary subtly in plumage but all are basically black above, white below, with conspicuous white wing bars and white flashes in the tail. All, that is, except for birds on the Snares Islands, which are entirely black. (Not to be confused with the black robin which is entirely confined to two islands in the Chatham group.) Females are nearly identical to males in pattern but differ in colour; essentially, they are drab brownish grey wherever the male is black.

Distribution Endemic to New Zealand, the tomtit is widespread on all three main islands and most of their associated offshore island groups, as well as the Chatham, Snares and Auckland Islands.

Habits Although common in most forest types, the tomtit especially favours beech forest. It is mainly a lowland bird, usually encountered in pairs, territorial and largely sedentary, although youngsters may wander far in their search for territories of their own. Males have a brief whistled song, the commonest call being a thin high *seee* or *see-see-see*.

Food Tomtits and robins (the two are closely related) are the two prominent 'pounce-feeders' of New Zealand forests — that is, whereas most insectivorous birds 'glean' their prey in foliage or 'hawk' it in midair, robins have the distinctive habit of perching on a log, post or fence-wire, from which they scan the ground, swooping suddenly to snatch any small creature that moves. Tomtits also catch insects on the wing and glean from branches and foliage.

Breeding The nest is a deep, bulky cup of small twigs, grass and similar material, lined with feathers and placed in a deep vertical tree-fork or broken stub. Three to five eggs form the clutch; hatching takes about 15 days and chicks fledge at about 19 days. Often two broods are raised in quick succession, the male assuming sole care of the first while the female lays and incubates a second clutch.

Order • Passeriformes	**Species** • *Petroica macrocephala*
Status • endemic; common; resident	**Maori name** • miromiro, ngiru-ngiru

New Zealand Robin

18 cm

Recognition Length about 18 cm; sexes similar. A drab, nondescript bird — look for upright stance, long slender legs and plain grey upper parts.

Distribution Confined to New Zealand, the robin is widespread but locally distributed on North, South and Stewart Islands and some nearby islands such as Little Barrier and Kapiti.

Habits Inconspicuous, solitary, territorial and sedentary, New Zealand robins are most common in beech or podocarp forest and kanuka or manuka scrub. Several characteristics may have prompted early settlers to link this bird by name with its European namesake (the bird of Christmas card fame), despite the lack of a red breast (although several of its closest relatives in Australia do have red breasts), but its extraordinary tameness was probably one of them. Both birds have the endearing trait of perching on a gardener's shovel handle when its user pauses to rest, pouncing on any worms unearthed. Even in the remotest forests a robin will fearlessly approach a tramper for tidbits at any campsite or lunchtime pause. Notwithstanding the parallel in names, the two birds are not at all related, but earn the similarity because they play similar roles (technically called niches) in their respective local forest songbird communities. The New Zealand robin is a member of a very large group of robin-like forest birds, widespread in, but more or less confined to Australasia.

Food Mainly insects and their larvae; most food is captured on the ground by pouncing, though they also forage by rummaging in leaf litter or by searching foliage in undergrowth,

shrubbery, and sometimes high in the canopy; prey varies from very small insects and spiders to large stick insects and even cicadas.

Breeding Nesting may occur as early as mid-July but mostly begins in September. The typical nest is a substantial cup of small twigs, moss and grass placed several metres from the ground in a deep vertical tree-fork, usually close to the trunk. The normal clutch is two or three eggs; incubation and fledging both take about 18 days. Only the female builds or broods, but her food requirements are met, and the chicks largely raised, on food fetched by her mate.

ORDER • Passeriformes	**SPECIES** • *Petroica australis*
STATUS • endemic; uncommon; resident	**MAORI NAME** • toutouwai

Silvereye

12.5 cm

Recognition   Length about 12.5 cm; sexes similar. The silvereye is a plain, light greenish bird with near-white underparts, blue-grey back and light tan flanks, most easily identified by a conspicuous narrow band of tiny white feathers rimming each eye.

Distribution   The silvereye is widespread in the south-west Pacific region from Australia to Fiji and the Tuamotu Archipelago. It was self-introduced to New Zealand in the 1850s, possibly the result of a storm-driven migrant flock from Tasmania surviving a trans-Tasman crossing. It is now common throughout all three main islands, as well as the Kermadecs, Snares, Campbell, Auckland and Chatham Islands.

Habits   Silvereyes occur almost anywhere there are at least a few trees, from coastal lowlands to at least 1200 m altitude, but they favour small trees and shrubbery and are most common in young, open, disturbed or fragmented woodlands such as orchards, suburban parks and gardens and forest fringes. Pairs mate for

life, spending much of the year in loose, wandering flocks, dropping out to nest and rejoining later. Silvereyes are mainly arboreal, only occasionally feeding on the ground. They have a light, formless, twittering song, the most distinctive call being a high, thin, rather peevish *cheee*.

Food   Nectar, spiders and small insects — especially small caterpillars — make up the bulk of the diet, frequently supplemented by fruit. Silvereyes sometimes cause damage in vineyards and orchards; they often visit garden bird-feeders where they will nibble almost anything.

Breeding   Nesting begins in early October with usually two broods raised in succession. The nest is a delicate cup of grass and similar material bound with cobweb, suspended by the rim from a slender tree-fork a couple of metres from the ground. Three eggs form the typical clutch, and incubation and fledging both take about 12 days. Both parents cooperate fully in the entire cycle.

Order • Passeriformes		**Species** • *Zosterops lateralis*	
Status • native; common; resident		**Maori name** • tauhou	

Stitchbird

19 cm

Recognition   Length about 19 cm. Males are easily recognised by their yellow-bordered black breasts and a conspicuous plume of white above and behind each eye. Females are mainly drab grey, with narrowly streaked grey and dingy white breasts.

Distribution   Originally the stitchbird was confined to the North Island where it seems to have been common and widespread. However, as early as 1885 it was virtually extinct and for decades survived only on Little Barrier Island. More recently it has been translocated by wildlife authorities to Hen, Cuvier and Kapiti Islands.

Habits   Stitchbirds are conspicuous, active, aggressive and frequently cock their tails. Common only on Little Barrier, they inhabit all types of native forest and scrub, especially those with an understorey of dense shrubbery. They also forage in flowering coastal flax. They are sedentary, strongly territorial and apparently form permanent pairs. Males utter a soft warbling song and a brisk three-note whistle,

but the most distinctive call, uttered by both sexes, is the dry *sti-tch* from which the bird gets its name. Like the tui and the bellbird, stitchbirds play an important role in native forest ecology, pollinating and spreading the seeds of many native shrubs. In earlier days the male's plumage was valued by the Maori for decorating ceremonial cloaks.

Food   The stitchbird relies heavily on nectar from such native flowers as puriri, kohekohe, and pohutukawa, supplemented by berries and small insects gleaned mainly from foliage.

Breeding   Breeding begins in October when the female builds a feather-lined cup-shaped nest of twigs, rootlets and stems in a tree cavity, 2 m or more from the ground. Little is known of its nesting, but four eggs make up the usual clutch and the female incubates alone while her mate defends the territory. Later, both parents rear the chicks and continue to feed them for a week or so after they have fledged and left the nest.

ORDER • Passeriformes
STATUS • endemic; restricted; resident

SPECIES • *Notiomystis cincta*
MAORI NAME • hihi

Bellbird

20 cm

the bellbird is common throughout all three main islands and their offshore small island groups, as well as the Three Kings, Auckland and Chatham Islands — although the Chatham Island population is now extinct.

Habits   It inhabits native forest of all kinds and also occurs in suburban gardens, orchards and plantations of exotic trees, especially where there is native bush close by. Some local migration occurs, especially from higher altitudes in the South Island, but for the most part bellbirds form permanent pairs that mutually defend a permanent territory. By pollinating many native flowers and spreading seeds the species has a prominent role to play in the ecology of New Zealand's natural forests. Both sexes sing loud, rich, rambling songs, often in duet or with neighbouring birds in concert. The birds usually sing with feathers fluffed and neck outstretched vertically. Bellbirds have three distinct songs, one of which — mostly sung at dawn — is the series of pure, bell-like tones from which the bird gets its name.

Recognition   About 20 cm in total length, the bellbird is predominantly olive-green with almost black wings and tail. The sexes are similar, except that males have a strong gloss of iridescent blue on the face, forehead and crown that is mostly lacking in the female. The female, however, has a narrow streak of white extending backwards from the gape, which is not present in the male.

Distribution   Like the tui, the bellbird is distinctive in its status as one of the most abundant and widespread of New Zealand's endemic songbirds. Confined to New Zealand,

Food   Nectar and fruit, supplemented with insects, usually captured by gleaning them from foliage or hawking in midair.

Breeding   Usually well hidden in a vine tangle or tree-fern, the nest is a loosely woven saucer of twigs, lined with feathers, and placed anywhere from ground level up to 15 m or so. Three or four eggs make up the normal clutch, and incubation and fledging both take about 14 days. Some males assist their mates, but mostly the female builds, broods and rears her chicks largely unaided by the male.

ORDER • Passeriformes		**SPECIES** • *Anthornis melanura*	
STATUS • endemic; common; resident		**MAORI NAME** • korimako, makomako	

Tui

30 cm

Recognition   In poor light or at a distance, the plumage appears plain black, but from close range it is strongly glossed with metallic violet, copper, green and blue. Two large, curled white plumes on the lower throat suggest an old-fashioned frilly cravat, and the neck is adorned with dense, narrow white shafts that curve down and forward. Length about 30 cm; sexes similar.

Distribution   The stitchbird, bellbird and tui are New Zealand's three representatives of the honeyeaters (Meliphagidae), a family of songbirds widespread throughout Australasia but with the bulk of its approximately 170 species confined to Australia and New Guinea. A New Zealand endemic, the tui is common throughout all three main islands, including offshore islands, as well as the Auckland, Kermadec and Chatham Islands.

Habits   Tui are common in most native forest habitats, suburban parks and gardens, and come readily to back-yard bird-feeding stations. They frequently perch at the very tops of dead trees, or fly high from one patch of forest to another. Pair bonds may endure from year to year with territories vigorously defended through summer although they are usually abandoned in winter. The tui is perhaps the most persistent of all the songbirds in the New Zealand bush, the first to tune up at dawn and the last to fall quiet at dusk; it often sings on moonlit nights. Both sexes sing, often in duet, and sometimes in concert with neighbouring birds. Songs are extremely variable, some being hard to distinguish from those of the bellbird, and include mimicry of various bush sounds and the songs of other birds.

Food   Nectar is an important component of the diet, and tui congregate in considerable numbers at flowering trees and flax. They also eat fruit and insects.

Breeding   The nest is a bulky, loosely woven bowl of twigs, lined with moss or leaves, usually high in a tree. Often several nests are built before laying begins in one. Three or four eggs constitute the usual clutch. The incubation period is about 14 days, and the chicks fledge and leave the nest at about 11 days. The female builds, incubates and rears the chicks unaided, but both parents feed and escort the youngsters.

ORDER • Passeriformes
STATUS • endemic; common; resident

SPECIES • *Prosthemadera novaeseelandiae*
MAORI NAME • tui

Redpoll

Recognition A small, pale brown, sparrow-like bird, streaked above and below; males have a small black chin patch, raspberry-red crown, and pale pink breast and rump. Females and immatures are similar but with colours very subdued, the crown a dull red.

Distribution The natural range of the redpoll encircles the globe at high latitudes, from the Arctic Ocean south to southern Canada, Russia, Scandinavia and the British Isles. With several introductions to New Zealand between 1862 and 1875, it is now common over much of the North Island high country and throughout the South Island and Stewart Island.

Habits For much of the year redpolls favour rugged, bleak, open highlands up to about 1500 m altitude, but they frequently visit coastal lowlands in their winter wanderings; at this season they may appear in suburban gardens, orchards, farmland or sand dunes. Strongly gregarious; even 'off-duty' nesting birds may join neighbours in temporary feeding groups.

They form large flocks in winter, often with other finches. Winter roosts are communal. The most common call is a light, metallic twitter, and the song is a brief, undistinguished trill.

Food Seeds constitute the chief food, supplemented with small insects. Redpolls sometimes damage fruit crops, especially by deftly picking the seeds from ripening strawberries, and through an unexplained but persistent habit in early spring of systematically working over apricot or peach trees, pecking at every swelling bud.

Breeding As is characteristic of several close relatives (such as greenfinches), redpolls form pairs in their winter flocks even though nesting does not begin until early November. Both partners participate in building the neat, compact, cup-shaped nest, but the female carries out most of the construction while the male escorts and supervises, only occasionally gathering material. The usual site is about 2 m up in a small, dense shrub.

ORDER • Passeriformes
STATUS • introduced; common; resident

SPECIES • *Carduelis flammea*
MAORI NAME • none

Goldfinch

13 cm

Recognition Length about 13 cm; sexes similar. The goldfinch is easily recognised either perched or in flight: at rest its bright red face, white cheeks and black nape are diagnostic; in flight it reveals a white rump and broad, bright yellow band across each black wing. The typical goldfinch flight is nearly as distinctive — light, fluttering and deeply undulating, almost dancing through the air.

Distribution The goldfinch is native to western Eurasia and North Africa, but it has been widely introduced elsewhere in the world, including Bermuda, Argentina, the United States and Australia. Introduced to New Zealand in the 1870s, it is now common on all three main islands, from sea level to about 1000 m.

Habits The goldfinch is most common in open rural environments, avoiding forest and scrub. In winter it also visits stubble, dunes and coastal saltings, and is often abundant in vacant lots and along roadsides. It is strongly gregarious, forming large flocks in winter and sometimes even nesting in loose colonies. As they feed, goldfinches keep up a constant light '*tswitt-itt-itt*', the cheerful song a liquid, twittering series of notes.

Food It feeds mostly on seeds but, unlike other introduced finches, takes them from the plant in preference to gathering fallen seeds from the ground. It has a great fondness for thistles, but it also forages many other weeds and grasses.

Breeding As in several other introduced finches, goldfinches form pairs in their winter flocks, but most nesting begins in November when seed crops begin to peak. The nest is a frail but compact cup of grass and small twigs, down-lined and placed in an outer tree-fork 2 or 3 m from the ground. The female builds the nest and incubates her clutch of three to five eggs alone, but the male escorts her as she builds, feeds her on the nest, and later fetches food for her to give to the chicks. Incubation and fledging both take about 14 days.

Order • Passeriformes	**Species** • *Carduelis carduelis*
Status • introduced; common; resident	**Maori name** • none

Greenfinch

15 cm

Recognition   With his stout conical bill, bronzed olive-green head and body, and bold flashes of yellow in the wings and tail, the male greenfinch is easy to identify. Much duller, females are easily mistaken for the similarly sized (about 15 cm) female house sparrow — look for the dull *green*, not grey, rump.

Distribution   Native to western Eurasia, the greenfinch was brought to New Zealand in the 1860s and rapidly established itself across all three main islands and the Chatham Islands. Vagrants stray to Campbell Island and the Kermadecs from time to time.

Habits   The greenfinch avoids the two extremes of dense forest and wide open spaces, but it is common wherever groves of trees, orchards, shrubbery, pine plantations or copses are interspersed with meadows, croplands, stubble or abandoned, weed-choked fields. It visits gardens and sometimes forages amid the stormwrack on beaches. Greenfinches are gregarious birds: nesting pairs tolerate close

neighbours in summer and they congregate to form large flocks in winter, often mixed with yellowhammers, sparrows and other finches. Its calls, including a rapid jingling twitter and a drawn out *tsueeep*, rather suggest those of a canary, and its song is a rambling elaboration of its calls, sometimes delivered during a display flight.

Food   The staple diet is seeds, supplemented with insects and fruit. Much of its food is gathered on the ground, though it sometimes aggravates farmers with its habit of stealing ripening grain, snipping off fruit buds, and breaking apart small fruits and berries such as rose hips and crab apples to get at the seeds inside.

Breeding   Pair formation occurs in the winter flocks, nesting usually begins in mid-October. The nest is a bulky open cup of twigs, lined with down or hair, usually placed several metres from the ground in a shrub or sapling — a young conifer is especially favoured if available.

ORDER • Passeriformes
STATUS • introduced; common; resident

SPECIES • *Carduelis chloris*
MAORI NAME • none

Chaffinch

15 cm

Recognition Length about 15 cm; male has a rust-pink face and breast, with a powder-blue crown, nape and rump; female has a dull brown head and breast, with a pale green rump. In flight, both sexes reveal black wings, with white wing bar, shoulders and outer tail feathers.

Distribution The chaffinch's ancestral range extends across Eurasia from Siberia to the British Isles, Spain and Morocco. Introduced to New Zealand several times from 1862, it is now abundant throughout the three main islands and most outlying groups, including the Snares, Campbell, Auckland and Chatham Islands.

Habits Chaffinches are common wherever people live. They have also penetrated natural environments, perhaps to a greater extent than any other introduced bird — in the South Island for example, chaffinches are common in beech forests and alpine scrub far from any human habitation. They live in pairs during the summer but form large flocks in winter, when they often visit stubble, ploughed fields or open

wasteland — habitats normally shunned in summer. It has a loud, brief song, usually delivered from high in a tree; the most distinctive note is a metallic *pink, pink*.

Food Mainly seeds, gathered on the ground or from the plant, insects and occasionally fruit.

Breeding The nesting season begins in mid-September when males establish territories and use persistent song to attract mates and warn off rivals. The female builds the nest alone and may leave it empty for a week or more before laying her clutch of three to five eggs. The nest is a neat, compact bowl of moss and dry grass, decorated with lichen, lined with hair, and usually placed in a tree-fork a few metres from the ground. Incubation takes about 14 days and the chicks leave the nest at about 15 days. At first the male helps only casually, but he takes on a greater share of food gathering after the chicks are a few days old. Both parents continue feeding the chicks for about three weeks after they have left the nest.

ORDER • Passeriformes
STATUS • introduced; common; resident

SPECIES • *Fringilla coelebs*
MAORI NAME • pahirini

Yellowhammer

16 cm

Recognition   Usually encountered in open country, the yellowhammer is a small sparrow-like bird with a yellow head and breast and a reddish rump. The total length is about 16 cm. The sexes are similar, except that females are much duller and more heavily streaked than males.

Distribution   The yellowhammer is a typical member of a large group of birds called buntings in Europe and sparrows in North America. In its native Eurasia it has an enormous range extending from Siberia westward to Iraq and the British Isles. After several introductions to New Zealand beginning in 1862, it rapidly became so abundant in the North Island that it was declared a pest and a bounty placed on its eggs. Now in lesser numbers, it is nevertheless widespread and common throughout the country, including the Chatham and Kermadec Islands, though relatively scarce in Fiordland and on Stewart Island. It has been recorded as a vagrant on Lord Howe Island and several subantarctic island groups.

Food   Seeds and small insects make up the diet, gathered mainly on the ground.

Habits   Yellowhammers live in resident pairs during the summer but normally congregate in large wandering flocks during winter. They mainly favour agricultural land but also inhabit sand dunes, salt marshes and the fringes of pine plantations; they sometimes occur in alpine scrub. In winter they often visit urban parks and gardens. The most distinctive call is an abrupt *tink*, and the song is an easily recognised high-pitched twitter of notes followed by a prolonged glide, like *chitty-chitty-chitty-chitty-sweeeee*.

Breeding   The nest is a neat, compact feather-lined cup of dry grass well hidden in a tussock, weed clump, bramble thicket or similar site, placed on the ground or close to it. Laying begins around mid-November. Three or four eggs make up the usual clutch, the incubation and fledging both take about 13 days. Mostly the female incubates, but both parents rear the young. Normally two broods per year are raised.

ORDER • Passeriformes
STATUS • introduced; common; resident

SPECIES • *Emberiza citrinella*
MAORI NAME • none

House Sparrow

15 cm

Recognition   With its black bib, white cheek and grey cap, the male is almost unmistakable: the female, however, is very drab and could easily be confused with several other birds, especially the hedge sparrow (page 94). Look for the pale eyebrow, boldly streaked back and stouter bill. Length about 15 cm.

Distribution   Originally the house sparrow had an extensive range across most of Eurasia and northern Africa: introductions by humans have given it an even vaster range on all continents except Antarctica. First released in New Zealand in 1867 to control insect pests, its population expanded with such vigour that only 15 years later special legislation was enacted, declaring it a pest. It is now common on all three main islands, and has been recorded on the Antipodes, Auckland and Chatham Islands. House sparrows are homebodies and seldom roam.

Habits   House sparrows are often abundant in all habitats associated with humans, from the centres of major cities to marginal grazing land,

but they usually decline abruptly at the fringes of undisturbed native environments. Loosely gregarious, they normally live in small groups when not breeding, but much larger flocks sometimes form in winter. Calls and songs are varied but undistinguished, consisting mainly of miscellaneous cheeping and chattering notes.

Food   The chief food consists of seeds gathered on bare ground, supplemented by insects and, in urban areas, crumbs and food scraps. House sparrows may do considerable damage to standing crops of young wheat or barley, to seedling vegetables such as lettuce and peas, and sometimes raid orchards.

Breeding   Although most breeding occurs in spring, the season is very vague and prolonged. House sparrows build loose, untidy, domed nests of straw or grass, lined with feathers and usually with a side entrance, placed in almost any convenient crevice in a building or tree. Incubation and nestling periods are both about 14 days, with both parents participating fully.

ORDER • Passeriformes	**SPECIES** • *Passer domesticus*
STATUS • introduced; common; resident	**MAORI NAME** • tiu

Starling

22 cm

Recognition Unmistakable; length about 22 cm. The plumage is entirely black, with a silky sheen and glossed with green and violet. In winter, each feather is tipped with rusty brown, but these tips quickly wear off to reveal the glossy black breeding plumage. Starlings walk, not hop, on the ground, where they share with their close relative, the mynah, an inimitable, confident strut.

Distribution The common starling is abundant across Europe and much of Asia. After widespread introductions elsewhere it is now almost equally abundant over much of North America, South Africa, Australia and New Zealand, where it is ubiquitous on all three main islands and wanders with some frequency to all outlying groups.

Habits Starlings avoid dense forest; they inhabit open country of all kinds but, like the mynah, are most numerous in urban, suburban, rural and mixed farming areas. Strongly gregarious, they live in flocks except when

nesting, and congregate at night in communal roosts that sometimes involve thousands of birds, especially in winter. Starling calls include a variety of chattering and twittering notes, while its long, rambling song, often delivered from a television aerial, overhead powerline or similar conspicuous perch, is an extraordinary jumble of whistles, clicks, and gurgles, some of them beyond the range of human hearing.

Food Ground-dwelling insects and their larvae make up the bulk of the diet, but starlings also eat snails, seeds, fruit and food scraps; they sometimes damage fruit crops in orchards and market gardens.

Breeding The nest is a rough untidy mass of grass, twigs, scrap paper and other debris in a cavity or crevice in a tree or a building, often forcibly commandeered from other birds. Both parents participate fully in the nesting cycle, incubating the four to eight eggs for about 12 days and rearing the chicks. Fledglings leave the nest at about 20 days.

ORDER • Passeriformes	**SPECIES** • *Sturnus vulgaris*
STATUS • introduced; common; resident	**MAORI NAME** • taringi

Indian Mynah

25 cm

Recognition   About 25 cm long, the Indian mynah is easily recognised by its mostly brown plumage, bright yellow legs, patch of naked yellow skin around each eye, and a large patch of white in each wing.

Distribution   This bird's natural home extends from Afghanistan and southern Russia to India and Malaysia, but it has been widely introduced elsewhere in the world, including South Africa, Australia, Hawaii, New Caledonia and New Zealand. Introductions in the South Island failed to establish, but it is common in the North Island, north of about Wanganui.

Habits   The mynah inhabits most kinds of open country but it is usually most common in suburban, rural and mixed farming areas close to human habitation. It lives mostly in pairs which become family parties in autumn, and often combine with others to form flocks through the winter. Although resident in summer, birds wander more widely in winter. At dusk, mynahs congregate from a considerable distance to join communal roosts of several hundred birds, which are maintained throughout the year, though used mainly by non-breeding birds during the nesting season. An isolated group of trees is favoured for the roosting site — a grove of decorative palms in a quiet suburb is a typical spot. Mynahs have a very wide vocabulary of loud and boisterous chattering, gurgling and whistled notes.

Food   Unusually versatile in their foraging, mynahs eat a wide range of insects, seeds, fruit, and discarded human food scraps. They occasionally raid the nests of other small birds for eggs and chicks, and sometimes cause damage in orchards and to other fruit crops.

Breeding   The nest is little more than a rough bundle of grass, twigs and miscellaneous debris, stuffed into any available cavity in a tree or a building. The clutch of three to six eggs is incubated by both parents until hatching at about 14 days. Chicks fledge and leave the nest at about 25 days.

ORDER • Passeriformes
STATUS • introduced; common; resident

SPECIES • *Acridotheres tristis*
MAORI NAME • none

Kokako

38 cm

churrs and cat-like mewing notes, but the kokako is especially notable for its extraordinarily rich, loud, complex, flute-like songs, often uttered in long, rambling duets, especially at dawn.

Distribution   Once common on all three main islands, it is now virtually extinct in the South Island; several populations survive in a few extensive forests in the North Island, especially the Bay of Plenty forests.

Food   Eating leaves, seeds, fungi and fruit, the kokako is largely vegetarian for much of the year — though it eats some insects in summer — and is therefore dependent on old, rich, undisturbed forests with an abundance of different kinds of plants coming into season, species by species, throughout the year. Parrot-like, it has a characteristic habit of clutching food in one foot as it breaks it up with its bill.

Recognition   About 38 cm in total length, the kokako is long-legged and almost entirely pale grey in plumage, with a small black face mask and bright blue wattles at the base of the bill. The sexes are similar.

Habits   Almost flightless, the kokako is confined to dense forests where it forages mainly in the lower growth, bounding up from branch to branch on its strong legs, fluttering feebly from tree to tree, or scuttling squirrel-like through the foliage. Like the saddleback, it forms life-long pairs that mutually defend permanent territories from which they seldom stray. Its calls include a range of soft clucks,

Breeding   The nest is a bulky structure of twigs, well hidden in dense foliage. Three eggs make up the usual clutch. Incubation, by the female alone, takes 20 days and chicks leave the nest at about 32 days. Both parents are fully involved in rearing the chicks. The kokako is severely challenged by predation from stoats, weasels and rats, and by competition for food from the introduced brushtail possum. Include habitat destruction and it is difficult to be optimistic about its long-term survival prospects. Of special concern is its apparently very low breeding potential — one three-year study revealed that, on average, only one independent youngster was reared in every ten nesting attempts (that is, an average of 0.1 birds reared per pair per year).

Order • Passeriformes		**Species** • *Callaeas cinerea*	
Status • endemic; rare; resident		**Maori name** • kokako	

Saddleback

Recognition   The saddleback is glossy black in plumage, with chestnut under the tail, a chestnut 'saddle' on the back, and fleshy, bright red-orange wattles at the base of the bill. The total length is about 25 cm.

Distribution   At the time of European settlement the saddleback was widespread on all three main islands, but by the turn of the century it was nearly extinct. The decline has been attributed to forest clearance and predation from stoats, but it was most noticeable in the 1880s and 1890s, before any appreciable effects from these causes might reasonably be expected, and rats have since taken centre stage as the prime suspects. The saddleback survived only on Hen Island and a few small islands off Stewart Island but, since 1964, wildlife authorities have successfully relocated some to several other islands, including Kapiti and Tiritiri Matangi.

Habits   Saddlebacks are long-lived, form simple pair bonds that persist for life, and occupy permanently defended territories. The vocal repertoire is extraordinarily varied and intricate; many songs are uttered by females as well as males, and several are not inherited, as in most birds, but learned from neighbours. Anatomically, the saddleback has an unusual arrangement of the muscles and bony structure of the jaw which allows the bird considerable power and versatility in levering bark from trees, splitting dead branches and digging in rotted logs for food.

Food   The diet includes some fruit but saddlebacks feed largely on insects, especially weta, seeking them out at all forest levels from the ground to the canopy, and using their unusual jaw structure to prise open bark crevices to uncover them. They batter away at bark and epiphytes with such noise and gusto that they flush insects from a wide area, often accompanied by fantails which snap up any small fry ignored by the larger saddleback.

Breeding   Nests are loose, shallow bowls of twigs, leaves and rootlets placed in tree hollows. Two or three eggs form the clutch. Incubation takes about 19–21 days, fledging 27–28 days, and both parents participate fully in rearing the chicks. Youngsters accompany their parents for several months after leaving the nest.

ORDER • Passeriformes	**SPECIES** • *Philesturnus carunculatus*
STATUS • endemic; restricted; resident	**MAORI NAME** • tieke

Australian Magpie

40 cm

Black-backed
magpie

Recognition   About 40 cm in total length, the Australian magpie is easily identifiable as the only New Zealand bird with a large white patch on the back of the head. The sexes are similar, and immatures much resemble adults except for their somewhat more scruffy appearance.

Distribution   The Australian magpie occurs across almost the entire Australian continent, including Tasmania, as well as southern New Guinea. It was introduced to New Zealand many years ago, several times and in various localities. Two distinct subspecies have since become well established and widespread: the white-backed magpie is common in most of the North Island and the northern half of the South Island, while the black-backed form is numerous in the Hawke's Bay district and in Canterbury.

Habits   Essential habitat requirements include open country on which to feed and clumps of trees in which to roost and breed, conditions that are often met in general farming country, as well as open spaces in towns and cities. Social

rather than merely gregarious, magpies normally live in stable groups consisting of a dominant pair and several generations of offspring, which jointly defend permanent territories used for feeding, roosting and nesting. The size of the territory depends on the quality of the habitat and the number of defenders, but is normally about 10–20 hectares.

Food   Gathered mostly on open ground, the diet includes insects of all kinds. Magpies often dig for grubs and earthworms, and they also eat skinks and other small animals they encounter.

Breeding   Nesting usually begins in early spring. The nest is a rough untidy basket of sticks in a tree, built mainly by the female, which incubates the eggs alone. The usual clutch is three to five eggs, which hatch in 20 days. The chicks fledge and leave the nest about 24 days after hatching, and then all group members contribute to their care and guardianship. Nesting magpies are extremely aggressive, often 'dive-bombing' humans.

ORDER • Passeriformes	**SPECIES** • *Gymnorhina tibicen*
STATUS • introduced; common; resident	**MAORI NAME** • makipai

Rook

45 cm

Recognition   The rook is easy to identify as the only big (length about 45 cm), all-black perching bird in New Zealand; especially diagnostic is the patch of naked, pale grey skin between eye and bill.

Distribution   The original home of the rook is western Eurasia. It was first introduced to New Zealand in 1862 to control insects but proved largely unsuccessful. Although well established and still spreading slowly in the Hawke's Bay district (where the estimated total population is around 25,000 birds), rooks remain uncommon and very local elsewhere in New Zealand. Soon after release it became clear that rooks damage crops more than they repay in harmful insects destroyed, and the rook was officially declared a pest in 1971.

Habits   Largely confined to cultivated land, rooks sometimes forage in open spaces in cities and along the coast. They avoid dense forest. They are strongly gregarious at all seasons and normally forage, travel and even breed in flocks,

often several hundred strong. The most common call is a loud, deep, distinctive *caaw* or *kaah*.

Food   Rooks are omnivorous, the ratio of the plant and animal components of their diet varying widely with the seasons. Most food is gathered on the ground: largely insects, spiders, grubs and earthworms in summer, seeds, nuts, cereals, fruits, tubers and similar items at other times. In autumn, rooks often bury food (especially walnuts), returning in winter to retrieve it.

Breeding   A typical rookery, or breeding colony, is an isolated grove of tall, mature trees such as elms or eucalypts with a broad vista all about. Nests are bulky, untidy bowls, built of sticks, bound with mud and lined with grass. Mostly the female builds while the male fetches the materials. The eggs are pale green blotched with dark brown, the usual clutch is three or four, and incubation takes about 17 days. The female broods while her partner feeds her at the nest, but both parents feed the young.

ORDER • Passeriformes	**SPECIES** • *Corvus frugilegus*
STATUS • introduced; uncommon; resident	**MAORI NAME** • none

Brushtail Possum

82 cm

Recognition Unmistakable — a cat-sized mammal with a long bushy tail, prominent ears and large dark eyes. The soft, close fur is brownish grey, but the exact shade varies widely. Possums weigh about 2–4 kg, with a total length of about 80 cm, about 30 cm of which is tail. Males are larger and heavier than females.

Distribution The most common and widespread of all possums in its native Australia, the brushtail is even more numerous in New Zealand. It was introduced in 1858 to establish a fur industry and is now abundant almost everywhere except Fiordland and the far north. An average density of 1–1.5 possums per hectare is considered high in Australian forests, but densities ten or twenty times as high have been recorded in New Zealand.

Habits Mainly solitary and active mostly at night, the brushtail lives almost anywhere there are trees — including inner city gardens and parks. Although it normally dens in hollow trees, it also uses the attics of houses and other buildings. It browses in the canopy of trees but also spends some time on the ground; it rummages noisily in garbage cans and often raids bird-feeders. Longevity is typically about 10 years. Males mark their territories with scent produced from glands on the chin, chest and anus — the chest gland produces a reddish secretion that often stains the surrounding fur. Possums can be quite noisy, uttering a variety of sharp hisses and deep, guttural coughs.

Food Possums occasionally eat insects, fruit, nectar and even meat, but the main food is tree foliage. They tend to browse nightly on a favourite tree, so persistently that the tree is seriously weakened, making it prone to disease. Favoured food plants — such as the magnificent rata tree — may be devastated over wide areas. The damage done by possums to New Zealand forests is enormous.

Breeding In suitably mild climates, breeding may occur at any time of year. Normally only one infant is reared at a time. The gestation period is 17–18 days; youngsters leave the pouch at about five months and are weaned at around six to seven months. Maximum mortality occurs in young males, aged 6–18 months, as they scatter widely in search of their own territories.

Order • Diprotodontia		**Species** • *Trichosurus vulpecula*	
Status • introduced; common; resident		**Maori name** • paihamu, pohima	

Wallabies

1.6 m

Bennett's
wallaby

Wallabies of at least six species have been introduced into New Zealand from their native Australia. Many were released on Kawau Island and some other islands in the Hauraki Gulf (where several still persist), but only two are at all common or widespread elsewhere.

Introduced to the Rotorua district around 1912, the tammar wallaby prefers very dense vegetation such as scrub or fern thicket, through which it commutes by a system of narrow runways between its hidden sleeping places and nearby forest glades. It is solitary, and active mainly at night. Small and dark, with white chest and rufous hints in the fur of limbs and haunches, tammar wallabies grow to just over 1 m in total length — though females are noticeably smaller than males.

The red-necked or Bennett's wallaby is about 160 cm long, about half of which is tail. Like the tammar wallaby, it lives a mainly solitary existence, feeding at night and sleeping by day under a bush or in some similar secluded spot. However, it favours much more open country — hilly tussock grassland with scrub-filled gullies suits it just fine — and it is much more likely to be seen emerging to feed in late afternoon, or in the very early morning.

By far the most significant population of red-necked wallabies in New Zealand is in the Hunters Hills and surrounding district of south Canterbury. Here three animals were liberated around 1874 and successfully established themselves with such vigour that by 1947 they were deemed a pest.

Smaller cousins of the kangaroos, wallabies are marsupials, a group of animals best represented in Australia, but with many species in South America and elsewhere. This group's most conspicuous characteristic lies in giving birth to considerably 'premature' young who continue their early development in a pouch on the mother's abdomen.

Some macropods (kangaroos and wallabies), such as the tammar wallaby, exhibit 'embryonic diapause', an adaptation for coping with the erratic Australian environment. Under this regime, an embryo may suspend development and remain 'on hold' as long as any earlier youngster remains in the pouch, coming to term only when that joey either dies or outgrows the pouch. This ingenious backup system means that females can quickly resume breeding after any setback, without the prior delay of finding and courting a mate.

Long-tailed Bat

28 cm

Recognition Although the long-tailed bat is confined to New Zealand, it has several close relatives in Australia and New Guinea belonging to a worldwide family of bats comprising some 300 species. They are often called 'wattled bats' from the distinctive fleshy lobes or wattles along the sides of the lower jaw. The long-tailed bat has a wingspan of about 28 cm, has smaller ears, more delicate 'papery' wings, and darker, richer brown fur than New Zealand's only other bat, the rare short-tailed bat. Identification features are to some extent academic because the long-tailed is the only bat likely to be encountered by the casual observer.

Distribution Both this species and the short-tailed bat occur together on Little Barrier Island, on Stewart Island and perhaps one or two other offshore islands, but only the long-tailed bat remains at all common on the main islands. It is widespread but very local in the North Island, but much more numerous in the South Island, especially in Nelson, Westland, and on Stewart Island.

Food The long-tailed bat feeds on fairly large, night-flying insects such as beetles and moths, mostly captured in flight, although it occasionally snatches caterpillars or resting insects from tree foliage.

Habits Both bat species are similar in mainly inhabiting forests and in sleeping by day in small groups in hollow trees, emerging shortly after dark to hunt over quiet rivers or forest clearings. Using biosonar (uttering very high frequency 'squeaks' and being guided by the echoes) to locate and intercept insects, the long-tailed bat is noticeably swifter and more agile in flight than the short-tailed bat. The long-tailed bat is also much more adept at snatching insects in the cluttered forest environment. Unlike the short-tailed bat, the long-tailed hibernates in winter. Little is known of breeding behaviour in this species, but other bats of this group mate in autumn, and the female stores the sperm throughout winter for a sort of 'auto-fertilisation' in early spring — the only animals known to do so.

ORDER • Chiroptera
STATUS • endemic; uncommon; resident

SPECIES • *Chalinolobus tuberculatus*
MAORI NAME • pekapeka-tou-roa

Short-tailed Bat

28 cm

Recognition Almost impossible to identify at night (except possibly by its relatively low, slow and direct flight), the short-tailed bat is a tubby, well-built little bat, a little over 6 cm in total length, weighing about 15 g, and with a wingspan of about 28 cm. Its close, velvety fur is dark brown in colour, speckled with white, and it has prominent pointed ears. When not flying, the bases of its unusually thick, leathery wings are tucked into a sort of protective pouch on each side of the body.

Distribution Confined to New Zealand, the short-tailed bat is believed once to have occurred all over the North and South Islands and the closer offshore islands, but is now very rare and local. It remains fairly common on Little Barrier Island and on Stewart Island (especially on nearby Codfish Island), and has been reported in recent years in the Nelson District and the Omahuta Forest, Tararua Range, and Rotorua district of the North Island. There were once two species in this uniquely New Zealand family (Mystacinidae); however, live specimens of the greater short-tailed bat are known only from Solomon and Big Cape Islands off Stewart Island, where it has not been seen since 1967, so it is probably now extinct.

Food The short-tailed bat occasionally catches night-flying moths and similar insects in midair in the same way as 'ordinary' bats, but what is unusual is that much of its food is captured on the ground. It crawls and even scampers nimbly over boulders, tree trunks and forest leaf litter in search of insects and other small animals; it frequently eats fruit, sips nectar from flowers, and has even been observed scavenging at carcasses, such as slaughtered muttonbirds left hanging up to dry.

Habits The short-tailed bat lives in small colonies that roost in cavities in trees, mainly in beech or kauri forest, and scatter at night to feed. Its most distinctive habit is burrowing — the only bat known to do so. It rummages under leaf litter for prey, and often hollows out its own roosts in dead wood.

ORDER • Chiroptera
STATUS • endemic; rare; resident

SPECIES • *Mystacina tuberculata*
MAORI NAME • pekapeka-tou-poto

Rabbit

40 cm

Recognition   The rabbit can be confused only with the hare, despite being substantially smaller (total length up to about 40 cm), having shorter ears, and being much less gangly.

Distribution   Native to Spain and Morocco, the rabbit was first domesticated around AD 500. By about AD 1500 it had established feral populations almost throughout Europe. It has since been widely introduced elsewhere in the world — most notoriously in Australia, with disastrous consequences. It was first released in New Zealand in 1777, mainly as a source of meat and fur. At first it did poorly, but 50 years later it was considered a pest. (In 1873, only 33,000 skins were exported from New Zealand; in 1882 the figure was nine million.) Today it is common and widespread in suitable habitat almost everywhere in New Zealand, including some offshore islands.

Food   Rabbits eat mainly green grass but they also nibble a wide range of herbs, flowers and other plants, and browse saplings and shrubbery if other food is scarce, feeding mainly at night and spending the day underground. Access to drinking water is normally not required.

Habits   Unlike the hare, rabbits are social animals that live in groups of about six or eight adults and their offspring, under the leadership of a dominant buck and doe that contribute most of the group's breeding effort. Pregnancy usually lasts about 30 days; four or five kits make up the usual litter, and these are born naked, blind and helpless in a grass-lined burrow especially constructed for the event. Often five or even six litters are reared in a year. The colony lives in a warren, consisting of an intricate network of underground burrows with several entrances. All adults participate in defending the communal territory against trespass from neighbouring groups, which in favourable circumstances can reach densities approaching 100 rabbits per hectare. As well as damaging pastures with their burrowing, rabbits also compete directly with livestock for food — ten rabbits eat about as much as one sheep.

ORDER • Lagomorpha
STATUS • introduced; common; resident

SPECIES • *Oryctolagus cuniculus*
MAORI NAME • rapeti

Hare

60 cm

Recognition   Built for sprinting, hares are larger than rabbits, being about 60 cm in total length, with longer ears and very long, powerful hind legs. Hares moult their fur twice a year, alternating between a reddish brown summer coat and a duller, greyer brown winter coat.

Distribution   The hare's homeland sprawls across much of Africa and Eurasia, eastward to China. It was first imported and released in New Zealand in the Canterbury region in 1851 and it has since established itself in open country almost throughout the main islands, from coastal pasture to alpine meadows at nearly 2000 m altitude.

Food   Rigidly vegetarian, in diet the hare almost exactly mimics the rabbit, eating mostly green grass, clover and a wide range of similar low herbage, supplemented occasionally by chewing bark and browsing shrubs and saplings, especially when other food is scarce.

Habits   Despite its nearly identical diet, the hare sits much more kindly on the New Zealand environment than the rabbit, largely because it is mainly solitary and does not dig burrows. Adults live in permanent territories some 300 hectares in extent, which they vigorously defend from trespass by neighbouring hares. Like the rabbit, the hare feeds mainly in the evening and at night, especially during the hours before midnight. During the day it rests in a scrape or form, consisting of a bed of grass in tussock or under a low bush, and relies largely on immobility to evade detection by predators.

Breeding   Most breeding takes place in early spring, but may occur at any time. Competing males engage each other in vigorous and lengthy boxing matches. Courtship in general involves much chasing, wrestling and gambolling about — the origin of the old English expression, 'mad as a March hare'. Females may rear up to six litters per year, each of three to five kits, born after a gestation period of about 32 days. Unlike rabbits, hare kits are fully furred and open-eyed at birth, and are mobile within a few minutes. The mother hides them individually in dense grass, then visits only to nurse them. Females have the unusual ability to conceive a second litter while still carrying the first. As in the rabbit, the male plays no part in rearing the young.

ORDER • Lagomorpha	**SPECIES** • *Lepus capensis*
STATUS • introduced; common; resident	**MAORI NAME** • hea

House Mouse

16 cm

Recognition   Unmistakable, as the only very small non-flying mammal of any kind in New Zealand — much smaller than a rat. Adults may reach about 16 cm in total length, of which about half is contributed by the long, slender tail. The fur is soft, short and greyish brown in colour. Like all rodents, the house mouse is also characterised by ever-growing front teeth that are kept sharp and at optimum length by constant gnawing.

Distribution   Several thousand years ago, the ancestral house mouse may have been a resident of central Asia, but it became a commensal of humans in prehistoric times and has accompanied us virtually everywhere in our travels ever since — usually inadvertently. It now has an almost global distribution, and occurs almost throughout New Zealand, including many offshore islands. The absence of any small furred competitors in New Zealand means that it has also been able to penetrate native habitats far from towns and farms and other human habitation.

Food   The house mouse is essentially a seed-eater, supplementing its diet with insects whenever opportunity offers. However, in its association with humans it lives on a very wide range of stored foodstuffs — especially cereals — as well as such items as bread, leftovers and other scraps.

Habits   Mice are strongly gregarious, living in groups or colonies that are active mostly at night. Part of their success is linked to their unusually high reproductive potential. Where food is plentiful, breeding is almost constant, with females rearing up to 11 litters a year, each consisting of four to eight young. Pregnancy lasts only about 20 days, and females may begin breeding within two months of birth. Under some circumstances, where cycles of superabundance of food alternate with famine, mouse populations can increase explosively, resulting in spectacular plagues followed by devastating population crashes. Fortunately such events happen infrequently in New Zealand's relatively equable climate.

ORDER • Rodentia
STATUS • introduced; common; resident

SPECIES   • *Mus musculus*
MAORI NAME • mauhi

Kiore

30 cm

Recognition   The kiore looks very similar to the Norway rat but is substantially smaller. Males are about 30 cm in total length (of which about half consists of tail) and weigh around 100 g; females are somewhat smaller.

Distribution   Kiore are widespread in the south-western Pacific region, and were brought by the Maori to New Zealand, where they remain common on many offshore islands. The fact that Maori commonly trapped them for food suggests that some introductions may have been deliberate but, on the other hand, kiore are absent from several important Maori settlements on offshore islands. At the time of European settlement kiore were widespread on the main islands; now they are absent or extremely rare almost everywhere except Fiordland.

Food   Kiore eat the seeds, buds, flowers, leaves and roots of a wide range of plants, but they are also partly carnivorous and include caterpillars, weta, spiders, earthworms, snails and occasionally small birds and lizards in their diet

whenever opportunity offers — with perhaps an overall trend to small animals predominating in winter, plant foods in summer.

Habits   Beech forests are important kiore habitats, but they also occupy other areas such as tussock grassland at least occasionally; they also fossick along rocky shores and regularly occupy buildings. Their dry, sheltered dens are sometimes betrayed by chewed snail shells, insects, seeds and similar discarded food remnants, but they are not known to burrow. Kiore are active mostly at night and tend to be solitary: family ties are loose and soon dissolved, and males associate with females only for mating. Males may wander far in search of mates during the spring breeding season, but otherwise kiore tend to be strongly sedentary. The gestation period is about 20 days, and the average litter is five or six, or occasionally up to nine. Females mate soon after giving birth, rearing up to three broods per season. Youngsters are weaned at about four weeks and reach sexual maturity within their first year.

ORDER • Rodentia
STATUS • introduced; rare; resident

SPECIES • *Rattus exulans*
MAORI NAME • kiore

Norway Rat

40 cm

Recognition   It is easy to confuse Norway rats with ship rats, but the Norway rat is slightly bigger (up to 40 cm long) and much heavier, with a comparatively short tail — which is usually pale, whereas the ship rat's tail is nearly black. Also, the Norway rat's shaggy fur is muddy brown, whereas the ship rat is sooty brown or black. Examined at close range, the clincher is the colour of the hind foot, which is uniformly pale in the Norway rat, blackish in the ship rat.

Distribution   Despite its name, the original home of the Norway rat lies in the region surrounding the Caspian Sea, from where it spread to Europe by unknown means sometime during the 1700s, and from there as stowaways on ships to almost every country in the world. It seems certain to have arrived in New Zealand with the earliest European settlers, if not the first explorers, and is now widespread in towns and cities throughout New Zealand, including several offshore islands. However, it is largely restricted to the vicinity of human habitation,

and is generally absent or rare in undisturbed native environments.

Food   The Norway rat eats almost anything humans eat, and it thrives essentially as a scavenger, living on scraps, leftovers, and various kinds of stored, spoiled or discarded foodstuffs; it also eats insects, spiders, seeds, birds' eggs and baby birds.

Habits   Active mainly at night, Norway rats live in loosely structured groups that normally consist of a dominant male with perhaps three or four females and their offspring. They usually live in burrows and take most of their food on the ground. Females rear several litters a year, each usually consisting of about 8–10 young, occasionally up to 18, born blind and naked after a pregnancy of 21–23 days. Norway rats are much clumsier and less frequent tree-climbers than the ship rat, but swim willingly and well. In New Zealand, stoats appear to keep the population in check, except in the centre of cities and ports where stoats are less common.

ORDER • Rodentia		**SPECIES**	• *Rattus norvegicus*
STATUS • introduced; common; resident		**MAORI NAME**	• pouhawaiki

Ship Rat

37 cm

Recognition   Often known as the black rat, the ship rat closely resembles the Norway rat but is a little smaller, with a proportionately much longer tail. The Norway rat is also much burlier and more powerfully built, weighing — on average — nearly twice as much as the ship rat (about 150 g against 300 g). Ship rats are variable in colour, with an overall trend towards black in the South Island and sooty-brown with white underparts in the North Island.

Distribution   From its ancestral home in the Middle East, the ship rat spread westward through Europe in the thirteenth century, inadvertently transported by armies returning from the Crusades. Like the Norway rat, its distribution is now almost global, and it probably arrived in New Zealand with the first European settlers. It is now common and widespread throughout New Zealand, including many offshore islands.

Food   Part vegetarian and part carnivore, the ship rat eats a wide variety of fruits, nuts, seeds and similar plant material, as well as preying heavily on baby birds, birds' eggs, insects and other small animals.

Habits   In the early 1960s, three endemic species of birds, the saddleback, the bush wren, and the subantarctic snipe, survived on tiny South Cape Island, off Stewart Island, as their last remaining toehold on New Zealand's main islands. Then in 1962 ship rats 'jumped ship' from a fishing vessel and got ashore — and within two years all three birds had vanished. Such stories are typical of the spread of the ship rat, which has played a more prominent role in the destruction of New Zealand's unique birdlife than any other introduced animal.

Like the Norway rat, the ship rat is active mainly at night, but differs strikingly in its more solitary habits and its mainly tree-dwelling behaviour. Like the Norway rat it is a prolific breeder and reproduction is almost constant throughout the year. A healthy well-nourished female can rear litters of five to ten young up to six times in a year.

Order • Rodentia
Status • introduced; common; resident

Species • *Rattus rattus*
Maori name • matapo

Hedgehog

20 cm

Recognition   Unmistakable — the only New Zealand mammal with spines. The overall colour is brownish grey, but each spine is creamy white, with a broad blackish band near the tip, giving the whole animal a brindled or speckled appearance. The spines are hollow, sharply pointed, and about 20 cm long.

Distribution   The original motive for bringing hedgehogs from their native Europe is unclear. The first pair were given to the Canterbury Acclimatisation Society in 1870. Hedgehogs were released all over the nation to control garden pests such as slugs and snails. They prospered, and now occur almost everywhere except very cold areas, such as the North Island high country and the Southern Alps, or very wet regions, such as Fiordland.

Habits   The hedgehog is active mainly at night and feeds on insects, snails, earthworms and similar small animals, captured on the ground. It is often noisy when foraging, snuffling and scuffling as it rummages among the leaves.

Perhaps its best-known attribute is its habit of curling itself into a prickly ball when frightened — fine when confronted by a curious dog, but not so clever when startled by an oncoming car.

Hibernation   Hedgehogs hibernate when temperatures fall below about 10–11°Celsius, and south of about Wellington they hibernate for several months through the winter. Curled up in its den, a hibernating hedgehog's heartbeat slows to about 20 beats per minute and breathing stops altogether for periods of up to an hour. The defining characteristic of hibernation is that the animal *wakes itself up* (other torpid animals merely revive as the temperature rises), which means it must have sufficient energy stored as fat to 'rev itself up' to regain normal temperature in spring. Hedgehogs entering hibernation weighing less than about 300 g are unlikely to survive, having too little fat to fuel the recovery process. Hibernating hedgehogs lose about one-tenth of their body weight through the winter, and many young, sick or starved individuals never awaken.

Order • Insectivora
Status • introduced; common; resident

Species • *Erinaceus europaeus*
Maori name • tuatete, hetiheti

Ferret

55 cm

Recognition Ferrets, stoats and weasels are very similar animals, with long sinuous bodies, short legs and long slender tails; weasels are tiny, ferrets big and burly, and stoats intermediate in size. The weasel has a slender, rather short brown tail, the stoat a longer tail with only the tip bushy, while the ferret is easily identifiable by its long, dark, much bushier tail, as well as a conspicuous black 'bandit' face mask. The coat is very variable in colour, ranging from white through brown to nearly black. Males often weigh twice as much as females (up to about 1.4 kg).

Distribution Like stoats and weasels, ferrets were introduced to New Zealand from Europe in the 1870s in an attempt to counter the rabbit plague. For many years the Department of Agriculture operated breeding ranches for their release into the wild, but the ferret population expanded with such vigour that the ferret itself was ultimately declared a pest and a bounty system introduced. Today, New Zealand has both the largest wild ferret population and the

largest ferret-fur (called fitch) export industry in the world.

There are no ferrets on Stewart Island or any of the offshore islands, but on the two main islands they are common almost everywhere there are rabbits, though they are rare or absent in most of Northland, Westland and Fiordland. They generally avoid dense forest and are most numerous in rough grazing country.

Food Ferrets will eat almost anything animal in origin, including insects, fish, frogs and birds' eggs, but they depend mainly on rats, mice and rabbits. The great size difference between the sexes means marked gender differences in diet: males tend, on average, to prey more on rabbits, females on rats.

Habits Ferrets are more rigidly nocturnal than stoats or weasels and tend to rely more heavily on scent than vision in their hunting — rabbits, for example, are hunted mainly underground in their warrens. They swim well but, compared to stoats, are much less willing to climb trees.

Order • Carnivora	**Species** • *Mustela furo*
Status • introduced; common; resident	**Maori name** • torihura, toritahae

Stoat

40 cm

Recognition   Stoats reach about 40 cm in length, of which about one-quarter consists of tail. A healthy adult male stoat weighs around 250 g, but females are much smaller. Stoats are mostly brown in colour, shedding and replacing their fur in spring and again in autumn: if the temperature is very cold then the new hair in autumn grows out white. In some localities, New Zealand winters are occasionally severe enough to provoke this reaction and some stoats may be white or pied in winter. The moult itself is triggered by day length, its timing unaffected by climate or other factors.

Distribution   Stoats were introduced into New Zealand in the 1870s as a deliberate government policy in response to complaints from sheep farmers of severe pasture damage caused by rabbits. Despite protests from other parties — such as bird-lovers — a vigorous import programme saw large numbers released nationwide over several decades, and it was not until 1936 that protection was finally repealed and further imports banned. Today, stoats occur virtually throughout the North and South Islands but are absent from Stewart Island and most offshore islands such as Kapiti, Little Barrier and the Chathams.

Food   Stoats are formidable predators, habitually tackling a wide range of prey, from insects to hares and possums (and occasionally carrion), but they rely heavily on rabbits and tend to be scarce wherever these are uncommon.

Habits   Although all their senses are acute, stoats tend to rely most on sight. They hunt mainly on the ground but they climb trees with ease; they also swim readily, and have no trouble crossing straits up to a kilometre or so wide in order to visit small offshore islands. Mostly solitary, they hunt by day or night. At times they can be quite vocal, employing a wide repertoire that includes a low hiss when nervous, high trills in greeting, a sort of explosive chatter in threat, and a loud wailing squeal under extreme stress.

ORDER • Carnivora	**SPECIES** • *Mustela erminea*
STATUS • introduced; common; resident	**MAORI NAME** • tori ura, toata

Weasel

30 cm

Recognition   The weasel is almost a carbon copy of the stoat except in its much smaller size (total length about 30 cm, weight around 100 g). It is every bit as bold and formidable a predator, and can climb and swim as efficiently as its larger cousin. Even the calls, signs and behaviour of the two are similar. The weasel's tail is short (proportionately much shorter than the stoat's) and it lacks the stoat's brush tip. Its fur is warm brown above, white below but, unlike the stoat, in New Zealand it never turns white in winter.

Food   The most significant distinction between these two predators lies in the smaller size of prey the weasel can successfully handle, tending to rely heavily on warm-blooded prey such as mice — although a weasel can easily handle a rabbit if a suitable opportunity presents itself.

Distribution   Weasels were introduced from Britain in the 1870s, at the same time as stoats and for the same motive, to control rabbits. They were released in much larger numbers than stoats (probably because weasels were more numerous than stoats in Britain at the time, and consignments were accumulated indiscriminately); at first they spread widely and bred in very large numbers. But within a few years populations collapsed and the weasel remains today a much scarcer animal than the stoat in all parts of New Zealand. Like the stoat, the weasel is widespread on both main islands — except that it is rare or absent in most of Westland and Fiordland — but does not occur on offshore islands.

Habits   Weasels hunt at any time of day or night, mostly on the ground. Mainly sedentary, they appear to stay in pairs living 'separate lives' — males and females seldom making contact except during the mating season, even though they may jointly occupy the same home range — or at least two broadly overlapping ranges. Females tend to tolerate male trespassers but vigorously repel other females, while the converse applies to males. Several litters of 4–9 young (blind and naked at birth) are reared per year.

ORDER • Carnivora	**SPECIES** • *Mustela nivalis*
STATUS • introduced; uncommon; resident	**MAORI NAME** • tori uaroa, tori whatere, wihara

Feral Cat

77 cm

Distribution Cats were brought to New Zealand as domestic pets with the very first European arrivals. A feral population was quickly established. Feral cats are widespread in almost all habitats on the main islands and numerous offshore islands, many of which have been the target of vigorous eradication programmes in order to rid them of cats and rats and establish new nature reserves for endangered indigenous species.

ORDER • Carnivora
SPECIES • *Felis catus*
STATUS • introduced; common; resident
MAORI NAME • ngeru, poti, puihi, tori

Habits Nocturnal, solitary and territorial, the feral cat is a resourceful predator that prefers small mammals such as mice and rats (up to the size of a rabbit) but readily exploits other resources such as insects, small reptiles and birds. Its ability to do without drinking water means it can survive in many areas inhospitable to other predators. The most common size of litter is four or five kittens.

Feral Horse

1.48 m

Distribution Released or escaped horses have formed the nucleus of feral herds since the very earliest days of European settlement, but their establishment is to some extent restricted by their habitat requirements. They seldom browse on foliage, and so require plentiful supplies of grass, as well as access to drinking water at least every few days.

ORDER • Perissodactyla
SPECIES • *Equus caballus*
STATUS • introduced; restricted; migrant
MAORI NAME • hoiho

Habits Horses are strongly social and live in herds of up to six adult females and several generations of their offspring, under the leadership of a single dominant stallion. Old males often live alone. Sometimes several groups combine to form larger herds, especially where food is abundant. Stallions don't mate until their fifth year, but mares can foal as early as their second year. Mares give birth in seclusion, rejoining the herd with their single foal a week or two later.

Feral Pig

1.6 m

Distribution   Pigs have been domesticated for at least 6000 years, and were among livestock which accompanied the first European settlers to New Zealand. Some escaped and formed feral populations. And, like the goat, pigs were often deliberately introduced to islands by exploring mariners as a source of fresh meat for later voyagers. (Captain Cook is reputed to have landed the very first pigs in New Zealand.) Generally rare in the South Island but common in the North, feral pigs still survive on some offshore islands but have been eradicated from others in the process of habitat rehabilitation.

Habits   Pigs are omnivorous and will eat almost anything organic. They sometimes form loose groups but they are mostly solitary and territorial. Pigs prefer well-watered forest country where they are most active around dawn and again at dusk.

ORDER •	Artiodactyla
SPECIES •	*Sus scrofa*
STATUS •	introduced; common; resident
MAORI NAME •	puaka, kapene kuki

Feral Goat

1.3 m

Distribution   The goat has been a domesticated animal for so long — at least 8000 years — that its origins are lost in obscurity. Goats accompanied the first European settlers and, like the pig, were often deliberately released on islands as a source of fresh meat. Feral goats still inhabit many islands off the coast of New Zealand but have been destroyed on others in the establishment of nature reserves.

Habits   Usually living in flocks of up to 20, goats generally dislike wet feet and seldom do well in areas of high rainfall or dense forest, but thrive in most other kinds of rugged country. They can survive on vegetation of almost any kind — they can even climb low trees for forage — and often cause very severe environmental damage by denuding an area of almost all vegetation.

ORDER •	Artiodactyla
SPECIES •	*Capra hircus*
STATUS •	introduced; common; resident
MAORI NAME •	nanenane, piri koti, nane koti

Chamois

80 cm

Recognition   Even at a distance chamois can easily be identified by their distinctive horns, carried by both sexes. About 150–200 m long, the horns are close-set at the base, their slender shafts rising almost vertically before bending sharply backward. Chamois stand about 80 cm at the shoulder and weigh up to 50 kg. The coat tends to tawny brown in summer, blackish in winter, with a distinctive white patch on the cheek. Chamois hooves are even more hi-tech than modern running shoes, imparting a nearly miraculous surefootedness.

Distribution   The native home of the chamois is Europe. For many years it was thought they would do well in New Zealand and boost the tourist industry by attracting wealthy sportsmen from overseas. But it was not until 1907 that founding stock of eight chamois became available, in the form of a gift from the Emperor Franz Josef of Austria. They were released near Mount Cook and are now widespread in the Southern Alps from about Lake Wakatipu to near Lake Rotoiti.

Food   During the summer chamois feed on a wide range of alpine plants, especially grasses, herbs and flowers, but in winter they browse shrubbery and eat lichens and mosses.

Habits   Chamois have superb eyesight and hearing, and are extraordinarily nimble, taking refuge when alarmed in the most inaccessible places. The alarm call is an abrupt, high-pitched whistle. Normal daily routine sees chamois remaining at their lofty sleeping places until the morning sun is high, then feeding for several hours as they move steadily down-slope. They 'siesta' through the afternoon as they ruminate, then feed again in the evening as they wander back up-slope to bed down again. Mature males live alone for much of the year, except during the rut in May, while females and young usually form herds of 15–30 individuals. A single kid (rarely twins or triplets) is born in a nest of grass and lichens after a gestation of 153–210 days. The kid is active within a few minutes of birth, and can run and keep up with its mother within a day or two.

Order • Artiodactyla	**Species** • *Rupicapra rupicapra*
Status • introduced; common; resident	**Maori name** • none

Tahr

1.45 m

Recognition   Tahr of both sexes carry short, massive horns, laterally flattened and curving sharply backwards. A mature bull has a huge shaggy mane, a slate-grey to straw-coloured coat (dark in winter, bleached in summer), and a small red-brown patch on the rump; females are less massively built, less shaggy and much smaller. Young kids are brown, and look very much like goats.

Distribution   Tahr were introduced by the New Zealand government with the aim of creating a hunting resource to attract overseas tourists. The first release was of three females and two males from the Duke of Bedford's estate in England, and took place near Mount Cook in 1904. The herds prospered and tahr now occupy about 5000 sq km of high country, centred on the original point of release.

Habits   Tahr favour rocky ridges, cliffs and screes at the upper limit of alpine scrubland, especially steep, sunny slopes with less snow and more forage. Although they occasionally wander lower, they generally favour the zone between 1400 and 1700 m altitude. Gifted with superb eyesight, tahr are inquisitive but very wary and are more likely to see you before you see them; they can sometimes be located by their alarm call, a shrill bird-like whistle. They live permanently in close-knit flocks intricately segregated by gender, age and season. The rut lasts about six weeks in midsummer; although physiologically capable much earlier, bulls must reach social — as well as sexual — maturity in their fifth year before having any real chance of mating. Competing bulls display to each other, exactly mimicking each other's movements, until the loser runs away. Such contests rarely end in combat.

Food   Tahr browse a wide range of subalpine plants, especially matagouri scrub and snow tussock. They tend to wander slowly down-slope, foraging as they go, until dusk, remain at lower levels through the night, then move back up-slope to spend midday hours at high-altitude loafing stations.

Order • Artiodactyla		**Species**	• *Hemitragus jemlahicus*
Status • introduced; common; resident		**Maori name**	• none

Fallow Deer

New Zealand were three from Richmond Park in England, released in Nelson in 1864. Other introductions followed. Some succeeded, some didn't, but there are now fallow deer herds in a dozen or more localities scattered across New Zealand. The largest populations are in the vicinity of Tapanui, Lake Wakatipu and Paparoa in the South Island and Wanganui in the North Island.

Recognition   Perhaps the most easily recognised of New Zealand deer, the fallow deer stands just under 1 m at the shoulder. Mature bucks carry 'palmate' antlers — that is, webbed and broadly flattened. Coat colour is variable, ranging from nearly white to very dark chocolate, but is typically light brown in summer, sooty brown in winter. The back and flanks are dappled with broad white spots in summer, which fade to obscurity in winter.

Distribution   The fallow deer originally inhabited Asia Minor, southern Europe and North Africa, but it has been widely introduced elsewhere in the world. The first to arrive in

Habits   In the grand old days of European aristocracy, few country estates were considered suitably opulent unless graced by resident herds of fallow deer. Their status was helped by four prominent behavioural characteristics displayed in suitable conditions. They are: active by day; strongly gregarious; grazers rather than browsers (which means they spend a lot of time in the open), and they are strongly sedentary. In combination, these traits make fallow deer highly visible, and they were seen as a suitably genteel expression of conspicuous consumption. However, where persecuted, fallow deer herds tend to fragment into smaller groups that tend to spend more time in dense cover and modify their daily routine to forage more actively at night.

Breeding   For much of the year fallow deer herds are mixed, but as their antlers reach full growth males tend to split off into separate bachelor groups. These in turn fragment during the rut as competing males drive away lesser rivals. The further away a victor can drive his rivals, the bigger his territory — and the bigger his territory, the bigger the harem of available females living within it. Pregnancy lasts about 34 weeks, resulting in the birth of single young in early summer.

Order • Artiodactyla		**Species** • *Dama dama*	
Status • introduced; common; resident		**Maori name** • tia	

Red Deer

1.8 m

Recognition   Except for the wapiti, this is the largest deer in New Zealand as well as the most numerous and widespread. Males have a pronounced mane around the neck and shoulders and carry broad, many-pointed antlers. As in other deer, the antlers drop off shortly after mating and are regrown each year during the weeks leading up to the rut. As they grow they are protected by very short, plush-like fur and described as being 'in velvet'. Does are substantially smaller than bucks and fawns are dappled with small, round white spots.

Distribution   Native to western Eurasia and north-western Africa, red deer were first brought to New Zealand around 1850 to provide hunting for sportsmen. They prospered, and were soon abundant in forests and highlands almost throughout the main islands. By the 1920s the need for control was obvious and the government employed professional hunters to reduce their number. Since the 1960s the population has easily withstood a thriving export industry in venison (mainly to Europe) and antler-velvet (mainly to eastern Asia, where it is regarded as an aphrodisiac). Red deer are now widely farmed in New Zealand, but feral deer remain common and widespread.

Food   Red deer are both grazers and browsers, favouring grass when it is available but readily shifting to a diet of leaves, buds and shoots at other times, such as winter. Deer inflict severe damage on beech forests, chewing saplings and browsing the lower branches of mature trees up to about 2 m.

Habits   Where persecuted, red deer feed mainly in the evening and at night. Strongly

gregarious, they live for much of the year in herds loosely segregated by gender, except that during the rut in March or April (six months out of phase with their ancestors in the Scottish highlands), males become antisocial and extremely aggressive. They use their antlers in fierce battles with rival males over females, and challenge each other with a sort of loud bugling roar. The strategy is to gain sexual access to as many females as possible, in conflict with the identical aims of rival mates. Regrown in February, antlers are cast by late November. Females give birth (mostly in December) to a single young following a pregnancy of about 33 weeks.

ORDER • Artiodactyla	**SPECIES** • *Cervus elaphus*
STATUS • introduced; common; resident	**MAORI NAME** • tia

Other deer

Sika deer

At least nine species of deer have been introduced to New Zealand at one time or another; several failed to establish and several others survive only as small, precarious remnants. The most obscure introduction was probably the little-known South American species, the guemal, three of which were landed at Auckland in 1907 and never seen again. Others, such as the moose, mule deer and axis deer, survived for a time but have not been seen for decades and are presumably extinct.

The four species mentioned here might be counted as borderline cases — species that succeeded in establishing self-sustaining populations, but only on a local scale, or in small numbers.

Imported from North America, nine whitetail deer, *Odocoileus virginianus*, were released at Port Pegasus, Stewart Island, in 1901, and another nine near Lake Wakatipu in the South Island in the same year. The Lake Wakatipu herd has declined in recent years, but whitetails remain very common in parts of Stewart Island. Their habit of fleeing with tail stiffly erect to display the prominent white underside, prompts both their name and a convenient identification mark.

Sika deer, *Cervus nippon*, were released near Lake Taupo in 1905 and are now reasonably common in scrub and mixed beech forest over the central North Island extending, approximately, from Tongariro National Park to the Maungaharuru Range. Sika resemble red deer but are much smaller (standing about 1 m at the shoulders) and have a heart-shaped patch of white, narrowly edged with black, on the rump.

The New Zealand population of sambar deer, *Cervus unicolor*, is mostly confined to the central North Island between Rotorua and Otaki — the descendants of a pair imported from India and released in 1875. Exceeded only by the red deer in size, they are most easily distinguished by their broad, rounded ears. Bulky and dark brown in colour, sambar are usually only seen when startled unexpectedly in dense thickets, when the pale rump and under-tail is a good field-mark.

Rusa deer, *Cervus timoriensis*, were brought to New Zealand from New Caledonia (although the species is native to Indonesia) in 1907 and released in the Galatea foothills in the Bay of Plenty — the district to which they remain confined today. Smallest of New Zealand deer, they have a white chin and throat; they are timid, wary, elusive, and nearly nocturnal in habit. Males and females congregate in gender-segregated herds that tend to coalesce in the breeding season.

Whales and Dolphins

Bottlenose dolphin

Collectively known as cetaceans, the world's whales, dolphins and porpoises are divided into two groups: the toothed whales (technically called Odontoceti) and baleen whales (Mysticeti).

As their name implies, toothed whales have jaws equipped with more or less conventional teeth, but baleen whales are toothless, having instead sheets of flexible, comb-like *baleen*, hanging like a curtain from the upper jaw. This apparatus functions much like a sieve, straining from the water the vast numbers of tiny shrimp-like sea creatures (called krill), on which these ocean giants feed. One of this group, the blue whale, is the largest animal that ever lived, reaching some 30 m in length and weighing in the vicinity of 100–150 tonnes. Baleen whales have two blowholes, but toothed whales only one.

The toothed whales vary widely in size — largest of them all, the sperm whale (page 143), is about two-thirds the size of the mighty blue whale, but the smallest are well under 2 m in length.

Historically the terms 'whale', 'dolphin' and 'porpoise' have been used indiscriminately for various species of toothed whales, with an erratic trend to call the big species whales and the small ones dolphins or porpoises. A relatively recent attempt at rationalisation encourages the reservation of 'porpoise' to just one of the several families of these smaller cetaceans.

As a very general rule of thumb, 'dolphins' have pointed teeth and the snout extended into a distinct 'beak', whereas 'porpoises' have blunt, rounded snouts and spade-shaped teeth. The waters around New Zealand contain only one 'true' porpoise, the very rare and little-known spectacled porpoise. This is in marked contrast to the eight species of baleen whales and nearly 40 toothed whales and 'true' dolphins that have been observed and recorded in New Zealand waters.

Apart from New Zealand's 'specialty' dolphin, the endemic Hector's dolphin (page 146), at least four others may be seen in New Zealand coastal waters (dusky dolphin, common dolphin, striped dolphin, and bottlenose dolphin). Several have striking patterns of black, grey and white, but a further crucial cetacean identification feature is the presence or absence of a dorsal fin and — if present — its size, shape and position.

Southern Right Whale

18 m

Recognition   Three obvious features quickly identify the southern right whale: a strongly arched mouth in which the long baleen plates are easily visible; the total lack of a dorsal fin, and a peculiar whitish callosity called the bonnet that looks rather like some grotesquely enlarged wart on the top of the head, with similar but smaller irregular growths along the jaw. (The exact arrangement of these growths is unique to each animal, which means that individuals can be reliably recognised and tracked.) Even a glimpse of the tail as the animal dives is distinctive because the flukes are uniquely blunt and round-tipped. Right whales grow to about 18 m in length and are mainly black in colour. Unlike most other New Zealand whales, the sexes are roughly equal in size.

Habits   The right whale lives alone or in small groups. Before the days of fully equipped ocean-going factory ships, this whale was easy and profitable to hunt from very small boats because it frequents shallow coastal waters. It is relatively slow and ponderous in movement; it

floats when dead, which reduced wastage; and it yielded vast quantities of oil and valuable baleen — in short, the 'right' whale to target. By the close of the nineteenth century it had been hunted almost to extinction, and the first tentative hints of recovery have appeared only in the past decade or two. (Except at Campbell Island, there were no sightings in New Zealand waters between 1927 and 1963.) The right whale spends most of the year in cold Antarctic waters, migrating northwards in July to breed in temperate waters, returning south in late September. Well adapted to coastal waters, it rarely strands — often 'dozing' on the bottom with only its blowhole breaking the surface.

Distribution   Widespread in the southern hemisphere, the right whale seems to be making a comeback in Australian and New Zealand waters. Females with calves are seen with increasing frequency — even along busy tourist surf-beaches. Sightings are especially numerous in the Great Australian Bight and along southern shores of New Zealand's North Island.

ORDER • Cetacea	**SPECIES** • *Eubalaena australis*
STATUS • native; uncommon; migrant	**MAORI NAME** • tohora

Sperm Whale

18 m

Recognition   Largest of the toothed whales (up to 18 m in length), the sperm whale is immediately recognisable by its enormous, box-like head (contributing nearly one-third of the total bulk of the animal), its narrow, underslung lower jaw, and the row of hump-like ridges along the finless lower back. Even the 'blow' — the visible, steam-like plume of oily vapour emitted as the whale exhales — is diagnostic: because the single blowhole is canted to the left, the blow is uniquely angled at about 45° instead of vertical as in other whales.

Habits   Highly social, most sperm whales live in herds commonly up to 50 or 60 strong. These are typically segregated by gender, with young males forming 'bachelor schools' and females, calves and adolescents forming separate 'nursery schools' — with the added complexity that nursery schools promptly shift status to 'harem schools' when joined by a mature bull during the breeding season. The sperm whale merits fame as one of the most extraordinary animals on earth thanks to its adaptations as the

ultimate deep-sea diver — if these were mechanical they would surely rival stealth bombers as cutting-edge technology. One well-supported hypothesis, for example, suggests that the huge head and the famous spermaceti oil (in fact a wax) that fills it, are components of a unique hydrostatic system — using blood flow to warm or cool the wax changes its density, which enables the whale to rise or sink much faster than it could swim.

Food   Hungry sperm whales don't spurn fish or other prey, but their main food is squid and octopus which are caught mostly near the surface. Old males, however, habitually stalk giant squid at incredible depths, in dives lasting up to 90 minutes and sometimes reaching 3200 m or more.

Distribution   Sperm whales have a patchy distribution spanning all oceans; they are reasonably common in New Zealand seas, especially in the deep waters between the Kermadecs and the North Island.

ORDER • Cetacea
STATUS • native; uncommon; migrant

SPECIES • *Physeter macrocephalus*
MAORI NAME • paraoa

Orca

9 m

Recognition   Widely known also as the killer whale, the orca is in fact a dolphin — albeit a very big dolphin, with an exceptionally massive, powerful build. Mature males may grow to 9 m in length. The intricate, sharply black-and-white pattern is distinctive and the flippers are rounded and paddle-shaped; even the large dorsal fin itself is instantly diagnostic: tall, vertical and sharply triangular. In males the dorsal fin may tower nearly 2 m above the back, but in females it is much shorter (0.9 m maximum) and slightly hooked.

Distribution   Orcas occur in all the world's oceans, with especially large populations around Hawaii, off the western coast of Canada and in several other places. Very common in New Zealand waters, orcas have often been reported in Wellington and Auckland Harbours and the Bay of Islands. With luck it can also be seen from the Cook Strait ferry. Orcas have also been known to occasionally strand on New Zealand beaches with more than 50 such events having been documented.

Habits   A highly social animal, the orca normally lives in permanent family groups ranging from five or six up to 40 or more, consisting of mature males and females and sometimes several generations of their offspring — although very old bulls may live alone, and sometimes single pairs are seen. New Zealand orcas have not been intensively studied, but herds elsewhere often seem to be more or less resident in any particular locality, regularly patrolling their 'patch' and stopping off for a few days wherever the hunting is especially rewarding.

Food   Although the orca's staple diet consists of fish and squid, the species is much better known for its habitual attacks on other dolphins, seals and even large whales, subduing them by concerted attack as a wolf pack might bring down a moose. In some parts of the world they will even deliberately beach themselves to catch seals entering the surf. Despite their fearsome reputation as a carnivore, there are no documented attacks on humans.

Order • Cetacea		**Species**	• *Orcinus orca*
Status • native; common; resident		**Maori name**	• maki

Long-finned Pilot Whale

5.5 m

Recognition Often known as 'blackfish', this species — abundant all around New Zealand coasts — is very similar to the less common false killer whale and the rare short-finned pilot whale. A key feature to note is the pilot whale's bulbous forehead, which often bulges beyond the point of the lower jaw. Aptly named, the long-finned pilot whale has flippers up to one-fifth of the total body length, whereas in the short-finned pilot whale they are much less than one-fifth the total length. The latter is also slightly smaller.

ORDER •	Cetacea
SPECIES •	*Globicephala melas*
STATUS •	native; common; migrant
MAORI NAME •	upokohue

Habits The long-finned pilot whale is strongly gregarious, travelling in pods of 100 or more. It also seems to be prone to mass 'strandings', in which an entire school runs aground on a beach where its members die of stress, exhaustion and exposure. Several thousand strandings have been documented in New Zealand.

Strandings

Why do whales strand? The question is difficult to answer definitively; many variable but interlocking contributing factors — weather, season, age, state of health, strong 'herd' or social instinct — probably all play a part. One intriguing hypothesis involves the possibility of navigating by using the earth's magnetic field, a method known to lie within the abilities of various migrants ranging from sharks to pigeons.

This field is influenced by surface features, such as cliffs, islands and mountain ranges and is undetectable by human senses. Blindly following magnetic signals 'on autopilot' makes sense in the open sea, where there is no such thing as an obstacle, but the tactic may come drastically unstuck if the 'path' should just happen to run right up onto a beach. Proof is hard to come by, but some degree of correlation between strandings and known geomagnetic anomalies has been found.

Hector's Dolphin

1.5 m

Recognition   This is a dumpy little cetacean only about 1.5 m in total length. Its head presents a blunt, almost beakless profile with a steeply sloping forehead and it has a striking and complex pattern of black, pale grey, and white. But one clear glimpse of its dorsal fin is all that's really needed to identify it. The fin is small and round and its trailing edge bellies *outwards* — unlike all other New Zealand dolphins in which the trailing edge of the dorsal fin is concave. Males and females differ negligibly in appearance.

Distribution   A member of a small group of dolphins confined to the southern hemisphere, Hector's dolphin is further confined to coastal waters of the two main islands of New Zealand, from about Kawhia in the north to Foveaux Strait in the south. Its centre of distribution is in the cold waters of Cook Strait. Seldom seen more than about 10 km from shore, it especially favours muddy or turbid waters off the mouths of estuaries. It is common in areas such as Greymouth and Cloudy Bay, and occasionally

they even mingle with holiday crowds bathing in water barely waist-deep.

Food   Mostly small fish, such as anchovies, stargazers, red cod, and horse mackerel.

Habits   Usually living in pairs or small groups of half a dozen or so, occasionally it congregates in much larger schools — pods of about 100 have been reported. Little is known of its breeding behaviour. It is much less spectacular in behaviour than many other dolphins. It seldom leaps clear of the water, rarely 'porpoises' or 'breaches' at speed as common dolphins and bottlenose dolphins do, and usually surfaces to breathe with the minimum of fuss, briefly exposing the head, back and dorsal fin before slipping unobtrusively below again. However, especially in rough seas, Hector's dolphins often ride the bow wave of small boats; in calm seas they sometimes laze idly at the surface. Known to be extremely inquisitive, these dolphins often approach to investigate stationary craft.

Order • Cetacea	**Species** • *Cephalorhynchus hectori*
Status • endemic; uncommon; resident	**Maori name** • tupoupou

New Zealand Fur Seal

Recognition Zoologists use the term 'pinniped' (meaning 'fin-foot') to gather together all the world's seals, sea lions, walruses and their kin in a single convenient heap. In New Zealand pinnipeds come in two kinds: seals and sea lions (which includes fur seals). Sea lions have small but obvious ears, seals don't; and sea lions can stand — or even gallop, when pushed — on all four flippers, whereas seals are functionally legless on land, and can only sort of hump along — though pretty quickly when pushed. The New Zealand fur seal can be confused only with the sea lion, but it is much smaller (weighing only half as much), much less 'craggy', and with a more delicately modelled head and pointed snout.

Distribution Unlike sea lions, which favour sandy beaches, fur seals prefer surf-washed rocks on which to haul out and loaf, but within this constraint fur seals are common all around the coasts of New Zealand, as well as all the outlying islands such as the Chathams, Campbell and Auckland Islands. Breeding sites are mostly in the South Island. The species also occurs in Australia.

Food Mostly fish and squid.

Habits Fur seals are strongly gregarious and have a breeding regime similar to that of sea lions, in which males have as many mates as they can deny rival males. A successful bull in his prime might have exclusive access to about a dozen females. Most live close to their breeding colonies all year but the rookeries themselves are occupied only during the season, beginning in October. Males arrive first to establish territories and females follow a few weeks later to give birth to their pups, mating about eight days after that. Pups first enter the water about four weeks after birth, but are six or seven months old before they are weaned. Unlike so many other New Zealand animals, these pinnipeds seem to be maintaining and even increasing their numbers, after having been decimated by sealers during the nineteenth century — the population at Macquarie Island was almost wiped out by 1820. Recent estimates place the total New Zealand fur seal population at something close to 60,000 individuals (including some 7000 expats that happen to live in southern Australia), increasing at about 2 per cent per year.

ORDER • Carnivora	**SPECIES** • *Arctocephalus forsteri*
STATUS • native; common; resident	**MAORI NAME** • kekeno

New Zealand Sea Lion

in the 1800s) and scattered haul-out sites extend up the east coast of the South Island almost to Dunedin, but the bulk of the breeding population is at the Auckland and Campbell Islands. Adults are sedentary, seldom travelling far from their breeding sites, but youngsters often wander much farther afield.

Habits In contrast to the New Zealand fur seal, the sea lion prefers sand or shingle beaches over rocky shores for hauling-out places, especially where dense overhanging vegetation provides shade. They sometimes penetrate several hundred metres inland (and even climb small hills) to find a suitably secluded spot to loaf, doze and groom. Although built for grace and speed in water, they are agile enough on land and can even manage a brisk canter for short distances, bounding along on all four flippers. Mature bulls tend to be solitary when not breeding, but females are intensely gregarious.

Food Sea lions eat fish, crabs and molluscs, but their preference is for squid; they have also been known to occasionally prey on penguins and seal pups.

Recognition Also known as Hooker's sea lion, the New Zealand sea lion is closely related to the New Zealand fur seal but much larger. Bulls may exceed 3 m in length and weigh 400 kg or more; females are about 1.8 m long and weigh about 230 kg (this marked sexual dimorphism is obvious even at birth: new-born male pups average 7.9 kg, female pups only 7.2 kg). Males are much darker than females, with a shaggy, blackish-brown mane.

Breeding Like fur seals, sea lions have a 'harem' mating system in which bulls compete with each other for exclusive mating rights to the largest group of females they can defend from trespass by rival males. Bulls arrive first at the breeding colonies to establish their territories, followed by the pregnant females about three weeks later. Females mate about one week after giving birth. Pups are suckled for up to a year and the bond may persist for some time, even after weaning.

Distribution This sea lion occurs only in New Zealand, although wanderers occasionally reach distant Macquarie Island. It is not uncommon around Stewart Island (where breeding occurred

ORDER • Carnivora	**SPECIES**	• *Phocarctos hookeri*
STATUS • endemic; restricted; resident	**MAORI NAME**	• whakahao

Elephant Seal

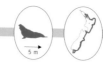

Recognition Unmistakable. Adult males are huge — up to 5 m in length and weighing 3500 kg (this is the largest seal in the world). The fur is plain, dark grey; no external ears. Sinuous and graceful underwater, ashore it humps along like a cumbersome caterpillar, with hind flippers trailing behind. Sexually mature males are nearly ten times heavier than females. Males have a unique trunk-like proboscis (hence 'elephant'), which is inflated when the animal roars during sexual combat.

ORDER • Carnivora
SPECIES • *Mirounga leonina*
STATUS • native; common; visitor
MAORI NAME • ihu koropuka

Distribution The elephant seal is largely confined to Antarctic and subantarctic waters, but it is not uncommon as a casual visitor to the beaches of New Zealand, from Stewart Island north to the Bay of Islands. Occasionally elephant seals will haul out of the water for the duration of the summer moult, which can last for as long as three weeks.

Leopard Seal

Recognition Long, lean and sinuous, with large head and massive jaws. The coat is deep blue-grey above and silver below, irregularly blotched and spotted with slate-grey on the shoulders and flanks (hence 'leopard'). As in all 'true' seals, the leopard seal has trailing hind flippers and no visible ears (sea lions have small but obvious ears and can bend their hind flippers forward).

ORDER • Carnivora
SPECIES • *Hydrurga leptonyx*
STATUS • native; uncommon; visitor
MAORI NAME • pakaka

Distribution While largely confined to Antarctic and subantarctic waters, visits to New Zealand beaches in winter are not uncommon.

Food Although the leopard seal relies heavily on krill it is unique among seals in also hunting warm-blooded prey. It often catches penguins but doesn't like the feathers, so it first shakes its victim out of its skin with spectacular arcing slaps against the ocean surface.

Native Frogs

4 cm

Archey's frog

Recognition Length about 4 cm. The three species of native frog are among the most primitive living frogs in the world, surviving almost unchanged from fossil forms that are 140 million years old. Adults have fish-like vertebrae and retain their tadpole tail-wagging muscles, even though they have no tails to wag. They have no eardrums or vocal sacs, little or no webbing between the toes and they seldom enter water. Small and brown, they could perhaps be mistaken for the introduced whistling frog, but at very close quarters the lack of a tympanum — a taut circular membrane just behind the eye, obvious in all except native frogs — is diagnostic.

Distribution All endemic to New Zealand, the three native frog species have very restricted ranges. Hochstetter's frog, *Leiopelma hochstetteri*, occurs from Northland to East Cape; Archey's frog, *Leiopelma archeyi*, is confined to the Coromandel Peninsula; and Hamilton's frog, *Leiopelma hamiltoni*, inhabits only Stephens Island and Maud Island in the Marlborough Sounds.

Habits The three species have different habitat requirements: Hochstetter's frog can be found under stones near streams and seepages and is the only species likely to be found near water; smallest of the three, Archey's frog hides under damp logs and stones on cloud-shrouded ridge-tops; and Hamilton's frog occurs on mossy boulder banks under scrub and native forest. All three live entirely on the ground (although Hamilton's frog occasionally climbs trees), are active mostly at night and hide by day in damp, sheltered crevices under rocks or fallen timber. Captive breeding programmes have been initiated with a view to boosting their numbers, so far with indifferent success.

Food Native frogs feed on worms, spiders, insects and other invertebrates. They lunge at their prey with open mouth and swallow it whole. Any dangling excess is crammed into the mouth with their front legs.

Breeding Native frogs lack a free-swimming tadpole stage, each embryo undergoing its early growth in its own personal pond inside a large gelatinous egg. Males alone brood and, when the eggs hatch, the tiny tailed froglets wriggle up onto the father's back to complete their development.

ORDER • Anura	**SPECIES** • *Leiopelma* spp
STATUS • endemic; rare; resident	**MAORI NAME** • poko-poko

Whistling Frog

4 cm

Recognition Total length about 4 cm; tadpoles grow to about 5 cm (including tail). Difficult to mistake for any other frog within its range, the whistling frog varies in colour and pattern. Most individuals are pale greyish brown to rich brown, usually with a darker grey-brown streak behind the eye, and with orange inner thighs.

Distribution Called in its native Australia the brown tree frog, the whistling frog was introduced into the South Island in 1875 and is now common over much of the South Island, from Westland and the Waiau River system southward.

Habits Needing shade and moisture, the whistling frog is most common in forest and scrub, where almost any small wetland — a pond, a quiet stream, a roadside ditch, or even a water-tank — provides a suitable home. In Australia it is as much at home in suburbs as in the bush, and over much of the populated south-east it is the frog with which most city dwellers are familiar. Although it sometimes

emerges on overcast days, the whistling frog is active mostly at night. It sometimes forages on the ground, but is equally likely to be found among the branches of shrubs or small trees. Courting males attract females with incessant, shrill, chirping calls, prompting the name whistling frog.

Food Tadpoles are mainly vegetarian, but adults prey mostly on insects and similar small invertebrates.

Breeding In warm regions breeding may occur at any time of year, whenever water levels rise following heavy rain, but elsewhere is usually in spring. Males congregate around ponds and mate with females as they arrive to spawn. The male hugs the female in a unique amphibian embrace known as amplexus and as the eggs are fertilised they are laid in water, in jellied blobs that each contain about 10–15 eggs. These hatch a few days later and the infant frog begins its first few months of development as an entirely aquatic creature, a tadpole.

ORDER • Anura
STATUS • introduced; common; resident

SPECIES • *Litoria ewingi*
MAORI NAME • none

Bell-frogs

10 cm

Green
bell-frog

Recognition   Two very similar and closely related frogs were imported into New Zealand in 1867: the green bell-frog and the southern bell-frog. About equal in size (up to 10 cm in total length), both are far larger than native New Zealand frogs and about twice the size of a whistling frog (page 151). The southern bell-frog is more brown than green, and has a pale streak running down the centre of its back. As its name implies, the green bell-frog (known in Australia as the green and golden bell-frog) is typically bright green, 'detailed' in golden yellow. The former also has a rough and warty skin, whereas the latter's skin is smooth.

Distribution   Native to south-eastern Australia, these two immigrants now jointly occupy almost all of the North and South Islands, and are by far the commonest frogs in New Zealand.

Habits   In behaviour and habitat, both differ substantially from their nearest relatives — these two species don't live in trees, they live in marshes. They are most active at night, and usually spend the day hidden under vegetation on swampy ground, among densely tangled marsh plants, or sometimes behind a slab of bark in a nearby tree. Despite their aquatic lifestyle, they betray their tree frog heritage in their front feet, which, like the human hand, have strong opposable thumbs that enable a tighter grip.

Food   Like other frogs, they feed largely on insects, but both species are large enough to also overpower the occasional small fish or skink. The tadpoles are vegetarian.

Breeding   The major aspects of their breeding cycle differ little from that of the whistling frog but, despite their abundance, surprisingly little is known of the details of reproduction. The tadpoles are unusually large compared to others of their clan, which prompts the suspicion that complete development to the mature frog may take more than a year.

Order • Anura	**Status** • introduced; common; resident
Species • *Litoria aurea* (green)	**Maori name** • poraka
Litoria raniformis (southern)	

Common Gecko

Recognition   Overall length (including tail) about 14 cm; sexes similar. The common gecko is variable in colour and pattern, although the basic colours are usually pale brown or putty-grey intricately marked with paler and darker shades, the markings forming streaks, bars or freckles. The mouth and tongue are pink. A conspicuous distinguishing feature of all geckos is a loose-fitting skin covered in minute scales without the sleek gloss of skinks.

Distribution   This is New Zealand's most widespread and abundant gecko, common almost throughout the North Island and most of the South Island except parts of Fiordland.

Habits   The common gecko can be found in all kinds of open country from boulder-strewn hillsides to coastal sand dunes and even stony beaches within a few metres of the surf — wherever there is an abundance of driftwood and cast seaweed. It is the only gecko likely to be encountered on a beach. It is much more at home on the ground than other New Zealand

geckos, which makes it unusually vulnerable to predation, particularly from rats and cats. Active mainly by night, it can usually be found during the day hiding under stones or fallen timber, sometimes emerging to bask in the sun. Common geckos are often solitary and territorial, but they may congregate in groups to hibernate through winter in any suitable deep, sheltered crevice. Geckos are vocal, uttering various sounds from soft chirps to loud barks and they have unique 'suction-pad' toes that give them an extraordinary ability to climb smooth hard surfaces — many species can easily sprint upside down across a ceiling.

Food   Mostly night-flying insects such as moths and beetles, occasionally supplemented by fruit and nectar.

Breeding   Like all other New Zealand geckos (and unlike geckos everywhere else in the world), the common gecko gives birth to live young, bearing twins in late summer. There is no parental care.

ORDER • Squamata	**SPECIES** • *Hoplodactylus maculatus*
STATUS • endemic; common; resident	**MAORI NAME** • mokopapa

Forest Gecko

19 cm

Recognition Total length about 18–19 cm; sexes similar. As in the common gecko, colour and pattern vary widely, and some individuals can be hard to identify. However, the mouth is orange (not pink), the overall colour generally tends to brown rather than grey, and the markings often form intricate patterns involving subtle shades of grey, black, green, gold and white. Chameleon-like, the forest gecko can also adjust its colour scheme to some extent, to merge more effectively with its background.

Distribution Almost throughout the three main islands of New Zealand, including several of the closest offshore island groups.

Habits The forest gecko is nearly as widespread and as abundant as the common gecko but it usually favours more shaded environments such as forest and scrub, leaving the common gecko in possession of more open environments such as tussock grassland. It has, however, been recorded above the tree line at 1700 m altitude in the Southern Alps. It is also much more rigidly arboreal than the common gecko, almost invariably found on tree-trunks. Although occasionally fond of sunbathing, during the day it seeks shelter under fallen timber, in holes or crevices or behind loose bark on tree trunks. Geckos are territorial but not necessarily solitary, and sometimes several may be found sheltering in the same crevice. Like skinks, geckos are often seen with 'hand-me-down' tails — they freely shed their tails when attacked by predators, and though the tail later regenerates it almost always does so imperfectly. Forest and common geckos have two very close relatives that are almost as widespread, but there are several others with very restricted ranges, including *Hoplodactylus chrysosireticus* on Mana Island, *Hoplodactylus kahutarae* in the Seaward Kaikoura mountain range, and *Hoplodactylus rakiurae* in the far south of Stewart Island.

Food The varied diet consists mainly of insects such as moths and beetles, supplemented occasionally by small berries and nectar from flowers.

ORDER • Squamata		**SPECIES** • *Hoplodactylus granulatus*	
STATUS • endemic; common; resident		**MAORI NAME** • mokopapa	

Green Tree Gecko

Recognition   In the warmer parts of the North Island lives an especially resplendent, vivid green gecko, often handsomely marked with yellow or white, that is easily identified but variously regarded as comprising one, two, or even three species. They are treated together here because they are very similar, they don't overlap and they are easily separated by geography. These geckos are slim-bodied and lumpy-headed, with very long, slender tails. The mouth is deep rich blue and the tongue varies from red to black; in the Northland district, males have blue flanks.

Distribution   Endemic to New Zealand, the green tree gecko occurs in three distinct and separate populations: one in Wellington and vicinity, another around Auckland, and the third in the far north of Northland.

Habits   Green tree geckos have a strong association with manuka and similar low, dense shrubbery, and they are most often found in trees rather than on the ground. They often spend hours perched in the topmost branches, sunbathing and snatching at passing insects especially in warm, calm and sunny weather. Unlike other geckos, they are more active during the day than at night. In cold weather they seek shelter under boulders or behind loose slabs of bark, spending much of the winter in a state of torpor. Like skinks and other geckos, they frequently cast, or slough, their skin, in a process that typically takes about two hours and occurs about every two months throughout the summer. At first the moulting gecko looks merely dull, its pattern clouded and faded as the outer layers of skin begin to loosen away from the deeper, pigment-bearing layers beneath. Eventually the outer skin splits behind the skull and part way down the back. The gecko then clambers out through the opening, leaving the shed skin inside out and often entire.

Food   The diet includes a wide range of insects and similar small invertebrates, supplemented by nectar, small berries and other fruit.

Order • Squamata	**Species** • *Naultinus elegans*
Status • endemic; common; resident	**Maori name** • kakariki

Jewelled Geckos

15 cm

Jewelled gecko
Naultinus gemmeus

Recognition   Echoing the green geckos in the North Island, these geckos comprise a cluster of about five further species in the widespread genus *Naultinus*, each confined to its own restricted area in the South Island. Like the green geckos, they are basically green in colour, spend much of their time in trees, and are most active during the day. Unlike ground-dwelling geckos, they have prehensile tails that they can coil around a perch to assist, like a fifth limb, in clambering among the branches or, if needs be, to support their entire dangling weight.

Distribution   The starred gecko, *Naultinus stellatus*, is restricted to the region between Nelson Lakes and Golden Bay; the jewelled gecko, *Naultinus gemmeus*, is restricted to scattered localities from Canterbury to Stewart Island and the rough-scaled gecko, *Naultinus rudis*, to the Kaikoura Ranges. The West Coast green gecko, *Naultinus tuberculatus*, and the Marlborough green gecko, *Naultinus manukanus*, are confined to the districts suggested by their names.

Habits   These geckos mostly inhabit dense native scrub and forest, but several also occur in exotic pine plantations. The rough-scaled gecko, in particular, is often common on scrubby, boulder-strewn hillsides. Although several forms have striking colours and patterns which are visible up close, these geckos are protectively coloured and usually very difficult to spot among green foliage. They are mostly solitary and territorial; males are especially aggressive and bark loudly as part of their displays toward rival males.

New Zealand is home to about 17 species of gecko, of which the largest is Duvaucel's gecko, *Hoplodactylus duvauceli*. This giant among geckos, which is confined to the Poor Knights Islands and a few other offshore islands, has been known to reach 30 cm in total length.

Food   In common with other geckos, green geckos are largely omnivorous, feeding mostly on small insects and spiders. However, they also supplement their diet from time to time with berries and nectar.

ORDER • Squamata	**SPECIES** • *Naultinus* spp.
STATUS • endemic; common; resident	**MAORI NAME** • kakariki

Nocturnal Skinks

Copper
skink

New Zealand has nearly 30 species of skink. Several are common but others rank among the most critically endangered members of all New Zealand's wildlife. At least seven are confined to very small offshore islands. Although a connection has yet to be proven, there is circumstantial evidence that perhaps these rare skinks owe their present much-reduced distribution to predation from kiore over the past several centuries.

Skinks differ little among themselves in general appearance, but they can be divided into two groups on other grounds. Although the distinctions are somewhat blurred, in general members of one group are active mainly by night and live mainly in forest and humid scrub. They belong to the genus *Cyclodina*, and might be termed 'the nocturnal skinks'. The body is chunky and usually squarish in cross-section, and although hardly a useful feature in the field, these skinks are also characterised by small scales on the lower eyelids. Usually they have a whitish 'teardrop' mark near the eye. All are confined to the North Island.

Skinks of this group include the following:

The copper skink, *Cyclodina aenea*, is very common over much of the North Island and is often the best known skink in suburban gardens. Sleek, glossy and coppery in colour, it grows to about 10 cm, with a very long tail.

Among the very smallest of New Zealand's skinks is the decorated skink, *Cyclodina ornata*, which is widely distributed in the North Island but very local and usually uncommon; it sometimes inhabits boulder beaches, but it usually favours low scrub.

Oliver's skink, *Cyclodina oliveri*, Whitaker's skink, *Cyclodina whitakeri*, Alan's skink, *Cyclodina alani*, and McGregor's skink, *Cyclodina macgregori*, are all confined to one or more of the small island groups off the east coast of Northland and in the Bay of Plenty, although Whitaker's skink also has a small population on a boulder bank at Pukerua Bay near Wellington. These are all large skinks, reaching 20 cm or more in length. Their abundance as subfossil remains at scattered localities across the North Island show they were once far more widespread, and may have been extirpated by rats on the main island.

All of these skinks are live-bearers, not egg-layers. Usually 3–7 in number, the young are born in February or March, and are often large at birth, sometimes up to half adult length.

Suter's Skink

18 cm

Recognition   With an overall length of about 18 cm, Suter's skink is sometimes known as the black shore skink but this name is misleading, because the ground colour varies from rich copper to dark grey, with prominent black markings on the sides.

Distribution   This skink inhabits the northern part of the North Island and many islands off the north-east coast, from the Three Kings to the Alderman Islands and Great Barrier Island.

Habits   Several other skinks inhabit the coast but Suter's skink is the only species totally confined to boulder beaches along the tideline, especially where driftwood and cast-up seaweed is abundant. Preyed upon by rats, cats and other predators, it is rare and local on the mainland but often common on predator-free offshore islands where its population density may sometimes reach 13 individuals per sq m — among the highest densities recorded for any skink. It is active mostly at night, but sometimes sunbathes on boulders during the day,

disappearing promptly into the nearest deep crevice when disturbed. Also unusual for skinks is its fondness for water and it is sometimes encountered swimming in tidal pools.

Food   Mainly small insects, spiders, and similar invertebrates.

Breeding   Suter's skink is the only egg-laying native species in New Zealand (all the others give birth to live young). The female lays a clutch of three or four eggs in a nest scraped in sand or shingle, or under a boulder. Mating probably occurs in October or November; egg-laying is usually in late December, and hatching takes place in March or April. The total development time, ovulation to hatching, is therefore about five months — among the longest for any skink. Suter's skinks also mature slowly: males are, on average, about 29 months old when they reach sexual maturity, and females lay their first clutch at about 33 months. There is also the possibility that females may in fact breed only every alternate year.

ORDER • Squamata	**SPECIES** • *Oligosoma suteri*
STATUS • endemic; common; resident	**MAORI NAME** • mokopapa

Diurnal Skinks

Otago skink

The diurnal skinks are those belonging to the genus *Oligosoma*, and they differ from the nocturnal skinks in being active mostly during the day, and in usually inhabiting drier, more open habitats such as tussock and rough grassland. Physical distinctions are few and subtle: the body is generally oval in cross-section, the toes longer than in the nocturnal skinks and the movable lower eyelid is covered with a transparent disc. Diurnal skinks are usually slimmer in build, longer-tailed, more agile and more quick and sudden in their movements than their nocturnal cousins. They typically reach about 20 cm in total length, but several species are much larger than the nocturnal skinks, and the group is best represented in the South Island.

Apart from the common skink (page 160), the three most widespread of the larger species are the speckled skink, *Oligosoma infrapunctatum*, the spotted skink, *Oligosoma lineoocellatum*, and the green skink, *Oligosoma chloronotum*. All three occupy the South Island, but the first occurs also in parts of the North Island, while the second extends southward to Stewart Island, which also has its own endemic species, *Oligosoma notosaurus*.

Three populations of the giant skink, each confined to small localities of rock-strewn tussock in the Canterbury-Otago region of the South Island, are now considered distinct species. Biggest and most striking of these is the Otago skink, *Oligosoma otagense*, reaching nearly 30 cm in total length. It is mainly glossy black, marked on the sides with irregular yellow or pale green blotches.

Most of the other diurnal skinks are confined to small offshore islands. Though generally common within their respective small domains, their total populations are very small and vulnerable to invasion by rats and other predators. Examples include *Oligosoma moco*, which is confined to islands in Hauraki Gulf; Falla's skink, *Oligosoma fallai*, which occurs only on the Three Kings islands, and *Oligosoma homalonotum*, which is endemic on Great Barrier Island. The only known populations of *Oligosoma acrinasum* are on several small islands in Breaksea Sound in Fiordland, living among boulders, driftwood and seaweed.

Like almost all skinks, diurnal skinks are mostly carniverous, incorporating a wide range of insects, spiders and small crustaceans in their diet, but they also exploit other food resources such as berries, and even spilt fish and stomach oil at seabird colonies. Small insect prey is captured with the help of a long, sticky, slightly notched tongue. Hearing, vision and smell all play a part in foraging.

Common Skink

14 cm

Recognition Overall length about 14 cm. Like other skinks the common skink is variable in colour and pattern, but is commonly a rich glossy grey, with a bold side-stripe. The sexes are virtually identical in appearance.

Distribution The common skink is widespread throughout the South Island and in the Wellington and Hawke's Bay regions of the North Island; it occurs on most of the closest offshore islands, as well as the Chatham Islands.

Habits One of New Zealand's most abundant and familiar skinks, this species occupies a wide range of habitats from seashore to suburban gardens and open country inland. It favours places with abundant ground cover in the form of deep litter, fallen timber or rock piles. It is fond of basking in the sun but is very alert and wary, diving for cover at the slightest disturbance. It spends most of its time on the ground but occasionally climbs into low shrubbery or even into trees. Mostly it forages among tussock or in leaf litter, retreating at night or when disturbed into cavities in fallen timber or in crevices between boulders. In winter it may become torpid in 'retreat dens' — sometimes in small groups — in deep cavities. Like all skinks, it sheds its tail readily when attacked, leaving the still-wriggling and twitching member to distract the predator while its owner makes good its escape. The tail is later regenerated, though never perfectly, and it is common to see skinks with obviously stunted tails betraying some previous narrow escape.

Food Mostly small insects and spiders, but the varied diet also occasionally includes berries, and even nectar from low flowers.

Breeding Skinks are worldwide in distribution but those inhabiting warmer climates usually lay eggs. The group's New Zealand members, however — with Suter's skink (page 158) the only exception — bring forth their young alive. This unusual behaviour seems to be an adaptation to colder climates and shorter seasons; eggs need warmth to hatch, and where summer is short, safe inside the mother's body seems the most effective way of providing it. The common skink gives birth to a litter of up to eight or nine young, usually in January or February. New-born young are barely 25 mm in total length but they grow rapidly, entering their first winter at nearly double their birth weight.

ORDER • Squamata
STATUS • endemic; common; resident

SPECIES • *Oligosoma nigriplantare*
MAORI NAME • mokopapa

Tuatara

38 cm

Recognition   Unmistakable — grey and prehistoric-looking, with baggy skin and spines down the back. Size varies with age: at about 20 years of age tuatara have a snout-to-vent length of about 18 cm. Females more or less stop growing at this age, but males continue, and reach about 25 cm at an age of 50 years, so that males are often twice the size of females.

Distribution   Subfossil remains show that tuatara once occurred on both main islands, but today they are confined to about 30 small islands off the north-east coast and in Cook Strait and the Marlborough Sounds. Stephens Island, in particular, supports a large population estimated at 30,000–50,000, but on many other islands the population is small or declining.

Habits   The tuatara is entirely unique. Although it has a fossil history extending back some 225 million years, it has no surviving relatives anywhere. Among many remarkable features, tuatara have no external ears, but they do have three eyes. Although hidden by opaque

scales, the third eye, in the middle of the forehead, is fully equipped with lens, retina and optic nerve. Tuatara are fond of basking in the sun, but they are active mainly at night. They live in burrows, each of which is home to only one tuatara. However, several of their island homes are also occupied by thousands of nesting seabirds, and many burrows have joint ownership with prions or storm petrels. Recently, DNA 'fingerprinting' techniques have revealed that tuatara comprise two species, indistinguishable in appearance but very different genetically.

Food   Tuatara are 'stand-and-wait' carnivores that snatch almost any small animal straying within reach, including weta, spiders, skinks, geckos, and even birds and their eggs or chicks.

Breeding   Females lay their clutches of 8–15 eggs in special nest-burrows, which are then filled in and abandoned. The tuatara has one of the longest incubation periods of any reptile, the eggs taking up to 15 months to hatch.

Order • Rhynchocephalia	**Species** • *Sphenodon punctatus*
Status • endemic; restricted; resident	**Maori name** • tuatara

Pouched Lamprey

67 cm

Recognition Despite their rather eel-like appearance, lampreys are not fish; their most obvious distinguishing characteristic is a complete lack of jaws — instead of a conventional mouth there is a sucking disc armed with numerous flat, overlapping teeth radiating from the centre in curved rows. Lampreys have a complicated life history, going through several stages that differ strikingly in appearance. Very young lampreys, called ammocoetes, live in fresh water, reach about 10 cm in length, and are eyeless, worm-like creatures, light sandy brown in colour, somewhat paler below. What might be termed 'adolescent' lampreys, called macrophthalmia, live in the sea, reach about 67 cm in length, have large eyes, and are bright silver, with two streaks of brilliant blue-green along the back. As adults, these colours fade to drab muddy brown. Adult males have a soft, baggy pouch on the throat.

Distribution This lamprey is common in fresh water in Chile, Argentina, southern Australia, and all three main islands of New Zealand.

Habits Young lampreys live in shallow wetlands of all kinds where the bottom is soft mud or sand, in which they bury themselves with a swift wriggle at the slightest disturbance. They are active mainly at night and not easy to find, and the species may be declining. Lampreys are highly valued as food by the Maori.

Food Ammocoetes are filter-feeders, living on very minute organisms sifted from the mud, but at sea the macrophthalmia feeds by clamping its sucker-mouth to the flanks of large marine fish, rasping a hole in the flesh, and absorbing its prey's body fluids.

Breeding Although the main stages of the life history have been established, little is known of the details: adults spawn in the headwaters of rivers and streams, where the ammocoetes live for some time before developing into macrophthalmia and migrating to the open sea. There they live for several years before becoming sexually mature and returning to fresh water to spawn and die.

ORDER • Petromyzontiformes
STATUS • native; uncommon; resident

SPECIES • *Geotria australis*
MAORI NAME • piharau, kanakana

Long-finned Eel

Recognition A very large eel in which the dorsal fin extends along the back to a point considerably forward of the level of the anal (belly) fin. The colour is very dark grey, paler below than above. Females are much larger than males, and may reach nearly 2 m in length and weigh nearly 20 kg, but most are much smaller — typically about 120 cm (females) and 65 cm (males). Eels forage mainly at night but can often be found by day lurking in the shelter of river banks or log jams.

ORDER • Anguilliformes
SPECIES • *Anguilla dieffenbachii*
STATUS • endemic; common; migrant
MAORI NAME • kaiwharuwharu

Distribution Common in wetlands of all kinds throughout the main islands of New Zealand. The spawning grounds remain unknown, but are believed to be somewhere east of Tonga. Once hatched, the baby eels drift back to New Zealand on ocean currents then — at this stage about 6 cm long — join the whitebait migration upstream.

Short-finned Eel

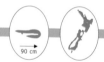

Recognition Very similar to the much larger long-finned eel in appearance, but more olive than grey, and the dorsal fin extends only a little forward of the level of the anal fin. Females are much bigger than males; some reach about 90 cm in length and 1.5 kg in weight, but most are much smaller.

ORDER • Anguilliformes
SPECIES • *Anguilla australis*
STATUS • native; common; migrant
MAORI NAME • hau

Distribution The short-finned eel is common throughout all three main islands of New Zealand as well as the Chatham Islands. It is also present in south-eastern Australia, Lord Howe Island, Norfolk Island, New Caledonia, and perhaps Fiji and Tahiti.

Breeding All freshwater eels have broadly similar life cycles. They mature over many years in fresh water (the former up to 90 years, the latter 34 years), then finally stop feeding and head for the open sea to spawn and die.

Banded Kokopu

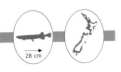

28 cm

Recognition   Total length about 20 cm, occasionally to 28 cm. Banded kokopu are slender, tube-shaped fish with the dorsal fin set far to the rear, near the tail. Their smooth, leathery skins lack scales and are covered instead with a layer of mucus. Mainly dull olive in colour, they usually have a row of brownish vertical bands along the flanks.

Distribution   Once common in forest streams throughout New Zealand, the banded kokopu is now rare or declining wherever forests have been logged or cleared for agriculture.

Habits   The banded kokopu prefers small, shallow pools in quietly flowing forest streams with rock or gravel beds, where the water is shaded by the foliage of trees meeting overhead, where there is little disturbance and where there is abundant shelter in the form of undercut banks and submerged logs. It feeds near the surface, mostly at night, and hides under logs or stones by day. Although often solitary in habits, it occasionally congregates in small, loose

shoals. Like other kokopu it is extremely sensitive to environmental changes, its populations prone to drastic collapse wherever its habitat requirements are eroded in any way, but tenacious wherever they are sustained — they remain common, for example, in some sensitively managed urban environments such as city parks and reserves. At the national level, banded kokupu are seriously threatened by habitat destruction, pollution, migration barriers and, perhaps, predation and competition from the introduced brown trout.

Food   Kokopu are largely insectivorous, feeding on the larvae of aquatic insects such as mosquitoes, and invertebrates such as caterpillars and spiders falling onto the water's surface.

Breeding   Adults are resident and spawn in autumn where they live but on hatching the larvae migrate downstream to spend their first winter at sea. The following spring they join the whitebait migration back to the pools and streams where they were born.

Order • Salmoniformes	**Species** • *Galaxias fasciatus*
Status • endemic; uncommon; resident	**Maori name** • kokopu, kopu

Giant
kokopu

Distantly related to salmon and trout, kokopu are slim, cigar-shaped, freshwater fish that lack scales and carry a rounded dorsal fin set far to the rear. Elsewhere known as *Galaxias* or jollytails, the group is widespread in the Australasian region but is especially well represented in New Zealand, where there are at least 13 member species, each of which differs from the others most significantly in the details of its habitat requirements. Some require quiet streams while others need more turbulent flows; some are confined to alpine brooks, while others live in swampy lowland pools. Common to most is the need for a shady forest canopy overhead. Making up the bulk of the whitebait fishery, and unusually sensitive to environmental disturbance, all are vulnerable to decline or extinction where the canopy is removed by logging or other development. Other threats include pollution, and predation or competition with the introduced brown trout. The most widespread species include the following:

Commonly reaching about 17 cm in length, the koaro, *Galaxias brevipinnis*, is widespread in New Zealand, including the Chatham, Auckland and Campbell Islands, and occurs also in south-eastern Australia. Solitary and secretive, it favours small, rocky streams with a vigorous, turbulent water flow.

The short-jawed kokopu, *Galaxias postvectis*, occurs wherever there are quiet, shallow pools in streams flowing through undisturbed old-growth forests other than beech. It remains common, for example, in podocarp forest streams between (approximately) Greymouth and Franz Josef Glacier, but is rare further south, where beech predominates.

Widespread throughout New Zealand and often called the native trout, the giant kokopu, *Galaxias argenteus*, is the largest of the whitebait species, occasionally reaching 58 cm in length and 2.7 kg in weight, though about 30 cm is average. Usually dark green to olive in colour, paler below, it is intricately marked with spots, bars, crescents or rings of gold. Its ideal habitat consists of shallow, swampy forest creeks not too far from the sea, with abundant shelter in the form of overhanging banks and submerged logs. Now rare, it has been severely affected by development, and struggles where brown trout are common. The young of most kokopu head for the open sea immediately after hatching, returning during their first spring, but a few species have entirely freshwater life cycles.

Inanga

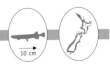

10 cm

Recognition A slender, streamlined kokopu with a slim tail, a rather small dorsal fin and a blunt, rounded head. The colour varies from a watery greenish grey to amber, silvery below and usually blotched or spotted along the back and flanks with darker olive. It occasionally reaches 19 cm in length, but most are under 10 cm.

Distribution Common in lowland wetlands throughout all three main islands of New Zealand, as well as the Chathams. Also south-eastern Australia (roughly from Brisbane to Adelaide), Tasmania; far south-western Australia, southern Chile, Argentina, and the Falkland Islands.

Habits The inanga is perhaps the most abundant native fish, making up the bulk of the 'whitebait' run migrating from the sea in spring. It is common in most unpolluted wetlands in coastal lowlands where the water is still or gently flowing, including lakes, ponds, streams, rivers and marshes. In summer, it usually occurs

in small schools, and feeds close to the surface, mainly at night.

Food Inanga feed largely on the larvae of midges and similar insects, minute crustaceans and small insects and spiders that fall onto the water's surface.

Breeding In autumn adults migrate downstream to spawn in salt marshes and estuaries when they are inundated by extra high tides. The eggs are left moist but stranded in the vegetation above water for about two weeks, hatching when the next spring tide flushes them into the water again. The young inanga spend the winter at sea, then re-enter fresh water as 'whitebait', migrate upstream to adult habitats, maturing during the summer to renew the cycle in the following autumn. Females lay several thousand eggs, each about 1 mm in diameter; the hatchlings are about 7 mm long. When they return from the sea in spring the slender, transparent juveniles are about 50 mm long. Most adults die after spawning.

Order • Salmoniformes	**Species** • *Galaxias maculatus*
Status • native; common; resident	**Maori name** • hiwi, inanga

Mudfish

15 cm

Canterbury
mudfish

Recognition Related to kokopu but usually inhabiting much shallower water, the mudfish make up a group of three uniquely New Zealand species: the Canterbury mudfish, *Neochanna burrowsius*; the brown mudfish, *Neochanna apoda*; and the black mudfish, *Neochanna diversus*. The last two average about 11 cm in length but the Canterbury mudfish grows a little larger — to about 15 cm. All three are slender, tubular fish, generally muddy brown in colour, variably mottled with darker brown; the Canterbury mudfish has small pelvic fins, which are lacking in the other two species.

Distribution The brown mudfish inhabits Westland and the southern part of the North Island; the black mudfish is confined to the North Island (north of about Pirongia); the most critically endangered species is the Canterbury mudfish, which is confined to the Canterbury Plain where virtually all suitable habitat has already been reclaimed for urban development or agriculture. Only a handful of small remnant populations are known.

Habits Though mudfish are closely related to the kokopu they have a very different lifestyle. Living their entire lives in fresh water, they have evolved a survival regime that enables them to live in shallow wetlands prone to drying out in summer — in fact some of the earliest specimens were discovered not in a pond but in a sodden potato field, prompting a wag in Britain to remark on the good fortune of antipodean farmers, able to procure a meal of fish-and-chips complete on a single shovel! They occupy wetlands of all kinds, from extensive marshes to small swampy streams, where the bottom is either peat or mud, where the surface is sheltered by abundant overhanging vegetation, and where the water is little more than a few centimetres deep in winter and often dries up altogether in summer. As water levels decline, the mudfish bury themselves deep into the mud — often as much as 2 m below the surface — and remain there in a state of torpor, or aestivation, throughout the summer months, emerging to spawn in autumn rains.

ORDER • Salmoniformes
STATUS • endemic; rare; resident

SPECIES • *Neochanna* spp.
MAORI NAME • hauhau

Bullies

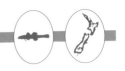

Giant
bully

Two groups of fishes, kokopu and bullies, make up the bulk of the New Zealand freshwater fish fauna. On the whole, kokopu tend to be slim, agile, quicksilver fishes that forage near the surface, whereas most of the six species of bullies are stockier, blunt-headed, sluggish fish that live and forage near the bottom. Especially during the breeding season, bullies are aggressive and strongly territorial. They feed mainly on insect larvae such as young dragonflies, caddisflies, and mayflies. Like kokopu, most bullies spawn in fresh water but the hatchlings move down to the sea for several months — although two species, Cran's bully, *Gobiomorphus basalis*, and the upland bully, *Gobiomorphus breviceps* — are entirely confined to lakes and alpine streams. Like kokopu, most species are adapted to forest-shaded streams and rivers, and are vulnerable to population decline when forest cover is removed.

The largest of the bullies is the giant bully, *Gobiomorphus gobioides*, which commonly exceeds 15 cm in length and sometimes reaches 20 cm. At the other extreme, the smallest, the

blue-gilled bully, *Gobiomorphus hubbsi*, rarely exceeds 7 cm in total length.

Most glamorous of the group is the red-finned bully, *Gobiomorphus huttoni*, in which the male's dorsal fins, flanks, and tail are stained bright scarlet — he reinforces the dramatic effect by turning deep velvet-black when spawning (the female is dull olive). This bully is characteristic of small, lowland forest pools in fast-flowing streams, and is severely threatened by habitat destruction.

In sharp contrast to any of the other bullies, the common bully, *Gobiomorphus cotidianus*, is an adaptable species that appears not to be threatened in any way, and remains ubiquitous and in some localities very numerous in freshwater wetlands of all kinds — swamps, lakes, and streams, with either rock, mud or sandy beds — throughout New Zealand. Their only obvious habitat preference is for still or quiet waters over turbulent flows. The common bully is typically about 10 cm long, and can be identified by the orange tip to the first (foremost) of the two dorsal fins.

ORDER • Perciformes
STATUS • endemic; common; resident

SPECIES • *Gobiomorphus* spp.
MAORI NAME • pako, kopu, koputea

Quinnat Salmon

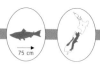

75 cm

Recognition   Largest of all salmon, in New Zealand waters quinnat salmon average about 75 cm (length) and about 8 kg (weight). They are mainly silver while at sea, but flush bright pink as they move up to their spawning grounds.

Distribution   Also known as the king or Pacific salmon, the quinnat salmon's native home extends from the Yukon River in Canada south to the Sacremento River in California and west across the Pacific Ocean to central China. Released into New Zealand in the late 1800s, it is now well established in several major rivers along the east coast of the South Island, from the Waiau south to the Clutha, and a few rivers in south Westland.

Habits   Salmon evolved to exploit the foaming, glacier-fed torrents that were a feature of arctic regions throughout the ice ages. Such rivers are high in dissolved oxygen but low in food, and salmon have an impressive arsenal of adaptations for mastering such an environment.

However, these same adaptations make them vulnerable in the modern, human-dominated world of pollution and habitat destruction. One of these is the development of a life cycle based on spawning in fresh water but maturing at sea. Another is their remarkable homing ability: after several years at sea, salmon are able to find their way back to the very gravel bank where they were hatched. Yet another is their trim, muscular, athletic body form, enabling them to force their way up foaming rapids and leap waterfalls as high as 3 m.

Food   Salmon are carnivores, feeding mainly on other fish.

Breeding   In March breeding salmon enter rivers, stop feeding, and begin their upstream migration to the spawning grounds, reached about late April. The female lays her eggs into a scrape in a gravel stream bed, her mate fertilises them, and she covers them with gravel. Both parents die within a day or two, and the eggs hatch about 60–200 days later.

Order • Salmoniformes	**Species** • *Oncorhynchus tshawytscha*
Status • introduced; common; resident	**Maori name** • hamana

Rainbow Trout

50 cm

Recognition   The rainbow trout is a more colourful clone of the brown trout in almost every aspect of its appearance, behaviour and lifestyle. The colour is basically silver instead of bronze, there is a variable flush of rose pink along the sides, and the tail is densely spotted (clear in the brown trout). The rainbow trout may grow to very substantial weights, but 50 cm (length) and 3 kg (weight) is about average.

Distribution   The rainbow trout is a native of North America but, like the brown trout, was introduced into New Zealand in the early years of European settlement. It is widespread in both the North and South Islands but is far less tolerant of warm water than the brown trout. It is much more common in the South Island, where it tends to be characteristic of high country lakes rather than rivers or streams.

Habits   Populations of rainbow trout that mature at sea are known as steelheads; they are typically larger and more silvery than lake trout. Like brown trout, they are usually the dominant

fish predator where they occur — kokopu and bullies have been introduced to many lakes to serve as food for trout. They are strongly territorial, usually solitary, and prey on small aquatic animals of almost any kind, ranging from insects to quite large fish. As formidable predators, rainbow trout have unusually acute senses: their sharp eyes are liberally supplied with cones, implying full colour vision; their sense of smell plays a major role in their extraordinary homing abilities (although experiments have shown that they can find their way back to their spawning grounds even without it); and the well-developed lateral line (a row of minute sensory pits along each side of many kinds of fish) functions as both a pressure sensor and as a sort of sophisticated 'passive-sonar' prey-detection system. They are also unusually trim, muscular, athletic fish — a characteristic fitting their status as top predators, adding to their value as a prime sporting fish, and well suiting them to the arduous trials of the upstream spawning run — they can readily clear waterfalls of 3 m or more.

ORDER • Salmoniformes
STATUS • introduced; common; resident

SPECIES • *Oncorhynchus mykiss*
MAORI NAME • taraute, tarautete

Brown Trout

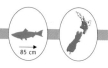

85 cm

Recognition Well-named, the brown trout is a distinctive shade of rich golden brown, profusely freckled along the back and sides with small black spots, each narrowly bordered with dull yellow. It attains about 3.6 kg in weight. A distinctive structural feature of both brown and rainbow trout is the small adipose fin between the dorsal fin and the tail.

Distribution A native of Europe, the brown trout has been widely introduced as a sporting fish elsewhere in the world, including New Zealand, in the very early days of European settlement. It is now the most widely distributed freshwater fish on both main islands, north to the Coromandel Peninsula.

Habits The brown trout is often the dominant predator in freshwater fish communities in New Zealand. It is strongly territorial, frequently adopting a suitable pool in a river or stream and driving all rivals away. Like its close relative the salmon, the brown trout also has specialised equipment for dealing with a lifestyle that

involves living part of its life in fresh water and the other part in the sea: it has glands in its gills that dump excess salt and very efficient kidneys to maintain an appropriate internal water balance regardless of external salinity. This equipment is so efficient and flexible that brown trout can thrive equally well in an entirely freshwater, landlocked environment such as a lake or — as a form called the sea-trout — in a salmon-like mode that involves maturing many years at sea and returning to fresh water to spawn.

Food Mainly other fish.

Breeding The trout's reproductive cycle is very similar to that of the salmon: spawning takes place in gravel or shingle shallows in cold, clear streams. The egg — about 5 mm in diameter — is heavier than water, which makes it less likely to be swept away from its original oxygen-rich laying site; and is abundantly supplied with yolk, which means the young trout hatches at a relatively advanced stage of development.

Order • Salmoniformes	**Species** • *Oncorhynchus trutta*
Status • introduced; common; resident	**Maori name** • taraute-pakaka, tarautete

Planarians

50 mm

Land flatworms

Recognition   Search patiently enough in any weed-choked pond and you are very likely to find minute, flattened creatures that look like small earthworms except that their bodies are entirely smooth, lacking any sign of the 'ringed' or segmented appearance that distinguish earthworms and their kin. Similar animals occur under rotten logs or stones in the garden, sometimes proving difficult to find. These are planarians, a group of free-living flatworms related to parasitic tapeworms. A typical planarian is dull greenish in colour and less than 20 mm in length, but land-dwelling forms are often more colourful and sometimes larger than aquatic forms. One colourful and fairly common soil inhabitant, *Artioposthia triangulata*, is pointed at both ends and about 50 mm long at rest, but may stretch to 200 mm when in motion. Its back is chocolate brown, often with a band of rich purple down the centre, and the underparts are yellowish, freckled with brown.

Distribution   Planarians are found worldwide with many species distributed throughout New

Zealand. Several native species have been accidentally exported elsewhere: *Artioposthia triangulata*, for example, is now widespread in the British Isles, having been discovered in a Belfast garden in 1963, apparently imported in a shipment of potted plants.

Habits   Planarians can raise their heads but lack a fully integrated muscular system: slug-like, they rely on cilia and a carpet of mucous to move over the ground or even upside down over a film of water. They are among the simplest animals with a brain, which makes them popular research subjects in the behavioural sciences. They can be taught to negotiate simple mazes, and they respond to light, heat, magnetic fields, gamma radiation and a variety of chemical stimuli.

Food   Many planarians are carnivorous: they thrust a unique nozzle-like organ called a pharynx into the body of a victim and, like a petrol bowser in reverse, use it to slurp up body fluids.

Order • Tricladida
Status • native; common; resident

Maori name • toke, ngata

Leaf-veined Slugs

Pseudaneitea papillata

Recognition   New Zealand has at least 24 species of native leaf-veined slugs, members of a family (Athoracophoridae) confined to eastern Australia, New Zealand and the islands of the south-western Pacific. They differ from other slugs by having only a single pair of retractable tentacles, and by an intricate pattern of reddish-brown, vein-like markings along the back. The size varies with the species, but several forms are about 10 cm long.

Distribution   Leaf-veined slugs occur throughout New Zealand, including many of the forested offshore islands such as the Three Kings and Little Barrier Island, as well as most outlying groups such as Snares, Campbell, and Auckland Islands. About 14 species are confined to the South Island but the most widespread species, *Athoracophora bitentaculatus*, is common on all three main islands of New Zealand.

Habits   Slugs are essentially air-breathing snails that have lost their shells; the last surviving shell traces remain as a few lime granules which are hidden below the lung. Slugs (and snails) both lack conventional jaws or tongue, but their distinctive feeding apparatus is perhaps easiest to visualise as a sort of 'cheese-grater' or 'cat's tongue' arrangement called a radula — a muscular strip covered with minute teeth, used to scrape off tiny particles of food. Leaf-veined slugs can be found in damp situations almost anywhere. They forage mainly at night, and spend the day hidden in sheltered places such as under logs or forest leaf litter, in wet tussocks, or inside the leaf sheaths of nikau palms.

Food   Leaf-veined slugs feed largely on fungi of various kinds.

Breeding   Little is known of the details of reproduction. Slugs in general are hermaphrodites; mating involves the *exchange* of sperm rather than its donation, and both parties subsequently lay a clutch of small, round, gelatinous eggs.

Order • Sigmorethra	**Species** • *Pseudaneitea* spp. and
Status • endemic; common; resident	*Athoracophorus* spp.
	Maori name • putoko-ropiropi, matuatua

Flax Snails

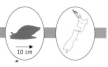

10 cm

*Placostylus
ambagiosus*

Recognition Flax snails are large (up to 10 cm long) snails with a long, elegantly tapered coil, very unlike the tight, flattened shell of the kauri snails (opposite). They are somewhat variable in colour (even within different populations of the same species) but most are plain, dark reddish-brown to chocolate, usually without any conspicuous pattern.

Distribution All four forms of flax snails are endemic to New Zealand, where they are confined to the far north of the North Island, south to about Whangarei and Great Barrier Island. Very closely related forms occur in New Caledonia, Vanuatu, the Solomons, Fiji, and Lord Howe Island.

Habits If the large numbers of subfossil shells to be found scattered through the sand dunes on the northern coast are any guide, flax snails were once abundant. Now, however, all four species are critically endangered, threatened by a combination of forest clearance and introduced predators. Wildlife authorities have

introduced several to some offshore islands, such as the Poor Knights, in a last-ditch attempt to preserve them from extinction. These snails exclusively inhabit lowlands within a few kilometres of the coast — precisely those areas first to be cleared for agriculture in the wake of European settlement. As well, all the introduced mammal predators eat snails, at least sometimes. Mature flax snails seldom leave the ground, where they can often be found hiding among the roots and litter at the base of flax plants, but young ones can sometimes be found in trees.

Food Unlike the kauri snails, these snails are strictly vegetarian, feeding on fallen leaves on the forest floor, especially those of karaka.

Breeding Flax snails make a nest under dead vegetation and lay eggs about 5 mm long (but the species *Placostylus bollonsi*, confined to the Three Kings Islands, has a relatively enormous egg measuring about 15 x 12 mm), in clutches of 30–40; the eggs are white and limy, with a pale olive cuticle.

ORDER • Sigmorethra	**SPECIES** • *Placostylus* spp.
STATUS • endemic; rare; resident	**MAORI NAME** • pupu harakeke

Kauri Snails

4 cm

*Paryphanta
busbyi*

Recognition   Kauri snails look a little like ordinary garden snails in being round and tightly coiled, but are very much bigger — a shell 8 cm across and 4 cm high is about average. One species, *Paryphanta busbyi* (confined to the Northland peninsula), is plain, unmarked tawny olive to deep green to black, but others are finely banded, usually rich red-brown on a yellowish ochre background — although colour and pattern vary from species to species and place to place.

Distribution   About 20 species of giant land snails, all endemic to New Zealand, are distributed along the western regions of both North and South Islands. They follow the trend common in much of New Zealand's wildlife — the group is more diverse in the South Island than in the North (contrary to the global rule, which holds that animal diversity increases towards the equator). At least 17 species are endemic in the South Island, only three are confined to the North Island; peak diversity is reached in Marlborough and Nelson.

Habits   Sometimes called giant land snails, kauri snails are largely confined to native forests — especially beech — and coastal scrub such as karo. Their distribution tends to be clumped, existing in small, widely separated pockets where the right combinations of warmth, humidity and shade come together. Like most snails, kauri snails are active at night when humidity is generally higher, hiding in crevices or under leaf litter during the day. In some habitats kauri snails can be very numerous, but most species are either vulnerable or endangered, and their continued survival is a matter of grave concern.

Food   Only about 10 per cent of the world's land snails are carnivores, but the kauri snails stand out even among this elite as top predators. Although they often hunt other snails and slugs, earthworms are the chief prey.

Breeding   The dull white eggs are laid in clutches of 20–50 in a mulch-covered nest on the ground.

ORDER • Sigmorethra
STATUS • endemic; rare; resident

SPECIES • *Paryphanta* spp.
MAORI NAME • pupurangi

Pseudoscorpions

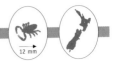

12 mm

Apatochernes
spp.

Recognition   The pseudoscorpions are a world-wide group of about 1700 species, of which several hundred occur in New Zealand. They superficially resemble true scorpions (which are absent from New Zealand), especially in having eight legs and a pair of venomous pincers at the forward end, but they differ most obviously in lacking tails and in being very much smaller — the giant of the group is barely 12 mm long.

Habits   Pseudoscorpions are obscure, inconspicuous animals that, although common, are unlikely to be encountered unless you go looking for them. Yet they have many fascinating characteristics. Like some mites, for example, they are among the few animals that habitually use a particular form of migration known as phoresy — which essentially means 'hitchhiking' — to move from one place to another by riding on the bodies of flies and similar small, mobile animals. And like spiders they use silk in various ways, but the silk-producing glands are on their chelicerae (food-

manipulating organs roughly comparable to jaws) instead of at the tip of the abdomen. They also carefully brood their young.

Many species of pseudoscorpions are found in the bush, hiding deep under leaf-litter, under rocks (carefully put the rock back the way it was!) or behind flaking bark on tree trunks or fallen timber. Another species, however, is very common in houses: the book-scorpion *Chelifer cancroides* is an introduced species about 4 mm long that lurks in the bindings of books and similar sheltered places and preys on such pests as the larvae of clothes moths and carpet beetles as well as bedbugs and book lice.

Breeding   Very little is known of the mating habits of pseudoscorpions but certain features are common to all known species: a packet of sperm is transferred from male to female (in some species in the course of an intricate courtship 'dance'), who then lays her eggs into a specially constructed 'pouch' that remains attached to her body until the young hatch, emerge, and wander off.

Order • Chelonethida
Status • native and introduced; rare; resident

Maori name • none

Harvestmen

5 cm

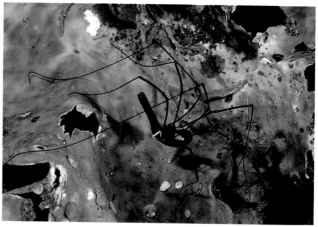

Long-legged
harvestman

Recognition   The folk-name 'daddy-longlegs' is widespread in English for three very different groups of animals: various species of craneflies (page 223); a common household spider, and the harvestmen. At a casual glance, harvestmen look like long-legged spiders but their bodies are made up of a single 'lump', without obvious sections, whereas the spider body is made of two very obvious parts — abdomen and a cephalothorax. Harvestmen are usually dull brown or grey, and rarely exceed 1 cm in body length. They vary widely in structure, some being grotesquely adorned with elaborate knobs and spines.

Distribution   New Zealand and its surrounding islands have several hundred species of this worldwide group, most of them endemic, and many of which are confined to single island groups such as the Kermadecs. However, the one most likely to be encountered in suburban gardens is an introduced species, the European harvestman *Phalangium opilio*, which arrived accidentally, presumably as a ship's stowaway

from England, but exactly when or how remains uncertain.

Habits   Harvestmen are common in most habitats, in town, country and wilderness alike but, unlike spiders and pseudoscorpions, they seldom enter houses. Vulnerable to desiccation, they live mainly in damp, shaded, sheltered situations such as leaf-litter, loose bark on tree trunks, or amid low, dense foliage.

Food   Harvestmen are partly predators, hunting insects and other small arthropods using the same 'touch-at-a-distance' sense that spiders rely on but, unlike spiders, they are also scavengers.

Breeding   Compared to other arthropods, harvestmen have extremely unusual reproductive behaviour. There is no courtship (sexes merely mate when they meet); males have a penis, and fertilisation is direct and internal. Females have an ovipositor, used to thrust eggs deep into moist soil, where they hatch in about two weeks.

ORDER • Opiliones
STATUS • native and introduced; common; resident

MAORI NAME • matua waeroa

Trapdoor Spiders

Recognition Trapdoor spiders are common but seldom seen, except that males in search of females occasionally wander into houses. Otherwise they rarely leave their silk-lined burrows in the ground, the entrance (in most species) protected and concealed by the camouflaged, silk-hinged flap or 'trapdoor' that prompts their name.

ORDER •	Araneae
FAMILY •	Migidae and Ctenizidae
STATUS •	native; common; resident
MAORI NAME •	pungakarirua

Habits Trapdoor spiders belong to a very ancient spider group known as the mygalomorphs, most easily recognised by their fangs, which operate vertically downwards, pickaxe-style (in contrast to 'modern' spiders such as orb-weavers, in which the fangs work inwards like pincers). Trapdoor spiders hunt at night, lurking in their dens with trapdoor open just a crack, alert to pounce with astonishing speed on any insect unwary enough to wander within range.

Black tunnelweb spider

Wolf Spiders

Recognition Wolf spiders are the cheetahs of the spider world, specialised to run down their insect prey on the ground and in the open. The various species come in all sizes up to about 20 mm in body length; lean-bodied and nimble-legged, they are clad in muted tones of brown, grey, ochre and fawn.

ORDER •	Araneae
FAMILY •	Lycosidae
STATUS •	native; common; resident
MAORI NAME •	pungawerewere

Habits Wolf spiders are extremely common, and easily found with a flashlight at night because their tiny eyes glow in the beam just like those of a cat — and for essentially the same reason. Cats and many other nocturnal creatures have a mirror-like structure (called the tapetum) in the back of the eye, which boosts night vision by reflecting light back through the sensitive cells a second time. Wolf spiders may bite if molested, but most species are too small to pose much of a threat — although several large species overseas are dangerous to humans.

Garden wolf spider

Orbweb Spiders

15 mm

Recognition As their name suggests, the orb-weavers build wondrously engineered webs looking like flimsy bicycle wheels slung between trees, to catch night-flying insects such as moths. Depending on its builder's species, webs are either rebuilt every night, or last several weeks and repaired only as necessary. During the day these spiders hide near their webs, carefully folding and packing their legs against their bodies to look as much as possible like a shapeless, inconspicuous chunk of debris. Fat-bodied and slender-legged, a typical orb-weaver has a body length of about 10–15 mm.

Order • Araneae
Family • Epeiridae
Status • native; common; resident
Maori name • punga matamatakupenga

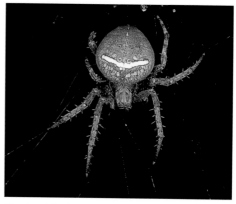

Distribution Orbweb spiders occur worldwide. The species most common in New Zealand gardens, the common orb-weaver *Aranea pustulosa*, probably migrated from Australia, but there are many closely related and very similar native species in New Zealand's forests.

Whitebanded orbweb spider

Nurseryweb Spiders

50 mm

Recognition Nurseryweb spiders are so-called from their distinctive habit of building special webs to shelter their young from the time they hatch until they reach independence. They are not easy to identify on appearance alone, lacking any obvious distinguishing features of structure, colour or pattern — dull brown or grey, rather long-legged, and with an egg-shaped abdomen, they might easily be mistaken for wolf spiders.

Order • Araneae
Species • *Dolomedes* spp.
Status • native; common; resident
Maori name • tuarahonu

Habits Many species are easily recognisable by their hunting behaviour. Often called water spiders, they lie in wait at the very edge of small pools or marshy shallows with the front pair of legs resting on the surface, alert for the faintest ripple which might indicate a meal. The spider dashes out onto the surface film, often plunging below the surface to snatch tadpoles, aquatic insects or tiny fish.

Dolomedes minor

Katipo Spider

10 mm

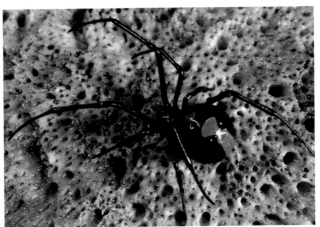

Recognition The katipo is easily identified by its long spindly legs and its glossy, black, globular abdomen — roughly the size and shape of a garden pea — with a bright red stripe down the middle. Females are about 10 mm in total body length, the males barely 3 mm long.

Distribution The katipo is a coastal species common on sandy beaches around the North Island and the northern part of the South Island, southwards, approximately, to Dunedin.

Habits The katipo is a close relative of the infamous redback spider of Australia and the black widow of North America, and all three are dangerous to humans. Although fatalities are now very rare since the advent of modern antivenenes, a bite can still incapacitate a human, at least temporarily. Fortunately, the katipo is restricted to sandy ocean beaches, rarely far from the sea, where it weaves its characteristically tangled webs amid driftwood, in tin cans or other debris, or at the base of marram grass. Since the 1970s its populations

have declined drastically; it is now absent along many beaches where once it was abundant, having been displaced, apparently, by an inadvertent introduction from South Africa, the spider *Steatoda capensis*. The Australian redback has also been accidentally introduced: first noted in 1980, it is now well established at Rotorua and various places in the South Island. Although timid, like the katipo, its threat is potentially greater because it is common in garden furniture and debris, and often enters houses.

Breeding The female katipo lays her eggs in a spherical, specially woven silk egg-sac or cocoon, some 10 mm in diameter, which she suspends from her web and shelters with a silken canopy. She may construct three or four such cocoons in quick succession, then guards them, clinging upside down, until the young hatch. The young disperse by 'ballooning' — each spiderling crawls to the tip of a grass blade, spins a long, single gossamer thread, and waits for a breeze to catch it and carry it aloft.

ORDER • Araneae	**SPECIES** • *Latrodectus katipo*
STATUS • endemic; uncommon; resident	**MAORI NAME** • katipo

White-tailed Spider

20 mm

Recognition   Body length about 2 cm (female) or 1 cm (male). The white-tailed spider is a member of a very large worldwide family (Gnaphosidae) of about 2000 species. In Europe they are called Mouse-spiders but are perhaps more widely known as sac-spiders from their habit of sheltering by day in a temporary 'pup-tent' of woven silk. This species looks a little like a wolf spider but with a longer, more cylindrical body. The colour varies from mottled pale brown through deep purple-brown to nearly black, depending on age or the time since the last moult, but a distinctive white tip to the abdomen usually makes identification easy. Like other sac-spiders, they have an unusual arrangement of the small eyes, which are in two rows of four. The tips of their feet are equipped with minute hairs which enable them to run up smooth, vertical surfaces with ease.

Distribution   The white-tailed spider is widespread throughout New Zealand; it also occurs across southern Australia, including Tasmania.

Habits   It inhabits woodlands of various kinds, usually sheltering under loose bark on tree trunks — though it sometimes enters houses, especially in late summer. Active mainly at night, it rests by day in a temporary retreat — the 'sac' — hidden wherever it happens to be at dawn. It can be aggressive, and easily provoked into delivering a painful bite. Its large fangs can inject a substantial quantity of venom, which is highly toxic to humans. Of greater concern is the fact that the bite is often infected with a bacterium, *Mycobacterium ulcerans*, causing severe ulcerous or necrotic sores around the wound which may stubbornly resist treatment and are very slow to heal.

Food   The white-tailed spider is unusual in preying, for preference, on other spiders; it specialises on those species that build snares or low webs near the ground — it stations itself at the perimeter of the web and tugs gently at the silk in imitation of the struggles of a captured insect, then seizes the spider when it comes to investigate.

ORDER • Araneae
STATUS • introduced; common; resident

SPECIES   • *Lampona cylindrata*
MAORI NAME • pungawerewere

Jumping Spiders

5 mm

Golden brown
jumping spider

Recognition   Jumping spiders are everywhere — the worldwide family to which they belong (Salticidae) is the largest of all spider groups (some 4000 species strong). Some are common in houses, but any garden or country hedgerow is as good a place as any to seek them out. Their jumping ability is their most prominent characteristic. The cephalothorax is characteristically bulky and box-like, and the arrangement of eyes is distinctive: one row of four, with the central pair very much larger than the others, and two rows of two below. Some species that live high in the forest canopy are colourful, but most are dingy brown or grey — except that, up close, nearly all species have striking colour patterns on the face, or bristly 'goggles', 'beards', 'whiskers' or similar facial adornments. Jumping spiders are usually very small — few species exceed 5 mm in body size.

Habits   With the keenest eyes of all spiders, jumping spiders rely on vision, not touch, to locate and catch their prey. They are much more long-sighted than other spiders, and have engagingly 'aware' eyes — if you examine one with a magnifying glass, it is quite likely to peer right back at you. Also in sharp contrast to other spiders, this group uses vision in its mating behaviour as well — a typical male jumping spider calling on a lady friend signals his intentions from a distance with elaborate 'semaphore' movements of his long forelegs. In many species, courtship involves intricate displays by both parties and males usually mate with several partners.

Food   Like all spiders, jumping spiders seek living prey, and usually hunt insects, especially small bugs, beetles and flies.

Breeding   When not out hunting, jumping spiders live in woven silk retreats hidden in crevices. These retreats are used for moulting and hibernating, the female laying her eggs within them, then sealing herself and her brood inside. There she remains until the eggs hatch into tiny spiderlings which break through the walls and wander off alone.

ORDER • Araneae	**FAMILY**	• Salticidae
STATUS • native; common; resident	**MAORI NAME**	• tupekepeke

Tadpole-shrimp

10 cm

Recognition   Deep vivid green in colour, this species gets its name from its superficial resemblance to a tadpole, being much the same shape and size (up to 10 cm in total length, of which about half is contributed by the long, slim 'tail' — actually two mobile, whisker-like appendages that serve much the same function as antennae in other crustaceans). It is the only member of its group (Notostraca) known in New Zealand. The group is often called shield-shrimps because of the relatively enormous carapace, beneath which the creature shelters as though under an umbrella permanently fixed to its back — you have to turn it over to examine its limbs and other body parts.

Distribution   The tadpole-shrimp is a cosmopolitan species that seems to be very local in New Zealand: much of its range is uncertain, but it has been recorded in Canterbury, Otago, the Wairarapa region, Hawke's Bay and the vicinity of Palmerston North.

Habits   The shield-shrimps are a small group of primitive crustaceans, distantly related to crabs, lobsters and shrimps but very different in structure. They live in wetlands of all kinds, but are more likely to be numerous in temporary pools such as stagnant flood-filled ditches or puddles — they have even be found in the waterlogged imprint of a horse's hoof!

Food   Like koura, the tadpole-shrimp feeds on minute particles of almost anything organic, ploughing through bottom ooze and sediment, filtering out edible bits with an incredibly complicated feeding apparatus. Occasionally it attacks larger animals such as tadpoles, insect larvae, and aquatic worms.

Breeding   No males have yet been found in New Zealand populations, which are self-fertilising hermaphrodites. Females lay their eggs into special brood pouches on their legs, carry them about for a few days then scatter them into the water. The tadpole-shrimp's life cycle is geared to rapid reproduction; the young have undergone several moults before they leave the egg and — in optimum conditions — they reach maturity, ready to breed themselves, within two weeks of hatching. This explosive population growth is an effective anti-predator device in ephemeral habitats such as floodwaters — by the time the predators can reach the outbreak, the new generation has scattered.

ORDER • Notostraca	**SPECIES** • *Lepidurus apus*
STATUS • native; rare; resident	**MAORI NAME** • kouraura wai maori

Freshwater Shrimp

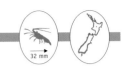

Recognition   This is the only New Zealand shrimp that occurs in fresh water, and then only in the lower reaches of lowland streams near the coast. Where the water is distinctly brackish, as in estuaries, its place is taken by various other marine shrimps, but this shrimp's identity can be confirmed by the minute bristles on the first two pairs of legs, which are part of an intricate feeding apparatus. It is common throughout New Zealand, and usually occurs in submerged vegetation. It feeds on minute particles of plant and animal 'sludge' that accumulate on underwater surfaces.

ORDER • Decapoda
SPECIES • *Paratya curvirostris*
STATUS • endemic; common; resident
MAORI NAME • tarawera

Habits   This shrimp is notable as the only member of its group that exhibits an extraordinary lifestyle known as protandry, in which gender is a function of age not genes — every individual is male as a youngster, then converts to female as it matures.

Freshwater Crab

Recognition   There is little chance of mistaking this inconspicuous species for any other crab, but the challenge lies in finding one in the first place — though fishermen not infrequently find them in the stomachs of their catch. The only freshwater species in New Zealand, it is a minute red-brown crab with a body a bit like a coin in shape but barely 10 mm across. Its large yolky eggs hatch directly into miniature 'adults' rather than minute larvae as in most other crab species.

ORDER • Decapoda
SPECIES • *Halicarcinus lacustris*
STATUS • native; rare; resident
MAORI NAME • papaka wai maori

Distribution   It has been recorded in only a few of Northland's coastal lakes and rivers, also in Lake Pupuke, Lake Waikare, the Waikato River, and a few lagoons on the Kaipara Peninsula, where it may be under threat from introduced brown trout. The species also occurs on Norfolk and Lord Howe Islands, and is widespread in south-eastern Australia.

Koura

16 cm

Northern
koura

Recognition   The southern koura and the northern koura differ little in appearance, except that the former averages slightly larger than the latter (maximum carapace lengths 80 and 72 mm respectively) — although the distinction is blurred by the fact that lake-dwellers also average larger than stream-dwellers. The northern koura has comparatively longer antennae than its southern relative, reaching well beyond the level of the fourth abdominal segment when bent backwards (in the southern koura they barely reach the third segment).

Distribution   Endemic to New Zealand, the two koura are separated by the Southern Alps-Kaikoura mountain ranges, the northern koura being common throughout the North Island and in Marlborough, Nelson, and Westland, whereas the southern koura is equally abundant along the eastern coastal lowlands of the South Island from north Canterbury southward, as well as on Stewart Island. Closely related species occur in Australia, New Guinea, Madagascar, and Chile.

Habits   Koura are bottom-dwellers with limbs well adapted for walking but not for swimming, although they can jet backwards at some speed by snapping the powerful tail forwards under the abdomen. They inhabit lakes, rivers and swamps of all kinds, but especially those with a moderately quiet flow and muddy or gravelly bottoms. By day they hide in burrows they excavate in the mud, or in crevices among boulders. At night in shallow water they can easily be located, with the aid of a torch, by their golden-red eyeshine.

Food   Minute animals and plants, living or dead.

Breeding   Their reproductive behaviour has not been studied, but females lay between 20–170 eggs (depending on age) along with a quantity of mucous from glands on the abdomen. The mucous serves to glue the eggs to her shell as she lies on her back with her abdomen curled forwards so that her body forms a sort of cradle.

ORDER • Decapoda		**STATUS** • endemic; common; resident
SPECIES • *Paranephrops planifrons* (northern)		**MAORI NAME** • koura
Paranephrops zealandicus (southern)		

Peripatus

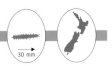

30 mm

*Peripatoides
novaezelandiae*

Recognition   One of the strangest animals in New Zealand's forests is a tiny creature barely 30 mm long that looks rather like a cross between a worm and an insect but in fact is neither. Peripatus, or velvet worms, are lonely survivors of a group that seems to have had its heyday some 500 million years ago; only about 130 species are known. The most common and widespread of several species in New Zealand is *Peripatoides novaezelandiae*, which is vivid smoky blue in colour, reaches about 35 mm in length, and has fifteen pairs of stumpy legs.

Distribution   Peripatus occur throughout the forested parts of New Zealand. Most are endemic, but closely related species occur in Australia, Africa, and South America.

Habits   Peripatus are restricted in the habitats they can occupy because, like harvestmen, centipedes and other 'primitive' arthropods, they lack mechanisms for controlling water loss. But they are often abundant in all kinds of damp or humid environments, such as mossy forests,

rotten logs, or under stones or wet leaf litter. They are rather sluggish in movement; the head is equipped with a pair of mobile antennae and small beady eyes, but peripatus rely mainly, like spiders, on a delicate sense of touch.

Food   Their inoffensive appearance is misleading, for peripatus are efficient carnivores with very unusual weaponry: they trap other small invertebrates with a device like a tiny water cannon, firing a stream of sticky mucous from turreted glands on the head. Knife-like jaws then slash open the helpless victim, it is injected with saliva, and the resulting partly digested broth is sucked back into the mouth.

Breeding   Little is known of the breeding behaviour of any New Zealand species, but *Peripatoides novaezelandiae* brings forth its young alive — as miniature adults that can immediately fend for themselves — whereas another species, *Ooperipatus viridimaculata*, a little smaller and confined to the far south, lays shelled eggs that take many months to hatch.

Order • Onychophora
Status • native; common; resident

Maori name • ngaokeoke

Springtails

Holacanthella
paucispinosa

Recognition Springtails are primitive, wingless, jumping insects. Most are barely visible to the naked eye, but New Zealand is home also to the largest known springtail, *Holacanthella paucispinosa*, about 14 mm long. The characteristic that prompts their name is a long, stiff, rod-like appendage, called the furca, at the tip of the abdomen. This is normally carried 'cocked', pointing forwards between the legs, but can be thrust downward into the ground very suddenly, which catapults the springtail backwards for several times its own length to escape danger.

Habits There are about 6500 species of springtails, of which several hundred occur in New Zealand. Springtails are probably the most abundant and widespread of all land animals. Several species are common in Antarctica, another has been found on newly fallen snow at an altitude of 7742 m in the Himalayas, and yet another occurs in vast numbers in Australian deserts. Some species feed on coastal mud flats at low tide, and one species, *Podura aquatica*, is

common on the water surface of ditches and puddles after rain. But the vast majority of springtails inhabit the soil and leaf litter of forests, where 50 species or more may coexist in numbers typically around 50,000 per square metre. Springtails are so minute that their vast numbers normally go unnoticed, but occasionally they swarm — an apparently capricious phenomenon, the cause of which is still not understood. The New Zealand black pasture springtail *Hypogastrura rossi*, for example, sometimes appears in unlikely places such as garden swimming pools in numbers so huge the results have been likened to piles of soot.

Food Most springtails feed on fungi or decaying plant material, some are carnivorous, hunting such minute animals as rotifers, nematodes and other springtails. A few graze on living plants, and at least one species, the lucerne 'flea', *Sminthurus viridis*, is a serious agricultural pest, reducing clover yields by up to 50 per cent in some circumstances.

ORDER • Collembola
STATUS • native; abundant; resident

MAORI NAME • tawhana

Centipedes

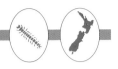

Common
centipede

Recognition The main visible differences between millipedes and centipedes are the obvious pincers at the head end of the centipede and just one pair of legs for each body segment, whereas the millipede lacks pincers and its segments bear two pairs of legs. Millipedes are usually round in cross-section, whereas centipedes are much flattened. Although it is true that most millipedes have many more legs than most centipedes, very few members of either group boast one hundred legs, let alone one thousand. There are many species of centipedes here, but by far the largest is the giant centipede, *Cormocephalus rubriceps*, of the North Island, which is often 150 mm long and — north of about Auckland — sometimes reaches 200 mm. It is a fearsome-looking beast, drab brown in colour, with yellowish legs, that is capable of delivering a very nasty bite — its venom is not lethal to humans, but a victim is not likely to forget the experience.

Habits Centipedes are mainly ground or soil dwellers, although many distinctive species live

in caves, others live in trees and even on sandy beaches. They hunt mainly at night, hiding by day in leaf litter, behind loose bark or under rocks — although many species are burrowers and live permanently in the soil. One striking characteristic of some larger species is the unusual soft swishing sound produced by their legs rubbing together as they run.

Food Centipedes are formidable predators, attacking a wide range of small animals including snails, worms, insects, and even other centipedes. When hunting they seem utterly fearless, sometimes charging unhesitatingly into burrows to tackle even large trapdoor spiders head-on, and several large overseas species habitually include scorpions in their diet.

Breeding There have been few studies on New Zealand centipedes and very little is known of their reproductive behaviour. Female centipedes generally lay their eggs in a bundle, then curl protectively around them, 'brooding' them until they hatch and wander off.

ORDER • Chilopoda
STATUS • native; common; resident

MAORI NAME • weri

Millipedes

Ophyiulus sp.

Recognition Like centipedes, millipedes are long slender creatures with a multitude of legs — two pairs for each body segment instead of only one as in centipedes. The distinction seems trivial but it imparts a very different appearance to the living animal and its movements. In a typical centipede the legs splay out to the sides, and the creature moves with a sort of slithery sinuousness. Millipede legs are short, and positioned directly under the body, so that there is a kind of steady, dead-ahead relentlessness to a typical millipede's movements — a bit like a tiny bulldozer. The short legs are adapted for generating forward thrust to force a path for the smooth, hard, compact body through loose soil and leaf litter. Despite the name, millipedes do not have 1000 legs — the maximum known count is 375 pairs. New Zealand has several hundred species of millipedes, ranging in size from barely 3 mm long to titans exceeding 100 mm. Few millipedes are conspicuous in colour or pattern, and most are plain black or dark brown in colour. Distinguishing one species from another is a job for specialists with

microscopes — and even then the specialists often have difficulty.

Habits Millipedes are abundant in most kinds of damp or humid environments. They are mostly nocturnal, inconspicuous in behaviour, and unlikely to be seen unless searched for — sifting carefully through a shovelful of soil in the garden is sure to yield several, while others shelter under rotten logs or stones, or behind loose bark on tree trunks. Millipedes, along with earthworms and springtails, play a pivotal role in the maintenance of soil ecology and the recycling of organic materials. When disturbed, many millipedes curl up into a ball or a tight spiral until the threat goes away, but many others rely on chemical defenses: several tropical species, for instance, can spray corrosive fluid for several centimetres — an effective defence against inexperienced birds.

Food Millipedes are mainly vegetarian, feeding on leaves, mosses, fungi and decomposing plant material of all kinds.

Order • Diplopoda
Status • native; common; resident

Maori name • weri mano

Damselflies

Blue
damselfly

Recognition Damselflies and dragonflies are similar in many respects — both are highly visible insect 'falcons' that hunt other insects in flight, relying entirely on superior speed and manoeuvrability in the air. There are exceptions, but the global rule of thumb is: if the creature keeps its two pairs of gauzy wings outspread while at rest, if the hindwings and forewings differ in shape, and if its enormous eyes seem to meet in the middle then it's surely a dragonfly, whereas if it folds its wings backwards and has widely separated eyes, it's probably a damselfly. In New Zealand, damselflies are mostly smaller and much more slender than dragonflies, and brilliantly coloured blue or red.

Distribution Damselflies are a worldwide group with about six species in New Zealand, the most widespread of which are *Xanthocnemis zelandica* and *Austrolestes colensonis*, both abundant throughout all three main islands. Several other species of damselflies have very restricted ranges.

Habits Like dragonflies, most damselflies are strongly associated with water at all stages of their life history — although some occasionally fly long distances from water. New Zealand damselflies are normally common wherever the water is shallow, clear and still or gently flowing. They are active during the day and rely heavily on vision in hunting (about 80 per cent of the total processing power of their brains is devoted to the analysis of visual images).

Food All species are carnivores, both as adults and immatures (nymphs).

Breeding Details vary between species, but the basic pattern of events is similar in most: the sexes copulate in flight, linked together for many minutes; the eggs are laid in, on, or near water; the eggs hatch into 'nymphs' — underwater predators that hunt other aquatic insects while they grow. The underwater sojourn commonly lasts for a month or so, but up to four years in at least one species.

ORDER • Odonata		**STATUS**	• endemic; common; resident
SPECIES • *Xanthocnemis zelandica*; *Austrolestes colensonis*, etc.		**MAORI NAME**	• tiemiemi, kihitara

Dragonflies

85 mm

Devil's
darning-needle

Recognition   New Zealand has eight native species of dragonfly, of which the most easily identified is the black and yellow devil's darning-needle, *Uropetala carovei*, with a wingspan of up to 13 cm. *Procordulia smithii* is also very common and nearly as large.

Distribution   Dragonflies are common on all three main islands of New Zealand.

Habits   A dragonfly is a minor miracle of aeronautical engineering. Like a tiny helicopter it can hover, fly backwards – or dart suddenly forward with astonishing acceleration. Both pairs of wings are independently manoeuvrable; they beat out-of-phase in flight but in-phase on take off, the wingbeats vary from 20–40 beats per second, and both pitch and amplitude are fully adjustable. A subtle forward angle (called the nodus) part-way along the wing allows flexure, and a tiny patch (called the pterostigma) near the wing tip — visible as a dark spot — functions as a balancing weight and a flight signal. Wing-loading is extraordinarily low which allows a dragonfly to keep hunting even with severely damaged wings. The huge flight muscles gobble up vast quantities of oxygen, and an ingenious pumping system in which the body wall of the thorax is made to flex like bellows by the flight muscles themselves, shunts oxygen directly to the muscles via a system of tiny tubes leading directly to the skin.

Food   Adult dragonflies feed entirely on other insects, mostly day-flying species such as bees, butterflies, flies and even other dragonflies, but they often continue hunting long after dark, sometimes including moths in their diet.

Breeding   As in damselflies, copulation takes place in a lengthy, complicated, tandem mating flight. In the rest of the world, dragonfly nymphs live mainly underwater, but *Uropetala* is unusual in that the group is adapted to bogs rather than streams; the nymph lives in burrows and emerges at night to hunt ground-dwelling animals such as spiders, cockroaches and beetles.

ORDER • Odonata	**STATUS** • native; common; resident
SPECIES • *Uropetala carovei*, etc	**MAORI NAME** • kapokapowai

Cockroaches

30 mm

Black cockroach

Recognition Viewed from directly above, the head of a cockroach is concealed under the top plate of the thorax (called the pronotum), which is much enlarged and extended forward — one of the most distinctive features of cockroaches. They can also run faster than most insects, and they have very long, slender antennae and two feelers, called cerci, at the tip of the abdomen. Apart from the familiar household pests, which are introduced, New Zealand has about 21 native species (mostly flightless), of which the best known is the black stinkroach. This species is glossy black in colour and just under 30 mm long. Several other species are smaller and range from amber to black in colour, a few with yellow markings.

Distribution The stinkroach is widespread in the North Island lowlands and northern South Island, extending up to 600 m altitude on warm, sunny, northern slopes. Another species, *Celatoblatta vulgaris*, is common under bark in beech forests of the South Island. Other species occur throughout New Zealand.

Habits Most of the native cockroaches live in native forest and woodland, and are usually active by night and hide under rocks, fallen timber and behind loose bark on trees during the day. Many species emit a vile odour when disturbed or handled, especially the well-named stinkroach.

Food Cockroaches have chewing mouthparts, like grasshoppers and mantids, and feed on almost anything organic, including paper, book-bindings, and wallpaper paste. Various species have, like termites, a symbiotic relationship with bacteria in their gut to enable them to digest the cellulose in wood.

Breeding Cockroaches have incomplete metamorphosis and hatch from the egg as miniature adults, maturing through a series of subsequent moults. Cockroaches typically lay their eggs in capsules called ootheca, which are gradually extruded from the tip of the female's abdomen and carried about for several days before being hidden in debris and abandoned.

ORDER • Blattodea
STATUS • introduced and native; common; resident

SPECIES • *Platyzosteria novaeseelandiae*
MAORI NAME • papata

Praying Mantis

40 mm

Recognition   Total length about 40 mm. Mantids of any kind are easily recognised by their long slender bodies, bulging eyes, triangular heads and spined, trap-like front legs held folded and poised to strike. Almost unique among insects, the mantis walks almost exclusively on its rearward four legs — the forelimbs are occasionally used in climbing but very seldom otherwise in locomotion. The common New Zealand species is green, with veined, leaf-like wing covers, and extremely difficult to detect amid foliage. The sexes are similar but the female is larger than the male and has a much plumper abdomen.

Distribution   The praying mantis is common throughout the warmer parts of New Zealand. It is often given the benefit of the doubt as a native species, although some suspect it may have been accidentally introduced from Australia — where it is also common — in the early days of European settlement.

Habits   Often common in gardens, the praying mantis spends much of its time lurking in the foliage of shrubbery and scrub. Mantids are unusual among insects in having a very mobile head, which can be freely rotated from side to side and up and down, enabling the large eyes, set far apart for extremely precise depth perception, to 'track' an approaching victim without unnecessary body movements. The mantis either waits in ambush for prey, or hunts it with all the stealth and intensity of a cat stalking a mouse. When prey is within range, the long, heavily armoured forelegs shoot out to snatch the victim which is devoured live.

Food   The mantis feeds entirely on other insects.

Breeding   Mantids are notorious for practicing cannibalism, with the female frequently eating the much smaller male during the act of copulation. However, this seldom happens in the New Zealand species, although the male approaches the female with due caution and is always careful to remain on her back, well out of reach of her claws, while mating — and retires promptly when mating is completed. The female lays her eggs in a soft, frothy, multi-chambered case, or ootheca, which she attaches to a twig and then abandons. The froth hardens like polystyrene to provide the embryos with a protective cocoon until they are ready to hatch as miniature versions of their parents.

Order • Mantodea		**Species** • *Orthodera novaezealandiae*	
Status • native; common; resident		**Maori name** • ro	

Migratory Locust

55 mm

Recognition   Length about 55 mm (female) and 35 mm (male). The locust is easily identified as the only fully winged short-horned grasshopper in New Zealand (all others are flightless).

Distribution   The migratory locust has a vast range across much of Africa and Asia, eastward to New Zealand, where it is occurs in many low-lying parts of the North Island and in the South Island south to the vicinity of Christchurch — mainly in isolated pockets or 'colonies'.

Habits   This grasshopper is most common on rough, flat, bare grasslands such as tussock fields and sand dunes. In New Zealand it is a solitary, secretive insect that feeds mainly in the morning and evening and hides in rough grass at other times. Yet it is the same species that has been the scourge of peasant farmers across North Africa and the Middle East for several thousand years. Swarms of plague locusts may cover thousands of square kilometres and contain billions of insects. In 1957 one swarm

destroyed enough grain — it was calculated — to feed 1,000,000 people for one year.

The locust exists in two phases, dubbed 'solitary' and 'gregarious', and it switches between the two states in response to a particular set of environmental and climatic conditions, which occur every few years in North Africa. Such conditions do not occur in New Zealand, so the species cannot switch to the gregarious or plague state and causes no significant agricultural damage. Several other grasshopper species in North America, South America and Australia also exhibit this extraordinary 'Jeckyll and Hyde' transformation.

Food   Entirely plant material, especially grasses and cereal crops.

Breeding   After mating, the female locust lays her eggs in soft ground and the young hatch as nymphs roughly resembling miniature adults, gradually achieving adult size and appearance through a series of moults spanning several weeks.

Order • Orthoptera	**Species** • *Locusta migratoria*
Status • native; uncommon; resident	**Maori name** • kapakapa, rangataua

Short-horned Grasshoppers

Sigaus villosus

Recognition The 'short-horn' in the name refers to the group's short antennae compared to those of the 'long-horned' grasshoppers (page 196). All New Zealand species are flightless and mostly drab in colour. Size varies with the species, and also with increasing altitude: for example, one species grows to 30 mm at an altitude of 1000 m, whereas at 1500 m the same species reaches 45 mm in length. Females are larger than males.

Distribution The short-horned grasshoppers are a worldwide group, but all but one of New Zealand's 15 species are endemic, and at least 10 of these are confined to the South Island.

Habits Elsewhere in the world, grasshoppers are usually associated with plains and low-lying grasslands but in New Zealand most of the endemic species are confined to the alpine zone above 900 m, living on high rock and scree slopes, shingle flats along rivers and tussock grasslands. Only a couple of species inhabit the lowlands. Their closest relatives are also alpine

species in Tasmania and southern Chile. This has prompted the natural speculation that they adapted to their unusual high-altitude habitat perhaps even before the breakup of Gondwana occurred around 100 million years ago, but more recent research has uncovered other possible scenarios (though the point is far from settled at the present time). These grasshoppers are well adapted to 'life in the freezer', but one of them, the hairy grasshopper, *Sigaus villosus*, has a truly remarkable way of escaping from predators. Instead of floundering about in soft snow, the grasshopper 'skis' from danger. Using its legs as ski-poles and its smooth abdomen as a snowboard, 'skiing siggy' is an excellent downhill racer.

Food Entirely vegetarian, feeding on a wide range of alpine herbs and grasses.

Breeding Like other grasshoppers, eggs are laid on the ground and hatch in a few weeks into nymphs resembling adults, which mature and grow over a series of moults.

ORDER • Orthoptera
STATUS • native; common; resident

FAMILY • Acrididae
MAORI NAME • mawhitiwhiti

Long-horned Grasshoppers

32 mm

Green
grasshopper

Recognition   The long-horned grasshoppers belong to a worldwide group with about 7300 members, of which nearly 50 species inhabit New Zealand. Members of the family are variously known as katydids, bush crickets, and long-horned grasshoppers — and many species do indeed strongly resemble 'true' grasshoppers (page 195) except for their extremely long, slender antennae. In general, the group is more numerous in woodland and shrubbery than in grassland, and most members are protectively coloured green to merge with the foliage in which they mainly live.

Distribution   Throughout New Zealand, including several of the outlying groups such as the Chatham and Kermadec Islands.

Habits   Common in lush grass, woodlands and shrubbery of all kinds, long-horned grasshoppers are wary, keen-eyed insects that rely first on crypsis to avoid danger and secondly on their strong hind limbs to leap from danger. In warmer climates, the tranquil,

pleasant sounds of katydids are a feature of summer nights in gardens – the famous author Nathaniel Hawthorne once likened them to 'moonlight made audible'. Most species produce sounds (called stridulation) in courtship, although the details vary from species to species. Even gender role is not universal, but usually males stridulate to attract females. The sounds are strongly species-specific to avoid attracting the 'wrong' mate. The stridulating apparatus consists of a small toothed area at the base of each wing cover, the sound produced by rubbing both together; katydid 'ears' are usually visible as small circular depressions just below the 'knees' on the forelimbs.

Food   Most species are herbivores, feeding mainly on the leaves of trees and shrubs.

Breeding   Typically the eggs are laid indiscriminately on the ground, and there is no parental care. Newly hatched, the young resemble miniature adults — though often with distinctive colour patterns.

ORDER • Orthoptera
FAMILY • Tettigoniidae

STATUS • native; common; resident
MAORI NAME • kikiki

Green Katydid

45 mm

Recognition Approximately 45 mm in total length, the green katydid is a slim, elegant 'grasshopper', almost entirely green in colour, that folds its wings tent-wise over its body to produce a shape markedly triangular in cross-section and tapering to a slender point at the rear. Even the long lanky legs are green, and the wing covers are intricately veined to produce a striking likeness to a leaf.

Distribution The green katydid is common at low elevations over much of New Zealand, but it remains uncertain whether or not it is a genuinely indigenous species: it may have been accidentally introduced from Australia — where it is also abundant and widespread — in the early days of European settlement.

Habits This is one of the commonest insect inhabitants of shrubbery and low foliage in many a city park or garden, yet finding one can sometimes take a great deal of patience thanks to its supremely effective camouflage and inconspicuous behaviour. Seldom seen in flight,

it usually moves slowly, constantly waving its antennae in all directions as though feeling its way, but it can make sudden leaps of a metre or so when alarmed.

Food Katydids feed on the green leaves of many kinds of shrubs and low trees, both native and introduced.

Breeding During copulation, the male deposits a capsule of sperm on the female's genital opening, where it is gradually transferred into her body to fertilise her eggs. Her response is to clean it off, to remove any hindrance to egg-laying and to prepare herself for further mating — but the male's counter-response to afford his own sperm the best chance of avoiding the cleaning response and achieving fertilisation is to bundle his sperm with a substantial quantity of mucous. The female then spends an hour or so getting rid of the mucous, giving the sperm ample time to do its job. She is equipped with a long ovipositor which she uses to thrust her eggs into bare ground.

ORDER • Orthoptera		**SPECIES**	• *Caedicia simplex*
STATUS • native or introduced; common; resident		**MAORI NAME**	• kikiki, kiki pounamu

Tree Weta

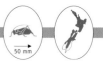

50 mm

Wellington tree weta

Recognition About 50 mm in body length, tree weta are most easily distinguished from other weta by the male's massive, heavily armoured head, powerful mandibles, and large, heavily spined hind legs. The head is usually reddish brown in colour, the abdomen striped with yellow and brown.

Distribution There are at least six species of tree weta, which together occur almost throughout New Zealand, although several species are confined to the South Island. All are endemic, but closely related species occur in southern Australia.

Habits Tree weta live in most kinds of native forest and woodland. They emerge to forage at night (they are easily found with a torch on humid, moonless nights) and spend the day in cavities in trees. They also take temporary refuge in almost any dry crevice, including stacked firewood and even footwear left outdoors. They enter their quarters head first, using their powerful, heavily armoured hind legs to block the entrance. They are nimble climbers but — unlike cave weta — they seldom jump. Several species live in treeless habitats. The mountain rock weta, for example, lives on scree slopes high in the Southern Alps, where it has the distinction of being the largest known insect able to withstand being frozen solid in winter and thawed out unharmed again in spring. Tree weta have an impressive threat display with the long spiny hind legs fully extended and held erect, and they defend themselves strongly when molested, biting, kicking and scratching vigorously. They often produce a scratchy *tsit tsit* sound by rubbing minute pegs on the inner surface of their hind legs against the abdomen — rather like a thumbnail run down a comb.

Food Tree weta feed mainly on leaves, but they also eat other insects whenever the opportunity arises; cannibalism is also not unknown.

Breeding Males meet in combat for mating rights to 'harems' of females, and the male with the larger head usually wins. The female has a huge curved ovipositor, not as a sting but for thrusting eggs, one by one, deep into damp soil. Eggs are laid mainly in April and take about eight months to hatch.

ORDER • Orthoptera	**SPECIES** • *Hemideina* spp.
STATUS • endemic; common; resident	**MAORI NAME** • weta

Giant Weta

9 cm

Poor Knights
giant weta

Recognition   The giant weta is easily recognisable by its awesome size alone — some tropical insects are considerably longer but this may well be the bulkiest, heaviest insect in the world. Some individuals reach 9 cm in length and weigh up to 80 g. Some tree weta are nearly as big, but they have huge, fierce-looking, heavily armoured heads and lack the benign expression of the giant weta. There are two species, similar in size: the wrinkled weta has a heavily sculptured back whereas the giant weta's is relatively smooth.

Distribution   Endemic to New Zealand, the two species were once common over much of the main islands; both are now gravely threatened. The giant weta remains common only on Little Barrier Island, while the wrinkled weta is effectively confined to Stephens Island and a few islets in Cook Strait.

Habits   Mostly nocturnal and foraging mainly on the ground, weta have an impressive and distinctive defence posture: when alarmed, they extend their hind legs vertically upwards and vigorously move them up and down, producing a rasping sound. New Zealand weta evolved in a land without mammals, other than bats. As a result their size and characteristic defence postures easily deter small birds, but were no protection against a hungry rat. The serious decline in ground-dwelling weta populations began with the introduction of stoats, weasels, rats and similar predators in the early days of European settlement. In Maori tradition the weta is viewed with abhorrence, and it was sometimes called taipo, which roughly translates to 'night-stalking devil'.

Food   Like other weta, these two species feed mainly on foliage but also scavenge a wide range of other organic materials, plant or animal, living or dead.

Breeding   Little is known of the reproductive behaviour.

ORDER • Orthoptera	**STATUS** • endemic; rare; resident
SPECIES • *Deinacrida heteracantha* (giant)	**MAORI NAME** • wetapunga
Deinacrida rugosa (wrinkled)	

Cave Weta

21 cm

Recognition   Elsewhere in the world cave weta are known as camel crickets because of their distinctive humped backs. Their bodies are small in relation to their extremely long spindly legs and incredibly long antennae — for example, *Gymnopletron edwardsii*, one of the most common and widespread species, spans about 21 cm from hind feet to antennae tips, yet its body is only 35 mm long. Cave weta lack both ears and wings.

Order	Orthoptera
Species	*Gymnoplectron* spp.
Status	endemic; common; resident
Maori name	tokoriro

Habits   Most species are abundant in caves but some members of the group live under rocks and similar dark, damp places both in forest and open country. Cave weta are scavengers, emerging at night to feed on fungi, tree foliage and animal remains. Unlike other weta, they are unaggressive, and can escape danger in amazing leaps — the larger species can cover 2–3 m in a single bound.

Wellington cave weta

Ground Weta

32 mm

Recognition   Two very different groups of insects are called weta, one of which is made up of the ground and cave weta. Most members are endemic but closely related species occur elsewhere. Ground weta somewhat resemble cave weta but have far more conventional proportions, without the extravagant length of limbs and antennae. Like the cave weta they are agile jumpers, lack ears and make no obvious noise, but differ most obviously in their spiny hind legs, with an array of longer spines around the 'ankle'.

Order	Orthoptera
Species	*Hemiandrus* spp.
Status	endemic; common; resident
Maori name	weta

Habits   They feed at night, mainly on other insects, and spend their days in tunnels in the soil, which they either dig themselves or else commandeer and modify those of worms or other insects. They have the distinctive habit of entering their burrows tail first so that their head faces any intruder.

Seaward Kaikoura ground weta

Crickets

35 mm

Black field cricket

Recognition Crickets look rather like small, squat grasshoppers and occupy similar environments, but many species are allocated, as it were, to the graveyard shift. Two kinds are common in New Zealand: the black field cricket *Teleogryllus commodus* — which may be an early introduction from Australia — and several native species of the genus *Neobius*. Despite their abundance, black field crickets can be difficult to find because they hide by day in cracks in the ground; native species are often more conspicuous. Exceptionally nimble on their feet, crickets leap, run and crawl with equal facility. Although fully equipped to fly, black field crickets seldom do so (except in annual dispersal flights in February and March), and many of the native species lack wings altogether. Black field crickets may be up to 35 mm long, but many native species are substantially shorter.

Distribution Crickets of one species or another occur almost everywhere in New Zealand, but the black field cricket is confined to the North Island and parts of the northern South Island. In many districts, especially Northland and south Auckland, it may reach densities of 40 per sq m, and it often causes severe damage to pastures.

Habits In general, crickets occupy tussock and grassland environments rather than forest and woodland. They are mostly active at night when their presence is obvious — especially on warm summer evenings — by their strident, monotonous chirping. Black field crickets are notable for their erratic population explosions, when very large numbers sometimes invade houses. Eggs are laid generally from February onwards, deposited about 20 mm deep in the ground. About 4 mm long at hatching, the nymphs mature rapidly, progressing through a total of 12 moults before reaching sexual maturity. A typical female begins laying about two weeks later, and may lay a total of 500–1500 eggs over her lifetime of nearly three months.

ORDER • Orthoptera		**STATUS**	• native and introduced; common;
SPECIES • *Teleogryllus commodus* (black field);			resident
Neobius spp. (native)		**MAORI NAME**	• pihareinga

Stick Insects

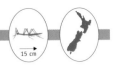

15 cm

Black-spined
stick insect

Recognition   New Zealand has about 20 native species of stick insects, all immediately recognisable by looking much as one would expect, only more so. About the largest is *Argosarchus horridus*, a spiny, grey-brown insect that grows to about 15 cm in total length. One of the most abundant is *Acanthoxyla prasinus*, which is mainly green in colour and about 8 cm in length, while another very common species, *Clitarchus hookeri*, is smooth-bodied (lacking spines), green with a yellow band along each flank. Among stick insects, females are often flightless, and they greatly exceed males in size.

Distribution   Stick insects occur throughout New Zealand, and are widespread elsewhere.

Habits   Reasonably common but extraordinarily difficult to find, stick insects are specialists in a category of camouflage that relies on shape and texture rather than colour. A typical stick insect is almost impossibly long and slender and its skin mimics in extraordinary detail the minute

grooves, bumps, and nodules of a twig. Most stick insects live in lowland forest and woodland — including parks and gardens — and feed in a variety of native trees and shrubs, but there are several alpine species that live in tussock. A notable trait of the group is that parthenogenesis (reproduction without fertilisation) is widespread, and males have not been found for several New Zealand species.

Food   Stick insects are entirely vegetarian.

Breeding   Mating among stick insects is a leisurely affair, and a male often remains mounted on a female's back for several days. The female broadcasts her eggs at random (some species lay 1000 or so in a season), and they simply fall to the ground below. In some species the eggs may lie for years before hatching, but in others incubation takes only a week or two. As in several other insect groups, metamorphosis is incomplete, newly hatched stick insects look superficially like tiny adults.

ORDER • Phasmatodea	**STATUS**	• native and endemic; common; resident
SPECIES • *Acanthoxyla prasinus*, etc	**MAORI NAME**	• whe kakariki

Earwigs

25 mm

European
earwig

Recognition Earwigs are recognisable as slender, flattened insects with a flexible, telescopic abdomen ending in two, slightly curved spines that function like forceps. Earwigs range from about 10 to 25 mm in length, and vary from reddish brown to black in colour. Many species are flightless (including all three native New Zealand species), but those with wings (such as the common garden pest, the European earwig) exhibit one of the group's most extraordinary characteristics — the folding of the wings. The performance is difficult to see because earwigs seldom fly to begin with and, on landing, the wings disappear with all the speed and panache of a conjuring trick. The large, fan-shaped wings are, in fact, folded in several pleats — just like a fan — then folded crosswise, and finally tucked under the very small, hard wing-covers with only the tips protruding.

Habits Earwigs are creatures of damp, confined spaces such as behind the bark of trees, under fallen logs and stones, and between the young leaves of palms and similar plants. The most widespread of the native species, the shore earwig, is often abundant along pebble beaches, hiding under driftwood and rotting seaweed, but the introduced European earwig is common in gardens, where it is often a pest, damaging vegetables and flowers (it seems to favour roses). They are active mostly at night, and flying species are often attracted to lights.

Food A wide range of plant and animal material, living and dead, is eaten.

Breeding Courtship is brief, and earwigs mate with the tips of their abdomens together, facing in opposite directions. Egg-laying may be several months after mating. The female lays her clutch of eggs (60–70 in the case of the shore earwig) in a burrow and remains with them until they hatch, frequently licking and gathering the eggs together if they should become scattered.

Order • Dermaptera	**Status**	• native and introduced; common; resident
Species • Species *Anisolabis littorea* (shore) *Forficula auricularia* (European)	**Maori name**	• mata

Green Vegetable Bug

15 mm

Recognition Bugs are characterised by their piercing, sucking mouthparts, in most species used to penetrate the skins of plants and drink the sap, almost like slurping a milkshake through a straw. Other species, as diverse as bedbugs and assassin-bugs, use the same equipment to drink animal fluids, either from other insects or even from mammals and other vertebrates. Belonging to a family known variously as shield-bugs (from their generally flattened, shield-shaped bodies) or stink-bugs (from the offensive chemical spray they use to defend themselves from predators), green vegetable bugs are easily identified by the shape and colour expressed in their name. They are up to 15 mm long.

Distribution A native of Europe but now virtually cosmopolitan, the green vegetable bug was first detected in New Zealand, feeding on beans, at New Plymouth in 1944. It has since spread virtually throughout the North Island and some parts of the South Island, notably Blenheim and Nelson.

Habits The green vegetable bug is common in parks, gardens and rural countryside generally. Mating flights occur usually around dusk, but otherwise they seldom fly. Adults tend to become most noticeable in gardens around January or February, and they have an average lifespan of about 4–6 weeks.

Food Both nymphs and adults of the green vegetable bug attack a very wide range of garden vegetables and field crops, including beans, turnips, cabbage, maize and tomatoes

Breeding A little over 1 mm in length, the egg resembles a tiny keg, capped with a circular lid that the larva pushes aside on hatching in order to climb out. The eggs are laid in neat, compact, multiple rows, in batches of 40–60 at a time, on the underside of leaves. Incubation takes about 10–20 days, and the larvae undergo a series of five moults, changing colour at each stage, before becoming winged adults. The complete cycle, from egg-laying to adult emergence, takes from about 56 to 100 days.

Order • Hemiptera	**Species** • *Nezara viridula*
Status • introduced; abundant; resident	**Maori name** • kirirakau

Leafhoppers

20 mm

Green planthopper

Passionvine hopper

Recognition Leafhoppers look a little like miniature cicadas, with broad heads, robust bodies, large conspicuously membranous wings and mouthparts pointing downwards. Elsewhere in the world they are often brightly coloured but New Zealand species are mostly drab yellow, brown or green. Some are very small, but most leafhoppers fall within the range of 10–20 mm in length.

Distribution The leafhoppers are a worldwide group of several thousand species, of which New Zealand has about 100 (about 90 endemic), together found virtually throughout the country including several outlying groups such as the Kermadec and Chatham Islands. About 20 species belong to the genus *Novothymbris*, endemic to New Zealand though related to several Australian groups, but several other species have their closest links in southern Africa or South America. As well, a few nearly cosmopolitan groups are sparsely represented, and there are several introduced species.

Habits Leafhoppers are all sap feeders, mostly attacking flowering plants. Most native species inhabit woodlands; only one occurs in beech forests. Grass-dwelling native leafhoppers are almost equally sparse, but there are many that specialise on rushes and similar marsh vegetation. Like most bugs, leafhoppers use their mouths almost like drinking straws to suck plant juices. More precisely, the mouthparts are in two pairs that together form twin channels, and salivary secretions are pumped down one while partly digested plant fluids are drawn simultaneously up the other. Leafhoppers are aptly named, and both adults and nymphs generally leap to avoid danger, although they may merely dodge, with equal nimbleness, to the far side of their perch when disturbed.

Breeding Eggs are inserted into plant tissue. Nymphs do not differ greatly from adults in appearance, except in lacking wings, and they reach maturity through a series of (usually) five moults spanning several weeks.

ORDER • Hemiptera	**FAMILY** • *Cicadellidae*
STATUS • introduced, native and endemic; common; resident	**MAORI NAME** • kiritaitea

Clapping cicadas

75 mm

Amphipsalta
zelandica

Recognition   The largest (wingspan about 80 millimetres) of all New Zealand's cicadas is so common, conspicuous and widespread that it was one of the very first insects encountered by Joseph Banks, the naturalist accompanying James Cook on his famous first voyage in 1769–1770. For nearly two centuries 'clapping cicada' was regarded as a single species, until it was noted that this 'species' has two quite different songs. Subsequent investigation finally confirmed that there are in fact two species, virtually indistinguishable in appearance but very different in several other aspects of their biology. Clapping cicadas are dull green, intricately marked with black.

Distribution   One of the species, *Amphipsalta cingulata*, is confined to the North Island but the other, *Amphipsalta zelandica*, is widespread throughout the North and South Islands.

Habits   Clapping cicadas differ from other cicadas in the unusually heavy, thickened leading edge to their wings, which the males use to 'clap' against their perches to augment their already extremely loud songs. Adult clapping cicadas live in the treetops all summer long, and the cicadas' most obvious feature from the human perspective is that very few other living creatures of any kind can produce quite such an ear-splitting din. Few other species 'sing' solo or space themselves sparsely (*Amphipsalta zelandica* is one of those few that do), with the result that the typical summer cicada sound is a massed chorus of thousands, reaching crescendos that may sweep wave-like across an entire valley and extend from mid-morning well into the night. Only the males 'sing', and the sound-producing apparatus is unique to cicadas. A ribbed membrane (called the 'tymbal') is set into a depression on each side of the abdomen, and made to vibrate very rapidly by a set of powerful muscles. The abdomen is largely hollow, thus producing a resonating chamber that enormously amplifies the resulting, extremely rapid, series of clicks.

ORDER • Hemiptera	**STATUS**	• endemic; common; resident
SPECIES • *Amphipsalta cingulata*	**MAORI NAME**	• tatarakihi
Amphipsalta zelandica		

Other Cicadas

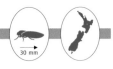

30 mm

*Maoricicada
nigra*

Recognition   Cicadas have broad, blunt heads, large, widely-separated compound eyes and four transparent wings. These are folded tent-wise and typically extend substantially beyond the tip of the short, broad abdomen, resulting in a distinctive 'inverted teardrop' outline. Cicadas vary widely in size, but several of the larger species are around 30 mm in total length.

Distribution   Cicadas of one species or another occur almost throughout New Zealand, although the large, noisy and especially conspicuous species tend to be more numerous in the north.

Habits   The noisiest cicadas tend to live in forests, but New Zealand has a rich and diverse cicada fauna that extends into most habitats from coastal sand dunes to alpine meadows: in fact the various species tend to fall into 'guilds' — the members not necessarily related — according to habitat type, so that it becomes useful to speak of 'tussock cicadas', 'rock cicadas', 'scrub cicadas' and so on.

Food   Both adults and nymphs live entirely on the sap of plants; adults generally take their food from the stems, nymphs from the underground roots.

Breeding   The most distinctive feature in the life-history of cicadas is that they spend their time as larvae deep underground, in some cases for many years, before emerging as adults. The female has a spear-like ovipositor that she uses to insert her eggs deep into plant tissue. Hatching takes anywhere from about 70–120 days, and the tiny nymphs then fall to the ground and quickly work their way under the surface until they can select a suitable spot in which to hollow out a chamber adjacent to the root of a plant and begin feeding. When almost mature, they leave the ground, climb a stem or trunk, and shed their nymphal skin — a laborious process that typically occurs several hours after sunset and may take about an hour to complete. The cast off skin — the exuviae — is left clinging to the bark, and is a common sight in woodlands in spring.

ORDER • Hemiptera
STATUS • endemic; common; resident

MAORI NAME • kihikihi

Spittlebugs

8 mm

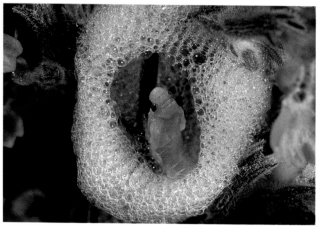

Meadow spittlebug

Recognition Spittlebugs are much like leafhoppers in lifestyle except that the larvae live within a large protective mass of froth or 'spittle'. They are sometimes known as froghoppers from the somewhat frog-like appearance of adults, but they also resemble small cicadas (if in doubt, count the ocelli between the compound eyes: cicadas have three, but spittlebugs only two). Perhaps the most common and widespread of New Zealand's five species, the meadow spittlebug, *Philaenus spumarius*, is yellowish brown with a blunt head and prominent eyes, and a little under 6 mm long. Another widespread species is the three-spotted froghopper, *Philaenus trimaculatus*, which is mainly green, flecked and marbled with reddish brown, and about 8 mm in length.

Distribution The spittlebugs are a large worldwide group most richly represented in the tropics. New Zealand has two native species (*Carystoterpa fingens* and *Pseudophronella jactator*) but those most often encountered are introduced: the meadow spittlebug, for

example, is a European introduction that was first noted in 1960 but did not become established until the 1970s.

Habits Like leafhoppers, spittlebugs feed entirely on the sap and other fluids of flowering plants, using their mouths as drinking straws (see page 205). The variety of plants attacked is large — at least 400 plant species have been documented in the case of the meadow spittlebug. Nymphs seldom move from good feeding positions but adults are more mobile and use their powerful hind legs to leap several centimetres to escape danger. Adult spittlebugs have wings but seldom use them.

Breeding Meadow spittlebugs lay their eggs in autumn in neat, compact rows of about 25 eggs each. These hatch in spring, and the pale yellowish nymphs begin feeding immediately, using a mixture of air and anal secretions to embed themselves in a large frothy mass of small bubbles. The nymphs moult five times, becoming darker and greener each time.

Order • Hemiptera	**Species** • *Philaenus* spp.
Status • endemic; common; resident	**Maori name** • kiritaitea

Backswimmers

8 mm

Recognition Perhaps the best known water bugs are the backswimmers, of which there are about 130 species in the world. Their common name conveys all the information needed to identify them: they have the unique habit of swimming upside down, often near the surface. There are two species in New Zealand, both of which belong to the nearly cosmopolitan genus *Anisops*, the commonest of which is *Anisops assimilis* — about 8 mm long and found almost throughout New Zealand.

ORDER •	Hemiptera
SPECIES •	*Anisops* spp.
STATUS •	endemic; common; resident
MAORI NAME •	hoe tuara

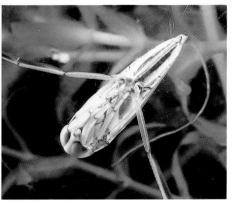

Habits Backswimmers are carnivores that hunt other aquatic creatures underwater, using their long hind limbs for swimming and their front legs for prey capture. The underside of the body carries a long keel flanked by hair-filled grooves, which trap the air needed to sustain them in their submarine forays. The eggs are thrust into small slits cut into the stems of waterweeds.

Common backswimmer

Water Boatmen

7 mm

Recognition Water boatmen are superficially similar to backswimmers but they have a much flatter body shape, much shorter front legs and they swim right-side up. New Zealand has three species, all fairly widespread, of which *Arctocorisa arguta* is by far the commonest. About 7 mm long, this water boatman is mainly brown in colour, liberally freckled with tiny dark-brown spots.

ORDER •	Hemiptera
SPECIES •	*Arctocorisa* spp.
	Diaprepocoris spp.
STATUS •	endemic; common; resident
MAORI NAME •	hoehoe tuara

Habits Like backswimmers, water boatmen live in clear, quiet waters such as ponds, pools and backwaters in gently flowing streams, and sometimes roadside ditches. They are generally less conspicuous than backswimmers because they tend to feed on or near the bottom, grubbing about in the bottom ooze for insect larvae and other small creatures. Water boatmen lay their eggs on water-plants, where the eggs stand clear of the substrate on slender stalks.

Common water boatman

Water Beetles

12 mm

Common diving beetle

Recognition   Water beetles are closely related to ground beetles (opposite) and are similar in general appearance and lifestyle, except that water beetles spend most of their lives beneath the surface and are strongly streamlined for underwater pursuit. The enlarged, oar-like hind legs are usually held stiffly angled backwards from the oval body, and are fringed with hairs to serve as paddles. New Zealand has about 14 species, most of which are black or brown in colour and about 12 mm or less in length.

Distribution   Throughout New Zealand. The largest and most common species, *Rhantus pulverosus*, may be an accidental introduction from overseas, but many others are endemic.

Habits   Although several species live entirely underground, in caves, deep wells and similar places, water beetles are generally common in ponds, ditches and similar quiet, shallow wetlands of all kinds. A few species, such as *Huxelydrus syntheticus*, are specialised

inhabitants of the fast-flowing shingle river systems of Canterbury, Otago and Southland. Adult water beetles breath air but they carry their supply, like scuba gear, in hollow tank-like containers formed by the close-fitting elytra (modified fore-wings). To refill its air-tanks, the water beetle thrusts the tip of its abdomen above the surface, opens its elytra slightly and draws in a fresh supply of air. Notwithstanding their aquatic lifestyle, water beetles often fly at night, either for mating or when their ponds dry up, and can often be seen zooming around porch lights or beneath street lamps

Food   Water beetles are predators throughout their lives; larvae, in particular, attack any aquatic animal small enough to overpower. Adults chew solid food but many larvae have non-functional mouthparts: instead, digestive enzymes are pumped into the victim's body through channels in the fangs, and the resulting 'soup' drawn back into the body via the same route.

ORDER • Coleoptera	**FAMILY** • Dytiscidae
STATUS • introduced, native and endemic; common; resident	**MAORI NAME** • tataka-ruku

Ground Beetles

40 mm

Mecodema trailli

Recognition   Ground beetles make up the enormous family Carabidae, with some 26,000 species worldwide (it is one of the largest of all animal families), of which there are several hundred in New Zealand alone. Built for running, most are fairly large — around 20 mm in length is typical, but some reach 40 mm — and often completely black, heavily armoured, usually glossy, and with a strong sheen of metallic blue, green or bronze. They have prominent biting jaws.

Distribution   Ground beetles of one species or another are common in all parts of New Zealand, and several are very widespread.

Habits   They are aptly named, and most species spend all life history stages on the ground or just under the surface; there are a number of flightless, burrowing species, as well as some that live in caves. Unlike the tiger beetles (page 212) they are active mostly at night, but most of the commonest species are

easily found sheltering under stones or fallen timber during the day. Abundant in forest and grassland alike, most terrestrial habitats support at least a few species. Ground beetles use their formidable jaws for hunting, but for defence most rely on chemical repellents, discharged through orifices adjoining the anus. This general form of defence reaches a pinnacle of sophistication in the extraordinary bombardier beetles, in which the chemicals are first squirted into what amounts to a reaction chamber, lined with a special enzyme that causes the chemicals to react so violently that they flash almost instantly to a corrosive vapour that is expelled at a very high temperature and pressure, full in the face of any attacker — the original 'mace' defence.

Food   Both larvae and adults are voracious predators. Some species specialise in hunting scarab beetles and other agricultural pests. Several exotic forms have been introduced into New Zealand as biological control measures.

Order • Coleoptera	**Family** • Carabidae
Status • endemic, native and introduced; common; resident	**Maori name** • kurikuri

Tiger Beetles

14 mm

some are olive, with yellow markings), but all are slim beetles with very long, slender legs, formidable sickle-shaped jaws and large, bulging eyes.

Distribution   Tiger beetles occur throughout New Zealand, but several have very restricted distributions.

Habits   Many species of tiger beetles, such as the common and widespread *Neocicindela tuberculata*, favour clay banks, but several others occur on beaches: *Neocicindela perhispida*, for example, is common on sandy beaches along the coasts of the far north of the North Island and occurs in several populations that closely match the colour of the sand on which they live. Some species live on the trunks of trees. The larvae are distinctive in that they live in vertical tunnels, lying in wait for prey. Often about 4– 5 mm in diameter, the tunnels are easily found on almost any patch of flat, bare, sandy soil. The larva's first body segment is armoured, camouflaged, and angled in such a way that it forms a sort of plug to the tunnel entrance, allowing the jaws to snap forward with lightning speed to snatch at any unwary insect straying within range. The larva is also equipped with a pair of prominent hooks midway along the back, which serves to anchor it firmly in its burrow during struggles with unusually vigorous victims.

Common tiger beetle

Recognition   Often popularly known as penny-doctors or butcher-boys, tiger beetles are easily recognised as active, sun-loving beetles that run with astonishing speed (they can sometimes catch even flying insects by running them down) over bare, sun-baked clay or sand, occasionally taking to the air for short, swift flights. Sometimes clad in brilliant, metallic colours, most are active only by day, but a few are nocturnal. They make up a worldwide family (Cicindelidae) with about 2000 known species. New Zealand has about 16 species, which range between about 10–14 mm in total length. The colour and pattern varies with the species (usually matching the substrate, though

Food   Both adults and larvae are carnivores, preying mainly on other insects.

Breeding   Little is known of the life cycle of most species, but the larvae probably take several years to mature.

ORDER • Coleoptera		**SPECIES** • *Neocicindela* spp.	
STATUS • native and endemic; common; resident		**MAORI NAME** • papapa	

Stag Beetles

40 mm

Helm's stag beetle

Recognition   There are perhaps 1250 species of stag beetles in the world, of which about 25 species live in New Zealand. At a casual glance they look much like ground beetles — especially in being typically black with a strong metallic sheen — but the abdomen characteristically looks a size smaller when compared to that of a typical ground beetle, the elbowed antennae can be folded away into special grooves on the sides of the head, and the sexes differ markedly in appearance. Size is very variable, even within the same species, but Helm's stag beetle, *Dorcus helmsi*, one of the best known New Zealand species, reaches nearly 40 mm in total length (females about 30 mm) and the common stag beetle, *Lissotes reticulatus*, another widespread species, is about 18 mm. Stag beetles seldom fly, some being entirely flightless.

Distribution   Helm's stag beetle is confined to native forests of Stewart Island and the west and south of the South Island, but the common stag

beetle is widespread on all three main islands. Other species occur throughout New Zealand.

Habits   New Zealand species are most numerous in native beech or podocarp forests where they can usually easily be found on the lower trunks of trees or sheltering amid, or under, rotten logs. Elsewhere in the world, stag beetles are notable for the enormous development of the mandibles in many species, often with elaborate spines and branches rather like the antlers of a stag — hence the name. In some species these 'antlers' are used in wrestling matches with rival males. Though large-jawed, the New Zealand species generally lack such extravagant equipment, and their somewhat smaller mandibles may be used in burrowing. The larvae of most species stridulate (see page 196) but, so far, no one knows why.

Food   Larvae feed mainly on very soft, decayed or rotten wood, aided by bacteria in the gut to enable the digestion of cellulose.

ORDER • Coleoptera	**SPECIES** • *Geodorcus helmsi*
STATUS • native and endemic; common; resident	**MAORI NAME** • none

Sand Scarab

25 mm

Recognition   Length about 25 mm. Largest of the New Zealand scarabs, the sand scarab is easily identified as a massive, burly beetle with very powerful legs and a short, blunt horn just behind the head, brownish black in colour with a sheen like highly polished leather.

Distribution   New Zealand generally.

Habits   The sand scarab is one member of a distinctively New Zealand cluster of beetles that are strongly adapted to a subterranean life in sand rather than soil. The shifting, almost fluid nature of loose sand dictates several characteristic body features, of which perhaps the most obvious is the unusually bulky, muscular legs. The sand scarab is confined to coastal sandy beaches. It has a close relative that occurs in river sands in the South Island, but otherwise lacks near relatives anywhere else in the world. The larvae — pallid, plump and curled, with a large brown head — can be found in cavities in driftwood. Like many other scarabs, adults form massed mating flights on

emergence, just after dusk, in late spring and summer.

The sand scarab is a member of the dung beetle group, named from their habit of laying their eggs in dung as food for their larvae on hatching. Details vary among species: typically the dung is from mammals, often it is first rolled into a convenient-sized ball and sometimes it is buried, but the group plays a vital ecological role in some parts of the world by recycling mammalian faeces back into plant fertiliser to promote the growth of more grass to feed more mammals. The cycle is also significant in ranching because, at any single point in time, several percent of a paddock's total area is hidden under cowpats. Pasture under a cow pat can't be growing grass and is therefore effectively out of production. In several countries, African dung beetles have been deliberately introduced to boost beef production by accelerating dung recycling, thus increasing carrying capacity. Native dung beetles are not numerous in New Zealand — until the last few centuries there were no land mammals to produce dung.

ORDER • Coleoptera	**SPECIES** • *Pericoptus truncatus*
STATUS • endemic; common; resident	**MAORI NAME** • mumutawa pango

Grass-grub Beetle

10 mm

Recognition   A member of the worldwide scarab family, some 27,000 species strong, the grass-grub beetle is nothing much to look at — a plump, brown beetle lacking especially obvious or striking markings, a little over 10 mm in total length. However, it has achieved considerable notoriety in New Zealand through the enormous damage it often causes to pastures and grazing land.

Distribution   Throughout New Zealand, including several outlying groups such as the Chatham Islands.

Habits   The grass-grub beetle was originally widespread in lowland and montane native tussock grassland but closely related species largely replaced it in alpine grasslands. Since European settlement it has also spread to improved pastures and introduced grasses of several kinds. Damage is caused by the larvae, which live underground and eat the grass roots. Clover, for example, is extremely vulnerable but lucerne relatively immune.

Breeding   Several days after mating, females lay their spherical white eggs in batches of 20–25 within about the top 15 cm of soil. These hatch after 15 days or so, and feed until early spring when they burrow deeper to form chambers in which to pupate, emerging as adults around October. Synchronisation is vital for mating, the peak period being just after sunset, lasting about half an hour. Just how the grub knows, several centimetres underground, exactly when sunset is remains a mystery, although it is known that some scarabs make advance preparations: the adult emerges but remains quiescent underground for up to nine days, waiting for the mystery signal – then burrows rapidly upwards to the surface and joins the familiar mating flight that often sees hundreds of beetles buzzing blunderingly about the lights on the back porch on a sultry summer evening.

Food   The grass-grub beetle and its close relations are entirely vegetarian, the adults eating mainly leaves of various trees and shrubs, while the larvae eat grass roots.

Order • Coleoptera	**Species** • *Costelytra zealandica*
Status • endemic; common; resident	**Maori name** • tutaeruru

Cromwell Chafer

18 mm

Habits The Cromwell chafer is a small brown flightless beetle with little to distinguish it in appearance from many other small beetles. Little is known of its life cycle, except that in summer adults live in soft sand from which they emerge at night to feed on scabweed, and larvae feed on grass roots. Threatened by habitat destruction and predation (owls and rats), the population is now reduced to only a few hundred individuals.

ORDER • Coleoptera
SPECIES • *Prodontria lewisi*
STATUS • endemic; rare; resident
MAORI NAME • mumu

Distribution Its only known home is a small area of inland sand dunes in the south-central South Island where the town of Cromwell now stands. When its acutely threatened status was realised, only 100 ha of suitable habitat could be found, but now a reserve of about 95 ha, established and managed by the Cromwell Borough Council as the first insect reserve in New Zealand, protects the only known population of the Cromwell chafer.

Manuka Beetle

10 mm

Recognition Common throughout New Zealand and strongly associated with manuka trees (*Leptospermum*) manuka beetles are gleaming, brilliant green beetles a little under 10 mm in length. They belong to the family Scarabaeidae, and their nearest relatives include chafers, dung-beetles and grass-grub beetles.

ORDER • Coleoptera
SPECIES • *Pyronota festiva*
STATUS • endemic; common; resident
MAORI NAME • kerewai, reporepowai

Habits The major features of the manuka beetle's life cycle differ little from those of its relatives. Eggs are laid in the soil, and larvae have a lengthy development underground, feeding on plant roots, especially manuka. The most conspicuous behavioural difference is that adults are diurnal rather than crepuscular or nocturnal and often swarm in great numbers around flowering manuka in early summer. Adults die shortly after mating. Their bodies often pile up in mud or shallow water below trees — an early Maori traditional delicacy.

Click Beetles

25 mm

Acutewinged click beetle

Recognition   Click beetles are immediately identifiable by simply picking one up by its abdomen and listening closely — if it's really a click beetle you will hear a quiet but distinct, sharp snapping sound. A worldwide group of about 7500 species, click beetles get their name from a unique mechanism by which the head and thorax are linked: if the beetle arches its neck backwards far enough, small prongs engage like cogs in special grooves on its back; when this mechanism is released, the head snaps instantly back into its normal position with a clicking sound. The beetle puts it to good use if you place one carefully on the ground on its back — the 'click' as the mechanism is released flips it bodily into the air, and it is quite likely to land right-way up. If not, it simply keeps clicking until it does, although many species also 'play dead' for some time before making any attempt at righting themselves. Click beetles vary widely in size, but most are dull brown or dark grey in colour, intricately marked and streaked and marbled.

Distribution   New Zealand has several species of click beetles, found throughout the country, although some have very restricted ranges; several others have also been introduced.

Habits   Click beetles occupy most terrestrial habitats. Generally common but often not easy to find, they are active mainly at night and adept at hiding by day in nooks and crannies of all kinds. However, they can sometimes be found on flowers, and are often drawn to outdoor lighting at night. Larvae are generally known as wireworms, several of which are among the most damaging of all agricultural pests. But the situation is complicated because some are also rapacious predators of other plant pests: *Agrypnus variabilis*, for example, introduced from Australia and common in New Zealand pastures, may cause severe damage to crops of maize, but it is also an important predator of two other common pests, the introduced Australian soldierfly, *Inopus rubriceps*, and the grass-grub beetle (see page 215).

ORDER • Coleoptera
STATUS • introduced, native and endemic; common; resident

FAMILY   • Elateridae
MAORI NAME • tupanapana

Rove Beetles

19 mm

Devil's coach horse

Recognition   The rove beetles, like ground beetles and click beetles, are a worldwide group of several thousand species, of which New Zealand has over two hundred. The largest is about 19 mm long, but many are much smaller. Their appearance is distinctive but difficult to describe: their bodies are generally long, slender and flat compared to most beetles, the wing covers are unusually small, revealing much more of the abdomen than is usual among beetles, the wings are packed and folded in an unusually compact fashion, and many species have a characteristic habit of holding the abdomen curled upwards. They tend to look a little like earwigs. A typical rove beetle is plain black in colour, often with a metallic green or blue sheen. Some have colourful markings: the common devil's coachhorse, *Creophilus oculatus* (introduced from Australia) is easily identified by its mostly orange head. Rove beetles typically give off an offensive odour when handled.

Distribution   Occurs throughout New Zealand.

Habits   Rove beetles occupy most habitats in forest and grassland alike, and are sometimes present in very large numbers: peak densities of 20 per sq m have been recorded in the widespread metallic-green rove beetles *Thyreocephalus chloropterus* and *Thyreocephalus orthodoxus* in pastures in Northland. Most live on or just beneath the ground. Some species are permanent inhabitants of ant and termite nests, where they live unmolested as scavengers. One especially interesting New Zealand species is *Staphylinus huttoni*, which can easily be found hiding under cast-up mounds of kelp on ocean beaches.

Food   Some rove beetles are predators: the metallic-green rove beetle, for example, is capable of reducing Australian soldierfly (a serious agricultural pest) populations by up to 60 per cent under favourable conditions. Most rove beetles, however, are scavengers — both as larvae and adults — feeding on a very wide range of dead and decaying organic material.

ORDER • Coleoptera	**FAMILY** • Staphylinidae
STATUS • introduced, native and endemic; common; resident	**MAORI NAME** • none

Ladybirds

10 mm

Recognition   Ladybirds are recognisable by their glossy, almost hemispherical body shape alone, with extremely short legs and antennae. The most familiar species are about 5–10 mm long, and boldly marked with black, red, or yellow. Although there are nearly 30 native species, the kinds most often seen are introduced. For example, the two most abundant species, the two-spotted ladybird, *Adalia bipunctata*, and the eleven-spotted ladybird, *Coccinella undecimpunctata*, are both introductions from Europe; the first is bright red, with a single large, round, black spot in the middle of each wing cover, while the second is similar but has eleven spots. One especially common native species, the yellow-spotted ladybird, *Coccinella leonina*, is black with seven yellow spots.

Distribution   Occurs throughout New Zealand.

Habits   Of more than 5000 species of ladybirds in the world, a significant number are important in controlling the populations of aphids and scale insects. Ladybirds eat astonishing numbers of aphids, but the situation is often not as clearcut as might seem at first sight. Aphids are relatively helpless against predation, and ladybirds don't so much hunt their prey as browse on it. Aphids 'win' against this particular threat by simply breeding faster than predators can reduce their numbers. And ladybirds are so cumbersome and slow-moving that an aphid outbreak has often done its damage long before ladybirds can get to the spot to clean it up. Even so, there are many exceptions to this generalised 'too-little-too-late' scenario, and ladybirds remain a vital biocontrol agent against many

Eleven-spotted ladybird

agricultural pests. Perhaps the most spectacular success story involved an outbreak of cottony cushion scale, *Icerya purchasi*, that very nearly wiped out the citrus fruit industry in California in the 1880s, but which was brought under control almost within weeks after release of the Australian ladybird, *Rodalia cardinalis*. New Zealand examples of exotic ladybirds used as control agents in this way include the steel-blue ladybird, *Orcus chalybeus*, the apple spider-mite ladybird, *Stethorus bifidus*, and the bluegum scale ladybird, *Rhyzobius ventralis*. Ladybirds often form flocks in sheltered places such as under loose bark to hibernate through winter.

ORDER • Coleoptera	**FAMILY** • Coccinellidae
STATUS • introduced, native and endemic; common; resident	**MAORI NAME** • mumutawa

Huhu Beetle

50 mm

Recognition   The huhu beetle is New Zealand's largest beetle, a member of the longicorn beetle family (Cerambycidae), which get their name from their enormously long, multi-segmented antennae – often considerably longer than the body. Huhu beetles are mainly dark brown in colour, intricately marked with straw-yellow; males are about 35 mm in total length, but females reach 50 mm.

Distribution   The species occurs throughout New Zealand.

Habits   The huhu beetle is most common in native forests of various kinds, but has also adapted to plantations of exotic pine trees with some success. The larvae represent a traditional Maori delicacy, served lightly fried in hot oil with a sprinkling of salt.

Food   Like stag beetles, the longicorn beetles are strongly associated with timber; the larvae eat mainly wood, relying on bacteria in their gut

to help them digest the cellulose. The many species are adapted variously to a diet of living, dead or rotten wood, in the roots, trunks or branches, either within the standing tree or once it has fallen to the ground. A dead tree often supports an entire community of longicorn beetle species, each occupying its own particular 'microhabitat'. How do the larvae obtain their symbiotic bacteria? The female beetle deposits a thin film of culture medium for the bacteria as a coating on each egg as she lays it, and the larva's first act on hatching is to eat its own eggshell, thereby transferring the necessary bacteria to its own gut. Adults eat nectar and sap.

Breeding   Huhu beetles lay their eggs on the bark of trees and the larvae burrow into the wood on hatching. They take several years to mature, ultimately reaching a total length of about 75 mm. When ready to pupate, they first bore an exit hole to the outside world, then retire a few millimetres back into the wood to form a pupation chamber.

Order • Coleoptera		**Species** • *Prionoplus reticularis*	
Status • endemic; common; resident		**Maori name** • tungarere, pepe tunga, pepe te muimui (adult), huhu (larva)	

Weevils

28 mm

*Lyperobius
spedeni*

Recognition   Weevils might be concisely defined as beetles with snouts. A typical weevil has its mouthparts at the tip of an extension, called the rostrum, emerging rather like a stiffened elephant's trunk from the front of its head, although it comes in a bewildering variety of sizes and shapes. The mouthparts are strongly adapted for boring rather than chewing.

Weevils constitute the family Curculionidae (and a few others of mostly technical interest) and together make up a worldwide group of about 60,000 species — by far the largest cluster of closely related living things on earth. New Zealand alone has about 1500 species and there are probably many more yet to be described and named. Some of the largest weevils are more than 60 mm long, but there is also a vast number of species barely 1 mm in length. Some are brightly coloured, but 'Persian carpet' patterns and sober hues tend to be more typical.

Habits   Few terrestrial habitats lack weevils of one species or another. They are mostly nocturnal and most species seldom fly. Many species play a vital role in recycling dead and decaying plant material, some pollinate flowers, and many others cause enormous damage to agricultural products of all kinds — before, during, and even after harvesting. One especially well-known species is the gorse-seed weevil, *Apion ulicis*. Barely 2 mm long, and living most of its life locked within the seedpods of gorse, the weevil was introduced to New Zealand in 1931 in an attempt to control this lovely but rampant weed, which at the time threatened to take over New Zealand entirely. Success has so far been limited, partly because — even though infestation can reach nearly 100 per cent in some cases — gorse has two generations per year but the weevil only one.

Breeding   Many weevils lay their eggs in chambers cut into living tissue; the larvae secrete irritants that provoke the plant into forming tumours or 'galls' within which the young weevils develop.

Order • Coleoptera		**Family**	• Curculionidae
Status • introduced, native and endemic; common; resident		**Maori name**	• ngututuroa

Giraffe Weevil

80 mm

Recognition   Identifying a giraffe weevil is no problem: it would be hard to find a more bizarre looking creature in New Zealand. The rostrum is extraordinarily long — nearly as long as the body. Size is variable but, sometimes reaching nearly 80 mm in total length, the male is New Zealand's longest beetle; the female is somewhat stouter and seldom exceeds 45 mm in length. In the male the long antennae arise near the tip of the rostrum, but in the female they emerge about halfway along it.

Distribution   The North and South Islands of New Zealand. Closely related species occur in eastern Australia, Madagascar, and southern South America.

Habits   The giraffe weevil is widespread in native forests and in spring can sometimes be found in swarms on the lower trunks of trees, especially pigeonwood and lacebark. The suggestion has been made that the adults sense in some way when a tree is about to die, and congregate to lay their eggs so that their larvae

can feed on the solid wood before it starts to decay.

Food   Larvae feed on dead wood, presumably — as in several other wood-boring beetles — with the aid of cellulose-digesting bacteria in the gut.

Breeding   Reproductive details are scanty but egg-laying has been described in detail. In a process lasting about 30 minutes from start to finish, the female bores a hole about 0.5 mm wide and 4.0 mm deep into the trunk of a tree, backing off every half-millimetre or so to clear the sawdust from the hole and from her jaws. While so occupied, the male mates with her, guards her, and occasionally helps to lever her rostrum from the hole if she gets stuck. When the egg-burrow is finally complete, the female inserts her abdomen, lays a single egg, then refills the hole and conceals the entrance with sawdust and bark fragments. The larvae probably spend a year or more tunnelling in the wood before finally emerging as adults.

ORDER • Coleoptera
STATUS • endemic; common; resident

SPECIES • *Lasiorrhynchus barbicornis*
MAORI NAME • tuwhaipapa

Craneflies

Recognition   Flies are unique in that only the forward pair of wings sustain flight; the rear pair are reduced to two small knobs on stalks, called 'halteres', which function as gyroscopes – a sophisticated flight control system that enables houseflies, for example, to casually perform such 'impossible' tricks as somersaulting in midair and landing upside down on a ceiling. By far the largest family is the craneflies or daddy-longlegs, with about 11,000 members worldwide. New Zealand has perhaps the richest cranefly fauna in the world, with at least 500 species. Apart from their enormous diversity, craneflies are also notable for their great range in size: many of the smallest species are nearly as minute as gnats, but at the other extreme *Austrotipula hudsoni*, the largest species in New Zealand, has a wingspan of nearly 76 mm. Whatever the size, craneflies are usually recognisable by their slim bodies and extraordinarily long slender legs.

Macromastix ferruginea

Distribution   Craneflies occur throughout New Zealand, including all of the outlying groups, most of which have endemic, flightless species, such as *Zaluscodes aucklandicus* on the Auckland Islands. Most species are endemic, but at least one (*Trichocera annulata*) is introduced, and many have close relatives in south-eastern Australia.

Habits   Craneflies generally prefer damp, shady places and are usually most numerous in forests, especially near rivers and streams, and are often most active in the early morning and evening; some are attracted to lights at night. Many larvae are aquatic or nearly so (though some

develop in decaying vegetation) and some are specialised to an alpine or montane existence in cold, rushing streams and torrents which are normally rich in dissolved oxygen but low in nutrients: the many small species of the genus *Aphrophila*, for example, live only in the spray of waterfalls. In many groups, including at least two New Zealand species (*Macromastix zeylandiae* and *Hudsonia heterogama*), the female has only vestigial wings.

Food   Larvae eat mainly roots or plant debris; adults feed on nectar or sap from bark-wounds.

ORDER • Diptera		**FAMILY** • Tipulidae	
STATUS • introduced, native and endemic; common; resident		**MAORI NAME** • matua waeroa	

New Zealand Glow-worm

15 mm

Recognition   The Waitomo Caves in the North Island have long been a world-famous tourist attraction for their glow-worm grottoes, where vast numbers light up the darkness with an ethereal sheen, each tiny creature emitting a bluish-green light from the tip of its abdomen. These caverns may well be the most impressive display of the phenomenon in New Zealand, but the animal responsible can be found in lesser numbers in almost any cave or sheltered cavity in the forested parts of both main islands. Places worth searching include undercut stream banks and even drainage culverts beneath forestry tracks.

Distribution   The New Zealand glow-worm (in fact a species of gnat) is endemic to New Zealand, but very similar and closely related species occur also in eastern Australia.

Habits   Glow-worm larvae are predators and the light they emit is part of a trap or snare. Adults mate and lay their eggs on the ceiling of caves and similar cavities, almost immediately on emerging from their pupae (neither sex lives more than three or four days). When the tiny larva hatches, its first act is to construct for itself a sort of nest or hammock, made of silk and mucus and suspended from the roof by several threads of silk. It then pays out a series of fine, dangling threads of more silk, each bearing at regular intervals a small droplet of mucous. The whole arrangement rather resembles jumbled rows of tiny pearl necklaces dangling for sale in some exotic eastern bazaar. These constitute its snare, and they may be of almost any length up to 50 cm or so, depending on the situation. As midges and other minute insects breeding in the mud or water below emerge as adults, they are attracted upwards in their first flight by the glow-worm's luminescence, and become ensnared amid the sticky mucous of its 'fishing lines', whereupon the glow-worm promptly hauls up its catch and eats it. Cannabalism is not unknown. The light-emitting organ is associated with the gut in such a way that the hungrier the glow-worm, the brighter its light, so the more likely it is to attract a victim.

ORDER • Diptera	**SPECIES** • *Arachnocampa luminosa*
STATUS • endemic; common; resident	**MAORI NAME** • puratoke

Sandflies

5 mm

Austrosimulium australense

Recognition   Allied to midges, gnats and mosquitoes, sandflies are small, plain black flies whose most obvious characteristic is to descend in barely visible hordes on innocent campers, trampers and picnickers, making life a misery with the ferocity of their bites, out of all proportion to their insignificant size. The largest New Zealand species has a body length of about 5 mm and a wing length of 4 mm. Other species are smaller, but otherwise virtually impossible to tell apart on appearance alone.

Distribution   Almost throughout New Zealand. There is a total of about 13 species, several of which are widespread in both the North and South Islands. Stewart Island, Campbell Island and the Auckland Islands each have one endemic species (the Kermadecs and Chatham Islands have none). All belong to the genus *Austrosimulium*.

Habits   Only two of the 13 New Zealand species attack humans readily, and one of these reaches its greatest abundance in beech forests

of Westland and Fiordland in the South Island. Only the female bites, requiring a meal of blood for the proper formation of her eggs. Active mostly by day, sandflies seem to attack most savagely on warm, sunny days, especially if the humidity is moderately high. Many groups of flies — notably mosquitoes — carry disease but sandflies, though a considerable nuisance, appear to present no serious threat in that no link has yet been established between their bites and any human disease.

Breeding   Eggs are laid in or near water and the larvae are aquatic. Insects have several distinct stages in their life histories, most simply summarised as egg, grub, pupa and adult, but in many insects the grub stages are themselves multiple, so that very intricate life histories are common. Most of the several thousand sandfly species around the world have six such stages (called instars), but one New Zealand species, *Austrosimulium tillyardianum*, is notable for having nine — the most extended life-history known in this group of insects.

Order • Diptera	**Species** • *Austrosimulium* spp.
Status • native and endemic; common; resident	**Maori name** • namu

Blowflies

10 mm

New Zealand
blue blowfly

Recognition   Blowflies look much like rather large (about 6–10 mm long), stocky houseflies except in being unusually hairy and often brightly coloured: the ubiquitous greenbottle or green blowfly, for example, has a glittering metallic-green abdomen, while the golden blowfly is yellowish.

Distribution   New Zealand has nearly 50 native blowfly species, many of which are endemic and several confined to outlying island groups such as Campbell Island and the Antipodes. Several others are restricted to particular habitats — *Ptilonesia auronotata*, for example, occurs only along ocean beaches. A number of species have been accidentally introduced, including ubiquitous pests such as the brown blowfly, green blowfly and hairy-maggot blowfly.

Breeding   Some blowflies lay eggs (oviparous) while other species give birth to larvae (viviparous). Otherwise their life histories are similar: the female deposits her offspring on

animal flesh (living or dead, depending on the species), the eggs hatch, the maggots burrow beneath the skin to feed on the flesh, then after several days emerge, drop to the ground, pupate, and about a week later emerge as adult flies.

Habits   In the case of the introduced blowflies, the target is usually a sheep, with serious consequences for graziers. Fly-strike results in a skin condition known as myiasis, a wound that is prone to infection, slow to heal and once healed leaves flaws that reduce the commercial value of fleece or hides. As well, sheep stop feeding when struck, rapidly lose condition, and only slowly regain it later. In the case of multiple strike, or in young lambs, such an attack often kills the animal. The green blowfly and the brown blowfly inflict the most severe damage; the hairy-maggot blowfly usually needs to find a pre-existing open wound before initiating a strike (the other two do not). It is estimated that 1–2 per cent of the national flock is affected by fly-strike at any one time.

ORDER • Diptera		**STATUS**	• native and introduced; common;
SPECIES • *Calliphora stygia* (brown blowfly)			resident
Lucilia sericata (green blowfly)		**MAORI NAME**	• rango pango, rango tuamaro

Hoverflies

10 mm

Melangyna
novaezelandiae

Recognition   Hoverflies superficially resemble bees but they are well named and are immediately recognisable by their distinctive habit of buzzing bee-like around flowers, frequently pausing to hover motionless in midair, like tiny helicopters. Moreover, the two New Zealand species — the large hoverfly and the small hoverfly — are easy to tell apart: the large hoverfly is about 10 mm long and shiny black with creamy white markings on its abdomen; the small hoverfly is similar but about half this size and its markings are much bolder and brighter — rich yellow or orange instead of creamy white. The dull brown or greenish larvae are slug-like but very active.

Distribution   The hoverflies are a worldwide group with hundreds of members. The two New Zealand species are endemic and abundant throughout all three main islands as well as many of the largest and closest offshore groups — although the smaller species is often noticeably the commoner of the two.

Habits   Hoverflies are 'advanced' insects in several respects: many species defend territories and are able to accurately assess course and speed of a trespasser in order to plot an efficient interception course some distance away — a sophisticated trick that few other insects have mastered. Some species of hoverfly even have lek mating systems (see page 80). Hoverflies are second only to bees as efficient pollinators of native flowering plants. They are most often seen during the middle of the day in hot, calm, sunny weather.

Food   Adults eat mainly nectar. The carnivorous larvae prey on aphids, gobbling them up at the rate of about 80 per hour, and small butterfly caterpillars, especially those of the introduced cabbage white (page 241). Up to 58 per cent of the total predation suffered by these caterpillars is by hoverfly larvae. However, the larvae are themselves the favourite target of a common New Zealand ichneumon wasp, *Diplazon laetatorius*.

Order • Diptera	**Status** • endemic; common; resident
Species • *Melangyna novaezelandiae* (large)	**Maori name** • ngaro paira
Melanostoma fasciatum (small)	

Native Bees

Leioproctus
fulvescens

Recognition   Native bees are much smaller than honeybees with few species exceeding 10 mm in length, many far smaller. They are seldom furry, usually black and easily overlooked because of their superficial resemblance to ordinary houseflies.

Distribution   New Zealand has no native bumblebees or honeybees (all are introduced) but has about 40 species of native bees mostly found nowhere else — although one Australian species, *Euryglossina proctotrypoides*, has been accidentally introduced. Common almost everywhere in New Zealand, they are most often encountered swarming in large numbers around pohutukawa, rata and other native trees.

Habits   Most native bees belong to the family Colletidae, a worldwide group not easily distinguished by appearance from other bee families, but clearly distinguished by the way they build their nests — each cell is lined with a transparent substance that resembles cellophane, a behaviour unique among bees.

Native bees are not as highly evolved in their social, nectar-harvesting lifestyles as honeybees and bumblebees. They have short tongues and are therefore unable to forage at flowers with deep corollas. They have neither queens nor workers, only males and females. Honeybees have small baskets, called corbiculae, on their hind legs in which they transport pollen back to the hive; many native bees lack corbiculae, and carry their loads of pollen internally. Female native bees have stings but seldom use them.

Food   Mostly nectar and pollen from flowers.

Breeding   Most species construct their nests in the ground or in hollow trees. The female lays a single egg on a small lump of pollen and nectar in a chamber at the end of a tunnel, then seals the chamber and departs. Details vary from species to species but, typically, females build twenty or thirty such nests in about six weeks, then die. The egg hatches in about three days, the grub feeds for ten days or so, then pupates until the following spring.

ORDER • Hymenoptera		**FAMILY** • Colletidae	
STATUS • native; common; resident		**MAORI NAME** • ngaro huruhuru	

Honeybee

28 mm

Recognition Honeybees are familiar to almost everyone — stout, furry insects about three times the size of a housefly, with a golden-brown, black-banded abdomen.

Distribution The honeybee is native to Africa, Europe and western Asia. The first documented occurrence in New Zealand was in 1839 when hives from England were landed at Hokianga. It is now one of the most abundant and familiar insects almost everywhere in New Zealand.

Food Mainly nectar and pollen from flowers.

Habits Honeybees have a very advanced social system and live permanently in colonies called hives. There are three casts: queens, workers and drones (males). As in other social insects, workers are genetically female but lack functioning reproductive organs. Although they vary seasonally in size, a typical colony in midsummer has one queen, several hundred drones, and perhaps 60,000 workers. The basic 'strategy' of the colony is storage — the accumulation of sufficient food in summer to enable the colony to survive the following winter.

Two honeybee characteristics are especially distinctive. One is the 'swarming' behaviour by which new colonies are founded: the queen abandons her old colony with a retinue of 'faithful' workers swarming protectively about her while scouts go in search of a suitable site for a new colony. Meanwhile the old colony carries on under the leadership of a new queen. The other characteristic is the unique 'dance' code by which one worker communicates to her fellows the range and bearing of a new source of nectar. On returning from her find, the worker performs a 'waggle' dance on a vertical surface at the hive, one component of which consists of running in a straight line while excitedly wriggling her abdomen: the length of the straight line conveys distance, its direction with respect to the vertical is the same as the angle between the source and the sun, thereby communicating the bearing, and the vigour of the 'waggle' expresses quantity and quality.

Order • Hymenoptera	**Species** • *Apis mellifera*
Status • introduced; common; resident	**Maori name** • pi honi

Bumblebees

Large earth bumblebee

Recognition Bumblebees look like big, fat, furry honeybees — up to 25 mm long. Four very similar species have been introduced into New Zealand, which differ mainly in the length of the tongue and the arrangement of the black bands on their golden-brown abdomens.

Distribution Bumblebees are native to Eurasia and North America where various species range from the tropics to the Arctic tundra — in Greenland bumblebees forage at wildflowers within 900 km of the North Pole. Several species were liberated near Christchurch in 1885 to improve the pollination of clover; they are now abundant throughout New Zealand.

Habits Bumblebees inhabit open country of all kinds, being especially well adapted to feeding at the small, low, scattered flowering plants characteristic of moors, bogs and tundra. They are closely related to honeybees and, like them, live in colonies, feed on nectar and pollen, and build their nests of wax produced by special glands on the abdomen. They differ most

significantly in making no attempt to store food for the winter. This sets limits to the life of the colony, but it also means that bumblebees can exploit a wider range of very small flowers and can also continue foraging under adverse weather conditions that confine honeybees to their hives (honeybees need enough surplus energy to carry a load back, while bumblebees need only enough fuel to make it to the next flower). For some flowers, such as clover, this characteristic also makes them more effective pollinators than honeybees — they visit more flowers for smaller reward.

Food Bees are essentially vegetarian wasps, feeding entirely on nectar and pollen.

Breeding Colonies are usually in the ground or close to it. Queens hibernate underground during winter and emerge in spring to seek a suitable site for a new colony. Each queen uses wax to fashion a pot into which she lays about 10 eggs which she incubates. The larvae emerge as workers about three weeks later.

ORDER • Hymenoptera	**SPECIES** • *Bombus* spp.
STATUS • introduced; common; resident	**MAORI NAME** • pi rorohu

Ichneumon Wasps

*Certonotus
fractiventris*

Recognition   In New Zealand any unusually slender wasp-like insect with a very long ovipositor is quite likely to be an ichneumon wasp of some kind (the ovipositor is a long, very slender egg-laying tube projecting from the rear of the abdomen). Like wasps, many species are black, boldly marked with yellow, white, or sometimes red, especially on the abdomen — although some also have brightly coloured antennae, or legs, or both.

Distribution   New Zealand has a number of native ichneumon wasps, but others have been introduced to combat various agricultural pests. Examples include *Apanteles glomeratus* and *Pteromalus puparum* against the cabbage white butterfly, and *Pterocormus promissorius* against the cosmopolitan armyworm.

Breeding   Details vary widely but several features are almost invariant: the female seeks a victim (commonly the larva of a beetle, fly or moth), injects it with a toxin that paralyses but does not kill it, lays her egg on its body and then leaves. There is no subsequent parental care of any kind.

Habits   Ichneumons belong to a very large, cosmopolitan and highly specialised group of insects often known as parasitic wasps — an unhappy choice because, unlike 'true' parasites, they invariably kill their hosts; parasitoid is the preferred technical term. The point is significant because the great 'web of life' becomes especially intricate and close-woven in the parasitoid arena. Many parasitoids are host-specific — that is, any particular species seeks its victims only within the population of a particular target species. Some parasitoids develop inside the victim, others outside; some develop alone, others in groups. There are even such creatures as parasitoids of parasitoids, called hyperparasitoids! Under favourable circumstances, ichneumons can devastate populations of their target species. Hence they attract considerable scientific interest in the quest for safe, effective biological control of agricultural pests.

Order • Hymenoptera		**Family** • Ichneumonidae	
Status • native and introduced; common; resident	**Maori name** • ngaro whiore		

Paper Wasps

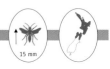

15 mm

Asian
paper wasp

Recognition   Paper wasps are about 15 mm long, mainly dark brown with pale yellow bands around the abdomen. The wings are faintly yellowish, with a bluish sheen.

Distribution   Two species have been accidentally introduced, the Australian paper wasp and the Asian paper wasp. Both are reasonably common but largely confined to the warmer parts of the North Island.

Habits   Paper wasps, together with the German and common wasps (opposite), are members of the worldwide wasp family, Vespidae, whose most distinctive characteristic is that their nests are made of paper. In a process that roughly parallels the manufacture of ordinary office paper, the wasp chews wood into a pulp by mixing it with saliva, using a resinous substance called propolis, obtained from plants, as a binding agent. When dry, the resulting material rather resembles thin, rough cardboard. Paper wasps are social but, despite their close

relationship, they differ from the common and German wasps in lacking castes — there are no queens or workers. After mating in autumn males die and females hibernate — sometimes merely clinging to the old nest — and build new nests in spring. Like common wasps, paper wasps will sting if provoked; the results are extremely painful and may have serious medical repercussions in sensitive people.

Food   Like other wasps, paper wasps live on a wide range of animal protein — especially caterpillars — as well as nectar from flowers. For the first few days the larvae are fed nectar, then weaned onto a diet of pulped insects.

Breeding   A typical nest is shaped rather like a toadstool dangling by its stem from some overhead support, often the eaves of a house or garage. A nest may contain just a few cells or as many as 400. A female lays a single egg in each cell. Hatching in a few days, the larva orients itself with its head at the cell entrance to be fed.

ORDER • Hymenoptera	**STATUS**	• introduced; common; resident
SPECIES • *Polistes humilis* (Australian)	**MAORI NAME**	• none
Polistes chinensis (Asian)		

European Wasps

20 mm

German wasp

Recognition   Two introduced wasps are common in New Zealand — the German wasp and the common wasp — but the differences between them in both appearance and biology are extremely subtle, and they are treated here together. Adults are about 20 mm long, and easily identified by the black and yellow abdomen — more black than yellow in the common wasp, *vice versa* in the German wasp.

Distribution   Accidentally introduced from Europe, the German wasp was first detected in New Zealand in 1922 and was common and widespread by 1944; the common wasp was first detected in Wellington in 1978. Both species now occur virtually throughout the country. (The common wasp swept through the beech forests of the South Island during the 1980s at about 35 km per year.) Originally widespread almost throughout western Eurasia, wasps have also established themselves in many other parts of the world, including Australia, South Africa and North America.

Habits   Wasps are now among the commonest and most familiar insects almost everywhere in New Zealand, but there is strong evidence that the common wasp is displacing the German wasp. Like bees, wasps have three distinct castes: queens, workers and drones. The wasp-paper nests are built in the ground, in trees, or in houses, and may reach several metres in length.

Food   Wasps owe much of their success to their omnivorous diet; they hunt insects and similar small animals at all levels from the ground to the canopy, they scavenge at carcasses and they exploit all possible sources of carbohydrates from honeydew and flower nectar to raiding bee-hives and stealing jam at picnics.

Breeding   Normally only the queen survives the winter, hibernating in any available sheltered crevice. In early spring she awakens, builds a nest of a few cells and lays an egg in each. These are all workers which, when grown, take over enlarging the nest and rearing young.

Order • Hymenoptera	**Status** • introduced; common; resident
Species • *Vespula vulgaris* (common)	**Maori name** • wapi, wapu, pi waikato
Vespula germanica (German)	

New Zealand Case Moth

10 cm

Recognition   The case moths are a worldwide family (Psychidae) of about 800 species, members of which are most easily recognised by their caterpillars. Case moth caterpillars live permanently in a sort of sleeve or case woven of silk and camouflaged with twigs, leaves, lichen or scraps of bark. A typical adult case moth is small, inconspicuous, does not feed, and lives only a few hours or days.

ORDER •	Lepidoptera
SPECIES •	*Liothula omnivoras*
STATUS •	endemic; common; resident
MAORI NAME •	kopa, kopi

Habits   In the common and familiar New Zealand case moth (as in many other case moth species), the adult female is degenerate — lacking limbs or wings — and continues to live in her case even after reaching maturity. The caterpillar extends its case as it grows, and it ultimately reaches about 10 cm in length. Cases can sometimes be found on fences and similar suburban and rural sites almost anywhere in New Zealand.

Looper Moths

35 mm

Recognition   Looper moths are members of the worldwide family Geometridae, with about 15,000 species. New Zealand alone has several hundred species, many of them diurnal and brightly coloured, especially among alpine species. The caterpillars, however, are obvious by their distinctive habit of 'looping' instead of crawling — they bring the tail end forward to meet the head, then anchor the tail to thrust the head forward.

ORDER •	Lepidoptera
SPECIES •	*Notoreas* spp.
STATUS •	endemic; common; resident
MAORI NAME •	none

Habits   One of the more distinctive New Zealand species is the yellow and brown looper moth. This attractive and widespread little moth is confined to the very highest shrubland on Mount Egmont in the North Island, is common anywhere above the beech forests in the Southern Alps, yet occurs as a lowland species around Invercargill, Dunedin and other scattered localities.

Declana egregia

Porina Moths

Wiseana
cervinata

Recognition Very closely related to the pururi moth (next page), porina moths are large, drab, stout-bodied and very difficult to tell apart. About 5 cm long, caterpillars are dingy grey-yellow with a brown head capsule; the pupae are dark red-brown.

Distribution Porina moths make up a uniquely New Zealand group with at least seven species. They are widespread in both the North and South Islands, though scarce and local north of Waikato, and are most common on the South Island. The most numerous and widespread species in low rainfall areas is *Wiseana cervinata* (individual species don't have English names), whereas the dominant high rainfall species are *Wiseana umbraculata* in Southland and *Wiseana signata* in the Wellington district.

Habits Porina moths are often seen fluttering against windows or milling around streetlights on summer evenings, particularly on warm, moist, cloudy nights, and in most kinds of open country. They are strongly associated with tussock grasslands, and several species may cause severe and sometimes permanent damage to rangelands and improved lowland pasture. Other species are confined to alpine meadows.

Food Caterpillars feed on the blades and stems of native grasses, but they also attack many of the introduced grasses of most interest to the farmer, including lucerne and cocksfoot. Adults lack mouthparts and do not feed.

Breeding Females live barely three or four days, only long enough to lay their eggs — about 500–1500 per female — which are scattered on the wing over grassland. Creamy white when laid but quickly turning black, the eggs hatch in about four weeks. The caterpillars spend a few days hidden in the grass, then construct vertical shafts some 20 cm deep, into the soil, from which they emerge at night to feed; the entrance is screened with a web of silk. Around August — after about 280 days of larval development — they pupate in their tunnels and emerge as adults about six weeks later.

Order • Lepidoptera		**Species** • *Wiseana* spp.
Status • endemic; rare; resident		**Maori name** • porina

Puriri Moth

15 cm

Recognition New Zealand's largest native moth, with a wingspan of about 10 cm (male) or nearly 15 cm (female). Variable in size, colour and pattern, it is mainly pale, vivid green; the forewings are freckled with dark brown in the female and white in the male, the hindwings variably washed with dull orange.

Distribution Often called the ghost moth, the puriri moth occurs in native forests of the North Island of New Zealand. It is a member of the worldwide family Hepialidae, elsewhere generally known as swift moths.

Habits Nocturnal, with a swift, vigorous but clumsy flight; easily attracted to lights. Emerging mainly from September to November, adults live only a few days, but caterpillars spend several years in tunnels bored into trees, grinding their food with the help of powerful mandibles. The tunnels are about 15 cm long and 1.5 cm in diameter, usually in the trunk of a tree but sometimes in the larger limbs. The entrance is usually shielded with a web of silk and concealed with scraps of bark. The tunnel has an abrupt elbow a few centimetres into the trunk, and continues vertically downwards; the elbow is sealed with a second web of silk.

Food The caterpillars feed on the wood of a number of native trees, especially puriri, titoki, and putaputaweta, but they also occasionally develop in exotic trees such as birch, oak, maple, willow and several orchard trees. Adults lack functional mouthparts and a digestive system, and do not feed.

Breeding Females lay a total of about 2000 eggs, widely scattered in flight by a vigorous twirling action of the abdomen. The eggs are glossy dark purple in colour and take about two weeks to hatch; the tiny caterpillars then feed on the ground before setting off in search of a suitable host tree. The caterpillar stages last about five years, followed by a pupation of about six months.

Order • Lepidoptera	**Status** • endemic; uncommon; resident
Species • *Aenetus virescens*	**Maori name** • pepetuna

Gum Emperor Moth

12 cm

Recognition Wingspan about 15 cm. Adults have bulky, hairy bodies and broad, velvet-brown wings, with pink spots on the forewings and one round, bright multi-coloured 'eye-spot' on each hindwing. Growing to about 12 cm in length, the larvae are plump, striking creatures, mainly bluish green but with a pale yellow line along each side, and bristly, blue-tipped orange and red tubercles scattered over the body.

Distribution The gum emperor moth inhabits northern and eastern Australia (roughly from Darwin to Melbourne), but was accidentally introduced — apparently as eggs — to New Zealand where it was first recorded in Taranaki in 1939. Now it is widespread in the eastern parts of the North Island and has been recorded in Nelson and a few other scattered localities in the South Island.

Habits Common in the vicinity of gum-trees in urban, suburban and rural habitats. Adults fly at night and are easily attracted to lights. Males are slightly smaller than females and have large feathery antennae with which they detect the fragrance of females from several kilometres away. Caterpillars feed during the day, but despite their arresting appearance they are well camouflaged in young, green foliage, and very difficult to find.

Food Larvae feed mostly on the foliage of gum trees (*Eucalyptus* spp.) but they will also feed on various exotic trees such as pepper tree (*Schinus molle*). Adults have incomplete mouthparts and do not feed.

Breeding Gum emperor moths overwinter as pupae inside brown, oval cocoons of hardened silk — which take about 10 hours to weave — suspended from twigs. Come spring, the emerging adult first secretes a fluid to soften the cocoon, then tears its way out using a hooked spine on the forewing. After mating, females lay their pale yellow eggs in neat rows on eucalypt leaves. When very young the caterpillar is black with orange tufts, but turns green after its second moult.

Order • Lepidoptera	**Species** • *Opodiphthera eucalypti*
Status • introduced; common; resident	**Maori name** • none

Cabbage Tree Moth

Recognition The cabbage tree moth is one of New Zealand's marvels of protective coloration, which is technically known as crypsis. The upper wings are a shade of pale yellowish brown that precisely matches the colour of dead cabbage tree leaves, among which the moths hide during the day. The wings are narrowly banded with drab brown to mimic the veins of the leaves as the moth rests with wings outspread, flattened against the leaf (so that it cannot be betrayed by its own shadow) and oriented so that the 'fake' veins on its wings line up with the real veins on the leaf. It is also careful to perch on dead leaves, never live green ones.

ORDER • Lepidoptera
SPECIES • *Epiphryne verriculata*
STATUS • endemic; common; resident
MAORI NAME • purere ti

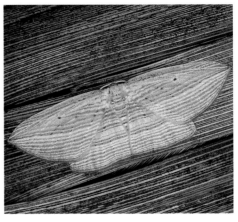

Distribution The cabbage tree moth is distributed widely throughout lowland New Zealand, and can be found wherever cabbage trees (*Cordyline australis*) grow.

Lichen Moths

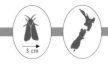

Recognition Often called zebra moths, these two species (one in the North Island, the other in the South Island) are striking moths about 3–4 cm in wingspan, with silvery white wings intricately marked with deep black.

ORDER • Lepidoptera
SPECIES • *Declana atronivea* (North Island)
Declana egregia (South Island)
STATUS • endemic; common; resident
MAORI NAME • purerehua

Habits They present a classic example of disruptive crypsis — a particular kind of camouflage that works by confusing the eye and destroying all impression of shape, rather than by matching background colours — you see the bits, but you can't easily put them together to form the familiar moth shape. Even the caterpillars are shaped and coloured to fool the eye: with yellowish bulges and grotesquely swollen head, they lie curled up when resting, to closely resemble bird droppings. Hatching in about eight days, the eggs are laid and the caterpillars reared on the host plant, the five-finger tree *Nothopanax arboreum*.

Declana egregia

Magpie Moth

4 cm

Recognition Adult magpie moths have a wingspan of about 4 cm; they have black bodies with yellow bands around the abdomen, and deep black wings with white spots. Males are slightly larger than females. The caterpillars grow to about 3 cm in length and are easy to find as they feed openly during the day. They are mainly black with white and orange markings along the sides, densely tufted with long black bristles (prompting the universal childhood name of 'woolly bears'). Pupae are black with dull orange spots.

Distribution Common on all three main islands of New Zealand, many of the larger and closer offshore groups and the Antipodes Islands; a very close relative is widespread in Australia and locally established in New Zealand. Sightings of hybrids between the two have been reported in Auckland.

Habits The magpie moth occurs in most urban and rural habitats. Its flight is feeble, fluttering, and seldom sustained. Like the monarch

butterfly (page 245), this moth takes up and stores in its tissues poisonous substances from the plants it eats and relies on its conspicuous coloration to advertise the fact to unwary or inexperienced predators. As a result of this, both moth and caterpillar are seldom attacked by birds — one observer noted a magpie moth snapped up but instantly spat out again by a gecko.

Food Magpie moths utilise a wide range of native and introduced host plants, including such weeds as groundsel, ragwort and especially cinerarias, which rarely escape attack.

Breeding About the size of a pinhead, the shiny, pale yellow eggs are laid in groups on the surface of leaves, and hatch in about a week. The larval stages last several weeks, then the caterpillar seeks out a sheltered spot such as behind a flake of bark, under a stone, even behind loose weatherboarding or tucked in a fence corner, and weaves a loose cocoon in which to pupate.

ORDER • Lepidoptera		**STATUS** • endemic; common; resident	
SPECIES • *Nyctemera annulata*		**MAORI NAME** • purere uri	

Cinnabar Moth

Recognition   The adult cinnabar moth is a striking insect with a black body about 12 mm long; its forewings are also black with a deep crimson stripe extending almost from base to tip and two crimson spots on the outer margins. Like many New Zealand moths it is active by day. Both adult and caterpillar can be identified by their close attachment to their host plant, ragwort.

Distribution   A native of Europe, the cinnabar moth was widely released in New Zealand throughout the 1930s. At first it became common and very widespread, but in many areas it ultimately failed to establish and seems to have died out. It is now common only in the vicinity of Wellington and Wairarapa in the North Island and in a few scattered localities in the north of the South Island.

Habits   The cinnabar moth is a member of the tiger moth family (Arctiidae), of which there are about 10,000 member species around the world. Tiger moths are conspicuous and boldly coloured, and absorb toxins from their food to deter predators. Some species are of interest because they emit loud high-frequency sounds when threatened by bats in flight as a sort of 'radar-jamming' tactic. Many tiger moths — including several native species — are also notable in that only the males fly; the females have only small flaps on the body in place of wings, and cannot fly.

Food   This moth was introduced from England in an attempt to combat infestations of its chief host plant, ragwort (*Senecio jacobaea*), a rampant introduced weed toxic to stock, especially cattle, and can be difficult to eradicate (its nectar also taints honey).

Breeding   The basic life history details are very similar to those of the magpie moth: the tiny yellowish eggs are laid singly on the surface of leaves, hatching takes about eight days, larval stages last about six weeks, and the caterpillar finds a sheltered nook or crevice in which to pupate. There are several generations per year.

ORDER • Lepidoptera		**SPECIES** • *Tyria jacobaeae*	
STATUS • introduced; common; resident		**MAORI NAME** • none	

Cabbage White Butterfly

5 cm

Recognition   Wingspan about 5 cm. Easily recognised by its pure white or creamy white wings; the sexes are similar but easily told apart if you examine them closely — males have one black spot near the middle of each forewing, females have two (the forewing also has a small black tip in both sexes).

Distribution   The white butterfly has an enormous range across the temperate parts of the northern hemisphere, and it may have made its way to New Zealand as a stowaway aboard refrigerated container ships from Europe (or possibly Hawaii), surviving the long sea voyage as pupae. First noted at Napier in 1930, within ten years it had become established and widespread throughout New Zealand, wherever its larval food plants occur.

Habits   Cabbage white butterflies are a familiar sight in gardens and farming country, but much less commonly encountered in native habitats. They can be a severe nuisance in gardens, but in New Zealand they seldom cause serious or

sustained damage in field crops, partly because their numbers are usually controlled by predation from harvestmen (page 177) and hoverfly larvae (page 227), as well as two ichneumons (*Apanteles glomeratus* and *Pteromalus puparum*, page 231) deliberately introduced in the early 1930s as a control measure.

Food   Adults feed on the nectar of a wide range of flowering plants; caterpillars eat only the leaves of brassicas — cabbages, cauliflower, sprouts, turnips, kale and related crops.

Breeding   Females lay their yellow eggs singly on the underside of cabbage leaves or related brassica plants. A female can lay up to 400 eggs, each measuring about 1 mm in length and hatching in about ten days. The larval stage takes about 30–40 days, during which time the skin is moulted four times. The caterpillar usually leaves its host plant to pupate, often selecting a fence or a low shrub. The entire cycle takes about 46 days in summer.

Order • Lepidoptera	**Species** • *Pieris rapae*
Status • introduced; common; resident	**Maori name** • pepe ma, pepepe ma

Black Mountain Ringlet

Recognition Sometimes known as the black butterfly, this is a true alpine resident, readily identified both by its habitat and as a black or very dark brown butterfly, marked only with a few small white spots. It has a distinctive flight style — erratic, aimless and lazy, low over bare, sun-drenched rock, with wings held outspread in a shallow V-shape.

Distribution This endemic butterfly is confined to the high mountains of the South Island, especially on bare boulder screes above 1200 m, where it is the only butterfly likely to be encountered — although it occasionally occurs on moraines or rocky slopes down to 800 m.

Habits It is on the wing from late November to early March, a calm, sunny day in January offering the best chance of finding it. The dark coloration absorbs radiant heat from the sun, which gives it a distinct survival edge over more brightly coloured butterflies at high altitudes. Like other high altitude butterflies, it is fond of basking in the sun with wings outspread wherever a rock surface offers full exposure to the sun but complete protection from the wind. The black mountain ringlet shares its environment with New Zealand's rarest butterfly, Butler's ringlet, which is known only from scattered localities above 1200 m in the Southern Alps.

Food Adults take nectar from a wide range of alpine flowers; caterpillars feed on the stems and blades of small grasses.

Breeding The black mountain ringlet differs from all other New Zealand butterflies in laying its sky-blue eggs on stones, which absorb heat from the sun better than plant surfaces. They hatch in about 12 days, and the tiny caterpillar first eats the eggshell before setting off in seach of a host plant — normally the small grass species *Poa colensoi*. The caterpillars are also unusual in that they feed at night, and hide under stones during the day. Full development takes two or three years.

ORDER • Lepidoptera		**SPECIES** • *Percnodaimon merula*	
STATUS • endemic; common; resident		**MAORI NAME** • pepe pouri	

Tussock Butterflies

Argyrophenga antipodum

Recognition Tussock butterflies are dusty brown with a large, rich, copper panel towards the tip of each wing; the diagnostic feature is six to eight long silver streaks on the straw-coloured underside of each hindwing. They are conspicuous in flight but very difficult to find in tall grass. The wingspan is about 4 cm.

Distribution The tussock butterflies are very closely associated with open, native tussock grasslands of the South Island, especially on the eastern side. There are three species, all endemic, all very difficult to tell apart, all with different but overlapping ranges.

Habits Abundant, big enough to be noticeable, and with a distinctive lazy, meandering flight style (seldom rising more than a metre above the ground), tussock butterflies are among the most familiar of New Zealand native butterflies. At high altitudes they are fond of sunbathing, basking with wings outspread but snapping them shut at any disturbance. Telling the three

species apart can be challenging, but location offers a tentative clue: in lowland rangelands of the east the common species is *Argyrophenga antipodum*; in montane and subalpine grasslands of Marlborough, Canterbury and Otago the species is likely to be *Argyrophenga janitae*; whereas the high-altitude snow grasses of northwest Nelson, Mount Owen and Lewis Pass are the home of *Argyrophenga harrisi*, the rarest and most restricted of the three.

Food Larvae eat only the stems and blades of rank grass, especially native tussock grasses.

Breeding Many details of the life history remain to be worked out, but the female lays her tiny, pale green eggs singly on blades of grass. The larvae chew their way out, and often eat the shell as their first meal. The caterpillars are long, slender, dull green, and very difficult to find in long grass. Pupation lasts about 12–18 days; larval development times are still uncertain — perhaps more than a year.

Order • Lepidoptera	**Species** • *Argyrophenga* spp.
Status • endemic; common; resident	**Maori name** • mokarakare

Common Blue Butterfly

Recognition   New Zealand's most abundant native butterfly is the common blue, which can be seen, often by the hundreds, in open country generally, but especially on coastal sand dunes, along stony river banks, or the grassy margins of country roads. It is most numerous in late summer. Females are brownish grey, but the male's upper wings are a delicate shade of sky blue. The underwings are drab grey and the wingspan is a little over 2 cm. Caterpillars are plain green with a reddish head, less than 15 mm long and very hard to find, as they shelter by day at the base of their food plant.

ORDER • Lepidoptera
SPECIES • *Zizinia otis*
STATUS • native; common; resident
MAORI NAME • pepe aouri

Distribution   This species is widespread across Australia and New Zealand, New Caledonia, the Loyalty Islands, Norfolk Island and Lord Howe Island. In New Zealand it is abundant in the North Island and the northern tip of the South Island.

Copper Butterflies

Recognition   As the name implies, the various species of the endemic copper butterflies are rich copper above, sometimes shimmering with deep purple iridescence in certain lights. With a wingspan of barely 2 cm, the smallest of all New Zealand's butterflies is the boulder copper and the most ubiquitous species is the common copper, which is abundant in coastal areas wherever pohuehue, its main food plant, grows. Especially in the North Island, coppers may be on the wing all year. Females are paler and duller than males, and seldom fly. The tiny caterpillars are dull red or green.

ORDER • Lepidoptera
SPECIES • *Lycaena* spp.
STATUS • endemic; common; resident
MAORI NAME • pepe parariki

Distribution   Copper butterflies are widespread throughout New Zealand in open habitats of all kinds; the boulder copper is more common in the South Island than in the North, and is especially characteristic of alpine and subalpine environments up to 1400 m.

Lycaena salustius

Monarch Butterfly

10 cm

Recognition   Wingspan about 10 cm; sexes similar. Easily recognised by its tawny red wings, bordered and veined in black, with many small white spots around the margins. The caterpillar is boldly patterned with black, yellow and white bands around its body.

Distribution   Originally a native of North and South America, over the past century the monarch — otherwise known as wanderer — has colonised much of the temperate world. It was first recorded in Australia in 1871, and in New Zealand even earlier, in 1840. For many years it was merely a rare visitor, but now it is well established and common throughout New Zealand, breeding south at least to Christchurch and wandering to many offshore islands.

Habits   The monarch is very common in suburban and rural areas, but seldom encountered in native bush or forest. In North America it is famous for its spectacular migrations, taking the butterflies — breeding as they go — northwards to southern Canada and

south again to California and Mexico, where they overwinter in enormous swarms on traditional trees, visited year after year by subsequent generations. Migration has not been demonstrated in New Zealand, but adults frequently overwinter (north of about Kaikoura) and several swarming sites are known, usually on pines or cedars. Swarming begins in April or May, but through the winter the butterflies often fly around on unusually mild and sunny days.

Food   Adults feed on nectar from flowers; caterpillars eat only the leaves of plants of the milkweed group, especially swan-plant, *Asclepias fruticosa*.

Breeding   The female lays her eggs on the underside of leaves, and they hatch in about five days. The tiny caterpillar chews its way out of the egg, and usually eats the shell as its first meal. Over the next three weeks it does little but eat, and moults its skin several times. It normally pupates on its host plant to form the pale jade-green chrysalis.

Order • Lepidoptera
Status • self-introduced; common; resident

Species • *Danaus plexippus*
Maori name • kahuku

Yellow Admiral Butterfly

Recognition   Wingspan about 5.5 cm. Very similar to the red admiral, but slightly smaller, and with yellow — not red — patches in the otherwise mainly deep brown wings. Both species often occur together.

Distribution   Southern and eastern Australia and New Zealand, where it is widespread throughout all three main islands, as well as on many of the closer offshore groups — although noticeably more common in the North Island than in the South Island.

Habits   Like the closely related red admiral, the yellow admiral is widespread in most lowland New Zealand habitats, commonest in gardens and farmland, and seldom penetrates native forest or alpine areas. Both admirals originated in Australia, the red probably many thousands of years ago, the yellow only recently. Indications that the yellow admiral is increasing in number suggest that it may still be in the process of establishing itself, but it seems equally likely that this might be due to the recent spread in

New Zealand of the introduced nettle *Urtica urens*, its favourite food plant. It is strongly migratory in Australia and its numbers in New Zealand are believed to be augmented from time to time by fresh arrivals from across the Tasman.

Food   Adults feed on nectar from a range of flowering plants (especially *Buddleia*); caterpillars eat only the leaves of various stinging nettle species, especially the introduced *Urtica urens*.

Breeding   Except for the difference in food plant preference, yellow and red admirals are extremely similar in almost every aspect of their reproductive cycles and it is not easy to tell the caterpillars apart. Caterpillars of both species share the unusual habit of drawing the tip of a leaf back onto itself, fastening it down with a few strands of silk to form a shelter. As in many other butterflies, hints of the adult's wing pattern can be seen through the translucent skin of the chrysalis for several days before final emergence.

Order • Lepidoptera	**Status** • self-introduced; common; resident
Species • *Bassaris itea*	**Maori name** • kahu-kowhai

Red Admiral Butterfly

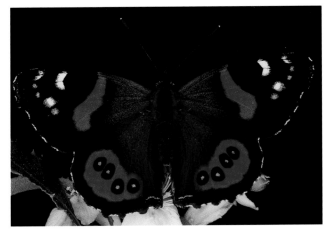

Recognition   Wingspan about 6 cm. Probably the most familiar endemic butterfly, easily recognised as a deep brown or black butterfly with a large, bright red blotch on the upper surface of each wing.

Distribution   Throughout New Zealand and wandering to many other outlying island groups. A closely related species inhabits the Chatham Islands.

Habits   The red admiral is common in almost all New Zealand habitats, from city parks to alpine meadows, including native old-growth forests where other butterflies are uncommon. It is most prominent from November onwards, but adults overwinter, hiding torpid in bark crevices, among dead leaves and other sheltered sites, and are sometimes on the wing on mild, sunny days right through winter. They often sunbathe on tree trunks, perched head-down with wings outspread. There are no detectable migrations within New Zealand, but the red admiral still retains its ancestral wandering

tendencies: an admiral, almost certainly this species, was once recorded on an American survey ship off the coast of Antarctica more than 5000 km from New Zealand.

Food   Adults take nectar from flowers or — especially in winter or early spring — the sap flowing from wounds in the bark of trees; in gardens they are especially attracted to *Buddleia* flowers. Caterpillars eat only the leaves of nettles, especially the stinging tree nettle or ongaonga, *Urtica ferox*.

Breeding   Females lay their eggs singly, usually depositing each one delicately on the side of a single stinging hair. Hatching occurs about eight days later; the tiny caterpillar chews its way free but does not normally eat the shell. It has the distinctive habit of tugging back the tip of a tender new leaf and anchoring it down with silk to form a sort of tent in which it shelters during the day. The caterpillar stage lasts about four to six weeks, and the adult emerges from the chrysalis after about 15 days.

Order • Lepidoptera		**Species** • *Bassaris gonerilla*	
Status • native; common; resident		**Maori name** • kahukura	

For more information

If you'd like to learn more about New Zealand's unique fauna and flora, there is a wealth of resources of every kind you can tap into, wherever you might happen to live in New Zealand.

If you're the active, gregarious type, you might consider joining a club, either local, regional or national. Many local clubs and societies organise regular field-trips, outings, and meetings of every kind. There are so many that a book like this cannot hope to list more than a handful of the more prominent, but your local public librarian ought to have all the details at his or her fingertips. If you feel you'd value a more structured approach, there are many courses you can take, designed for the entire spectrum of involvement — from beginner to advanced. Try making enquiries at The Open Polytechnic of New Zealand (see page 250). If you're the kind undaunted by computers, log onto the World Wide Web and do some surfing. The ESR, all national and regional museums, as well as a host of local and special interest groups, each have their own websites, which you can explore for all kinds of information. (If you don't know how to surf the Web, get your local librarian to show you that too. Do it right now, because you're missing something good.) If you're the sort that enjoys rummaging around in libraries, then you can pick from entire shelves of material, both popular and technical, published over the past century or so.

One source in particular that you should be aware of is the *Fauna of New Zealand* series, a project organised by ESR to cover all New Zealand animals in a series of inexpensive booklets (usually one family per volume), each written by the relevant authority on the group and each containing a popular summary of the group (in English and Maori), a checklist of all New Zealand species, and a technical synopsis of each. Something close to 40 parts have been issued so far.

The lists of titles, names and addresses that follow make no attempt to be comprehensive, instead seeking merely to call your attention to a few of the most useful, active or prominent resources you can call upon to find out more about New Zealand's wildlife — just enough to get you started.

References

Baker, A.N. *Whales and dolphins of New Zealand and Australia: an identification guide*, Victoria University Press, Wellington, 1983

Bishop, N. *From the mountains to the sea: the secret life of New Zealand's rivers and wetlands*, Reed Books, Wellington, 1994

Bishop, N. *Natural History of New Zealand*, Hodder & Stoughton, Auckland, 1992

Chapman, A. & Lewis, M. *An introduction to the freshwater Crustacea of New Zealand*, Collins, Auckland and London, 1976

Falla, R.A., Sibson, R.B. & Turbott, E.G. *Birds of New Zealand*, HarperCollins, Auckland, 1978

Forster, L.M. *Introduction to New Zealand spiders*, Collins, Auckland, 1973

Gibbs, G.W. *New Zealand butterflies: identification and natural history*, Collins, Auckland, 1980

Hutching, G. *The Natural World of New Zealand*, Reader's Digest/Penguin Books, Auckland, 1998

King, C.M. (ed.) *The handbook of New Zealand mammals*, Oxford University Press, Auckland, 1990

Kuschel, G. (ed.) *Biogeography and ecology in New Zealand*. Monographiae Biologicae vol. 27., Dr W. Junk Publishers, The Hague, 1975

McDowall, R.M. *New Zealand freshwater fishes: a guide and natural history*, Heinemann, Auckland, 1978

Meads, M. *The weta book: a guide to the identification of wetas*, DSIR Land Resources, Lower Hutt, 1990

O'Brien, C. *AA Book of New Zealand Wildlife: A Guide to the Native and Introduced Animals of New Zealand*, Lansdowne Press, Auckland, 1981

Reader's Digest Complete book of New Zealand birds, Readers Digest/Reed Methuen, Sydney, 1985

Robb, J. *New Zealand amphibians and reptiles in colour*, Collins, Auckland, 1980

Sharell, R. *New Zealand insects and their story*, Collins, Auckland, Sydney and London (revised edition), 1982

Sharell, R. *The tuatara, lizards and frogs of New Zealand*, Collins, Auckland (second edition), 1975

Useful addresses

The Open Polytechnic of New Zealand
Freepost 3797
Private Bag 31914, Lower Hutt
Freephone 0800 650 200
Fax 04 566 5633
http://www.TOPNZ.ac.nz

Te Papa
Cable Street
PO Box 467, Wellington Central
Phone 04 381 7000
http://www.tepapa.govt.nz

Auckland War Memorial Museum
Auckland Domain, Auckland
Phone 09 309 0443
Infoline 09 306 7067
http://akmuseum.org.nz

Canterbury Museum
Rolleston Avenue, Christchurch
Phone 03 366 5000

The Otago Museum
419 Great King Street
PO Box 6202, Dunedin
Phone 03 477 2372
mail@otagomuseum.govt.nz
http://www.otagomuseum.govt.nz

Auckland Zoological Park
Motions Road
Western Springs, Auckland
Phone 09 360 3800
Infoline 09 360 3819
Auckland Zoo@akcity.govt.nz

Wellington Zoo
200 Daniell Street
Newtown, Wellington
Phone 04 389 8028
http://www.zoo.wcc.govt.nz

Orana Park
McLeans Island Road
Harewood, Christchurch
Phone 03 359 7109

Royal Forest and Bird Protection Society of New Zealand
172 Taranaki Street
PO Box 631, Wellington
Phone 04 385 7374
Fax 04 385 7373
office@wn.forest-bird.org.nz
http://www.forest-bird.org.nz

Ornithological Society of New Zealand, Inc.
PO Box 316, Drury
Phone 09 294 8334

Natural History New Zealand Limited
http://www.naturalhistory.co.nz

Journal of the Royal Society of New Zealand
http://www.rsnz.govt.nz

NZ Education Online
http://www.cwa.co.nz/eduweb/edu/nzed2.html#
    museum

New Zealand Museums Online
http://www.nzmuseums.co.nz

Glossary

aestivation A form of torpor (q.v.) that typically occurs in summer, usually to evade the consequences of shortage of water rather than low temperatures, as in hibernation (q.v.).

allopreening Mutual grooming by birds.

amplexus A sexual posture used by frogs and toads during mating, in which a male wraps his arms round a female's body, clinging to her back, while he fertilises the female's eggs directly they are laid.

arboreal Living in trees.

ballooning A dispersal mechanism used by certain spiders, in which a baby spider climbs to the tip of a twig, blade of grass, or similar perch, then pays out a line of silk until it is long enough to be captured by the breeze and carry the spiderling off.

biosonar A prey-detection technique (used by many bats and dolphins), which, as in sonar, bounces high frequency sound waves off a target to assess its characteristics (range, bearing) by analysis of the resulting echoes.

commensal A description of two (or more) animal species characterised by any of several kinds of relationship that results in them seldom occurring apart.

crepuscular Active only at dawn or dusk.

crypsis A range of 'tricks' (not necessarily visual) by which an animal reduces the chance of being detected by a predator.

dispersal The act of travelling by any young animal, on reaching maturity, in moving from its parent's territory in order to establish its own territory.

diurnal Active mainly or entirely by day.

ecotone The boundary between two different habitats, such as forest and grassland.

embryonic diapause The hormonal interruption of the development of a foetus until an enabling environmental trigger is released – as in the departure of an older sibling from the mother's pouch among certain species of kangaroos and wallabies.

endemic A description of an animal or plant species that is native to a stated area but found nowhere else.

feral A description of a domesticated animal or plant that has reverted to the wild and established a population without any subsequent requirement for human care or husbandry

gregarious A description of an animal living usually in the company of others of its kind.

guild Any association of animal species characterised by common behavioural or environmental features rather than relationship.

hibernation A state of near suspension of bodily functions or 'sleep' adopted by certain animals to avoid cold weather in winter.

introduced A description of an animal or plant species brought to an area outside its normal range by human agency (inadvertent or deliberate), leading to the subsequent establishment of a viable population independent of further human intervention.

metamorphosis The progression of individuals of certain animals (notably insects) through several different physical states or body forms, as in (among butterflies) egg, caterpillar, chrysalis, adult.

migratory The opposite of sedentary (q.v.): typically (but not exclusively) a description of an animal that commutes seasonally between two or more distinct geographical regions.

mimicry A form of crypsis that relies on resemblance to another animal species (usually unpalatable or dangerous) to evade detection by predators.

native Not introduced (q.v.): a description of an animal species that has evolved and has always occurred in a stated area.

nocturnal Active mainly or entirely at night.

nomadic A form of migration in which there is no predictability in schedule, direction or destination.

ootheca A capsule produced by certain insects (such as cockroaches) to serve as a container for their eggs.

parthenogenesis Reproduction in the absence of male sperm.

polymorphism Literally 'multiple appearances'; certain bird species (and many other animal groups) occur naturally in several different colour states, without regard to gender, age, or locality.

rut Sexually aroused aggression in males of certain mammal species (especially deer) in competition with other males during the mating season.

sedentary Non-migratory: a description of an animal species that seldom moves far from its birthplace.

social A description of a gregarious (q.v.) animal species that also shows marked behavioural bonds between the various members of the group.

symbiosis Commensal (q.v.) behaviour in which the bonds are obligatory and neither species can survive in the absence of the other.

terrestrial Living mostly or entirely on the ground.

territorial A state in which a member of certain animal species attempts to evict all other individuals of its species (except a mate) from a given area.

torpor A sleep-like state characterised by marked reduction of physiological functions (metabolism, respiration, heart-rate).

Index

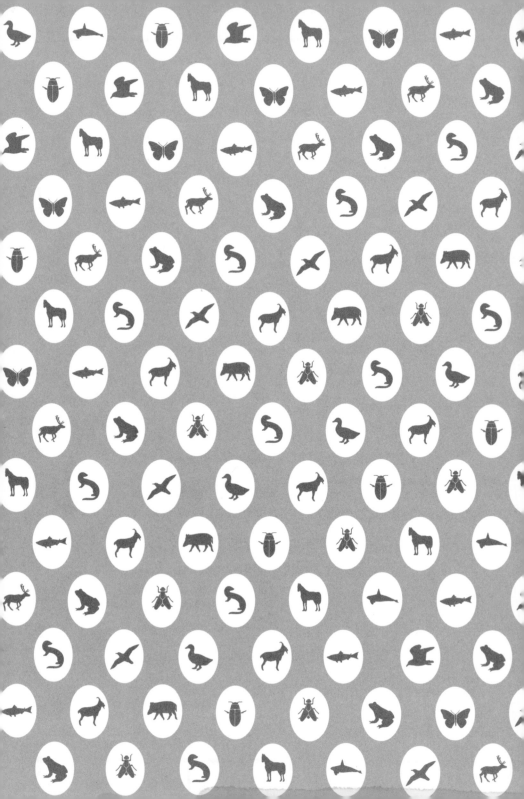